THE JFK ASSASSINATION EVIDENCE HANDBOOK

ISSUES, EVIDENCE & ANSWERS

by

Mike Davis

"The uneducated, when they engage in argument about anything, give no thought to the truth about the subject of discussion, but are only eager that those present will accept the position they have set forth."

Plato, *Phaedo* (Grube translation)

"It is of the highest importance in the art of detection to be able to recognize, out of a number of facts, which ones are incidental and which ones vital."

Sherlock Holmes, *The Reigate Puzzle*

"There comes a point when you have to start believing what some of these people saw. They can't all be wrong."

Deputy Sheriff Roger Craig
quoted by Barry Ernest in *The Girl on the Stairs.*

Preface

If the Kennedy assassination remains controversial more than 50 years after the event, this is certainly not because of a lack of evidence. From firearms and fingerprints to pubic hairs and poultry bones, the Warren Commission alone collected 26 volumes of hearings, depositions, documents and physical exhibits, running to more than 12,000 pages. These include files from the Dallas police department and Sheriff's department, as well as reports of interviews by the FBI and Secret Service, plus many items of physical evidence, such as a rifle, a revolver, bullets, documents, photographs, fingerprints, etc. In addition to the 26 volumes, the Commission received many thousands of pages of other documents, including reports from the FBI, Secret Service, CIA, and State Department. Since the Warren Commission was dissolved, other government panels have re-examined the assassination, producing their own collections of evidence in the form of hearings, interviews, and exhibits. Outside of government, numerous journalists have interviewed witnesses about the assassination, and some witnesses have published their own first hand accounts.

Despite this abundance of evidence, most people who have an opinion about the assassination are unable to buttress their views with citations from the original sources. There is simply too much of it for the non-specialist to master. Unless you are an assassination fanatic, you are not likely to devote the next ten years of your life to sifting through it all in order to find out what really happened. In this regard, the lone nut theorists have a distinct advantage. The government has already given them a handy reference guide outlining the evidence for their theory of the crime. Their handbook is called the Warren Report. A lone nut theorist who is familiar with the first 300 pages of the Warren Report will usually win a debate with a conspiracist who is not fully versed in the 26 volumes of the Warren Commission's Hearings and Exhibits, not to mention the thousands of pages of additional documents collected by the commission. This is because the evidence against Oswald has been cherry picked, organized, and convincingly presented in the Warren Report, but the much more voluminous evidence which undermines this theory remains spread out among thousands of unindexed pages in the 26 volumes and the National Archives. *The JFK Assassination Evidence Handbook*, equalizes the playing field, by providing conspiracists with a reference which sifts through the volumes of evidence to present a topical arrangement of testimony and documents proving that President Kennedy was the victim of at least three snipers in Dealey Plaza, and that Oswald was probably not one of these shooters. (Unfortunately for hard-core Oswald apologists, the evidence does show beyond a reasonable doubt that Oswald did indeed kill Officer J. D. Tippit.)

In *The JFK Assassination Evidence Handbook* the references for each topic are meticulously documented so that readers can look up each citation in the source materials to examine its full context. Under each topic, every effort has been made to be complete rather than selective. For example, instead of merely stating that

"Many witnesses saw Kennedy get hit in the right side of the head," I have listed every witness that I was able to locate who testified on that topic, identifying each by name, giving the relevant portions of their testimony, and the specific volume and page reference from the Warren Commission's Hearings and Exhibits, or other first hand source. One frustrating aspect of assassination research is that even some of the best books on the subject are thinly referenced, rarely citing any source evidence for their claims, or citing mostly secondary sources. It is difficult to have confidence in claims which cannot be traced back to original evidence. *The JFK Assassination Evidence Handbook* avoids this deficiency by citing extensively from the source evidence and by bringing the original evidence to bear upon the central questions of the case. Secondary sources are quoted only sparingly, usually on matters of historical context, but not to prove any essential facts. The point here is not to tell a story, but to make an argument, and to provide supporting evidence in the form of original testimony or interviews from first-hand witnesses. The topical arrangement means that it is not necessary for the reader to plow through 600 pages of narrative in order to gather up the evidence which applies to a particular issue.

Objective consideration of this evidence leads to a clear conclusion. The evidence proves that at least three assassins fired on Kennedy in Dealey Plaza, that Oswald was probably not one of the shooters, that the evidence against Oswald in the Kennedy case was probably planted in order to frame him, that Oswald probably did shoot officer Tippit (most likely in self-defense), and that Jack Ruby was closely tied to organized crime and the Dallas police department and was anything but a legitimate businessman trying to make an honest living by running a nightclub. Finally, the evidence will show that Oswald was not a real communist, but had ties to organized crime, U. S. intelligence agencies, and anti-Castro Cubans – the very groups who were most likely to have been responsible for conspiring to assassinate President Kennedy. All of these points can be proven beyond a reasonable doubt by the evidence cited in the following pages. Lone nut theorists may argue that there is a strong case to be made against Oswald in the President's assassination. They are right. There is a strong *prima facie* case against Oswald, and in fact we will present that argument in the first chapter, as a point of departure. But an examination of the source material will show that the evidence against Oswald in the President's murder suffers from many weaknesses, such as indecisive eyewitnesses, inconsistent logic, or faulty chain of possession for key physical evidence. We will see that the case against Oswald evaporates when we consider all of the evidence, rather than cherry picking the pieces that appear to incriminate Oswald.

In the course of presenting this evidence, many new arguments and facts will be presented based on evidential relationships not previously examined or emphasized in the assassination literature. For example: the Dallas police department's falsification of radio log transcripts, Oswald's family connections to organized crime, Sylvia Odio's acquaintance with Oswald *before* his visit to her apartment, and an FBI document which appears to corroborate an incident related by Judyth Vary Baker in her memoir, *Me and Lee*. Also, refutations are presented for several of the pseudo-scientific notions relied on by the Warren Commission and its defenders, such as the "delayed reaction" theory, the "neuromuscular reaction" theory, and the "jet effect", to explain away facts seen in the Zapruder film.

Evaluating the evidence

For a long time, the Warren Commission and its supporters relied on an old logical fallacy to support their claims against contrary evidence. This fallacy is the argument from authority. It presumes to establish the truth of a matter by appealing to the reputation of the person making the claim. So-and-so is a distinguished, respected, and honorable man. Therefore, what he says must be true. This is, of course, illogical. Surely we all know by now many examples where distinguished gentlemen have used their reputations as a cover for all kinds of self-serving misbehavior. But at the time of the Warren Commission, people were not yet so cynical (or realistic), at least not toward their own government. So the conclusions of this Commission of Distinguished Gentlemen with Excellent Reputations were given great deference by the populace and the news media, and the equally distinguished gentlemen who conducted the autopsy were believed when they said the evidence indicated that Kennedy had been shot twice from behind and that one of the shots hit him in the back of the neck and went all the way through to exit from the front of his neck and hit Governor Connally. Surely, it was claimed, you can't doubt the conclusions of these doctors who had the closest and most detailed look at Kennedy's wounds. Any witnesses who testified differently obviously did not have as good a vantage point as the autopsy team. And anyone who accepted the testimony of these contrary witnesses over the conclusions of the autopsy doctors was obviously not in touch with reality. Thus, if you concluded from the evidence that there were three assassins and that Kennedy was hit in the head from the front and that Oswald was framed, you were not only wrong, you were probably insane, and not very intelligent. Coverage in the national press continually drummed these themes into the public consciousness.

But in this book we will not grant any special concessions to the distinguished gentlemen. And we will make no disparaging assumptions about anyone's sanity based on the conclusions they draw from the evidence. We will set the testimony of the government's men against the testimony of other qualified witnesses and against the physical evidence. Where witnesses conflict, their testimony will be compared and weighed and conclusions drawn. In many cases, testimony which appears at first glance to be contradictory can actually be reconciled in a synthesis that provides new insights. We will not follow the lawyers' principle of "best evidence", which is a legal term meaning "pick the evidence you like and ignore anything that disagrees with it."

The Kennedy assassination evidence is such that you can prove anything you want with it, provided that you cherry-pick the evidence favorable to your side, and dismiss or discredit any opposing evidence. Therefore, it will be necessary to keep certain principles in mind that will help us assess witness testimony more objectively. As a general rule, a witness's testimony should not be discarded simply because it differs from a preconceived model. Instead, the preconceived model must be evaluated based on the testimony. Some basic guidelines for evaluating witness testimony are given below. The principles listed here are not intended to serve as ironclad rules, but only general rules of thumb, to help bring some order into one's deliberations on the evidence, and to reduce the chance of arbitrary decisions. In all cases we are dealing in probabilities, not certainties. It is very rare that one is justified in totally dismissing a witness as completely unreliable, or in accepting a witness as totally truthful in all circumstances.

Guidelines for assessing witness testimony:

Earlier statements from a witness are more reliable than later ones.
Earlier memories are fresher and uncontaminated by reports from press, police or other witnesses. This means we will not only be interested in a witness's testimony to the commission, which often occurred several months after the assassination, but also their statements to Dallas law enforcement officials and to the FBI. These statements often were taken on the day of the assassination, or shortly thereafter.

Consistent testimony by a witness repeated over time is more reliable than testimony which changes over time.
If a witness told the same story to the police, the Sheriff's department, the FBI and to the Warren Commission, this is justification for assigning great weight to what that witness is telling us.

Consistent testimony across multiple witnesses is more reliable than testimony from a single witness – provided that the witnesses are independent from each other.
We must guard against assigning more weight to witnesses who had the opportunity to get together and agree on their stories. But if witnesses who have had no contact with each other tell the same story, especially if they had different vantage points, then this is grounds for assigning more weight to their testimony.

The more detailed a witness's testimony is, the more likely it is to be true.
A witness testifying falsely is either lying or mistaken. A witness may be mistaken about a detail, but they are unlikely to be mistaken about a large number of details, especially when those details are internally consistent. For witnesses suspected of lying, it is much harder to tell a convincing lie packed with details than to tell a lie consisting of vague generalities.

Testimony that varies from the official view is more reliable than testimony which supports it.
This maxim may strike some as indicating bias, but there are sound reasons for following it. It is easier to go along with the prevailing orthodoxy than to go against it. Many of the witnesses in the Kennedy assassination reported threats or pressure to conform their stories to the government's preferred scenario. It

must be considered that those who did not succumb to this pressure may be resisting because they have a strong desire for the truth to come out. Other reasons may be imagined as well, but witness testimony must not be summarily discarded simply because it differs from what the majority are saying. It must be evaluated on its own merits.

A witness's incentive to tell the truth or a lie must be considered.

Does the witness have anything to gain by making a false statement? If so, we must discount their statement in proportion to this incentive. Conversely, a witness who makes a statement which clearly goes against their own interest, is to be granted greater credibility, because such a witness is more likely to be motivated by a desire to tell the truth, than by self-interest.

"Character" is a poor guide to the truthfulness of a witness's statement.

A common mistake is to evaluate a witness's testimony by asking whether he or she is a trustworthy *person*. According to this view, if the person is deemed untrustworthy then everything they say must be rejected. If the person is deemed credible then everything they say is believable. This is obviously a naïve and overly simplistic approach. In evaluating evidence we are concerned with the truth or falsehood of statements, not of persons. Even a habitual liar will tell you the truth most of the time. If you ask a habitual liar whether he wants fries with his cheeseburger, he will probably tell you the truth. For each of a witness's statements, the question must be asked, "Does this witness have any incentive to be telling a falsehood in the context of this particular statement?" To dismiss what a person says because of that person's presumed bad character is just another logical fallacy – the *ad hominem* argument. "This is a bad person, therefore what he says cannot be believed." Another example of the *ad hominem* fallacy is "Oswald was a loner, a loser, and a communist. Therefore, he probably shot the president." The Warren Report makes frequent use of this fallacy in trying to establish Oswald's guilt.

A witness should not be discredited by claiming that their testimony is motivated by a desire for fame or fortune.

A common tactic for discrediting a witness's inconvenient testimony is to claim that they are only making their statement for publicity, perhaps in the hope of obtaining a lucrative publishing deal, or even a movie. This tactic is based on the erroneous judgment that everyone wants to be famous and stand in the spotlight. From everyday experience, we all know that many, perhaps most, people have no desire to stand in the public spotlight. Several witnesses who have come forth with revealing personal stories about the assassination have in no way benefited from the publicity that resulted from their revelations. After confessing to being the grassy knoll shooter, James Files remained incarcerated in the Illinois State Penitentiary and did not become a rich and famous man. Judyth Vary Baker, who wrote a memoir about her relationship with Lee Oswald in New Orleans during the summer of 1963, received threats and had to move abroad to an undisclosed location out of fear for her life. Here again, no fame and fortune resulted from her revelations. Obviously, revealing groundbreaking information about the Kennedy assassination is not a strategy for financial success and public adulation. The argument that witnesses who tell sensational stories are merely seeking personal notoriety and financial gain is contradicted by our everyday experience and by these and other specific examples. Such revelations must be evaluated according to the same criteria as the testimony of other witnesses.

The Sources and abbreviations:

The evidence cited in this *JFK Assassination Evidence Handbook* comes primarily from the Warren Commission's own Hearings and Exhibits and their collection of commission documents, supplemented by subsequent evidence collected by other government bodies, such as the House Select Committee on Assassinations and the Assassination Records Review Board. In addition to these official evidence collections, we will occasionally cite works by journalists and researchers who have interviewed witnesses and participants, or first-hand accounts by witnesses and participants themselves. When citing these sources, the government publications are abbreviated as shown below. All of these collections are accessible online at maryferrell.org.

WCHE (Warren Commission Hearings and Exhibits – aka "the 26 volumes")

CE (Commission Exhibit) Within the WCHE, exhibits are identified by CE number.

WCR (the Warren Commission Report)

CD (Warren Commission Documents) These are filed apart from the WCHE, in a separate collection.

HSCA (House Select Committee on Assassinations) Final report plus twelve volumes of appendices.

ARRB (Assassination Records Review Board) Final report, medical testimony, medical exhibits, and document collections.

NARA (National Archives and Records Administration) Record numbers for records that are not part of a specific document collection.

Detailed summary extracts of testimony by many of the witnesses can be found in the author's *JFK Assassination Witness Index.*

Contents

THE SUSPECT

AN OPENING STATEMENT

After interviewing hundreds of witnesses and amassing thousands of pages of documents over the span of 9 months, the Warren Commission came to the same conclusion that the Dallas police took only 2 hours to reach on the afternoon of November 22, 1963: President Kennedy was fatally shot by Lee Oswald, acting alone, from the sixth floor of the Texas School Book Depository building. Nothing that the commission learned during its months-long investigation gave them any reason to differ from the initial assessment by the Dallas police. From the very beginning, Oswald was considered the prime suspect in the President's murder. But Oswald was not caught in the act of pulling the trigger. He was not apprehended at the scene of the crime, but was arrested some miles away in a movie theater. The assassination of President Kennedy leaves many loose threads which the Warren Commission failed to tie up. If the Dallas police could solve the case in two hours, why did it take the Warren Commission so long to confirm Oswald's guilt? Or was the commission merely putting on a show of thoroughness to justify a preconceived outcome?

By re-examining the evidence collected by the Warren Commission we will be able to assess the validity of their conclusions. We will find that the commission's own evidence contradicts the claim of the commission and the Dallas police that Oswald alone shot President Kennedy. The evidence will show that at least three assassins fired on Kennedy and that Oswald was, in all likelihood, not one of the shooters. We will find that much of the alleged forensic evidence against Oswald has no clear chain of possession and cannot be shown to be connected to the crime. In other words, it cannot be ruled out that the forensic evidence of Oswald's guilt was planted in order to frame him. We will find that the testimony of ballistics experts does not support the commission's claim that a single bullet ripped through Kennedy and Connally, and we will see that in firing tests conducted by the FBI and the U. S. Army their expert marksmen were unable to duplicate the feat ascribed to Oswald. In the Tippit case, the evidence will show beyond a reasonable doubt that Oswald killed officer Tippit, but it will also show that Oswald's movements and actions on the afternoon of November 22 were not such as to be expected from a lone assassin, but from a member of a conspiracy who realized he was being framed and who was desperately trying to escape his co-conspirators. Finally, the evidence does not allow us to rule out the possibility that Oswald was an undercover informant of the FBI who thought he had penetrated and exposed a plot to kill the President, but who was framed for the crime by the very contacts that he had trusted.

THE CASE AGAINST OSWALD

At first glance, the evidence provided to the Warren Commission appears to confirm Oswald's guilt in the assassination of President Kennedy. James Cadigan, FBI documents expert, testified that the order blank (CE773) for a rifle, sent to Klein's Sporting Goods, was in Oswald's handwriting, as was the envelope in which the coupon was mailed. (WCHE, v.7, p.420). The order form identifies the purchaser as "A. Hidell", an alias known to have been used by Oswald. The envelope addressed to Klein's carries a return address for "A. Hidell" at P.O. Box 2915, Dallas TX, a box which had been rented to Oswald. (WCHE, v.24, p. 419b and CE791) The Klein's catalog number (C20-T750) on the order blank was identified as referring to a 6.5 mm Italian carbine with a 4x scope, serial number C2766. The rifle was shipped on March 20, 1963 to the Dallas P.O. box indicated on the order form. (WCHE, v.25, p.807a) The money order for $21.45 which accompanied the order was determined by Cadigan to have been filled out by Oswald. (WCHE, v.7, p.423) While visiting the Oswalds shortly after April 10, 1963, Jeanne de Mohrenschildt observed a gun standing in a closet of the Oswalds' apartment, and told her husband George about it as he sat talking with Lee Oswald in another room of the apartment. Oswald's wife Marina told Jeanne de Mohrenschildt, "That crazy lunatic bought a rifle when we really need money for other things." (WCHE, v.9, p.315-317); In a search of Oswald's possessions, photographs (CE133) were found showing Oswald in the backyard of his previous residence brandishing a rifle and wearing a holstered revolver, while displaying copies of pro-communist newspapers. (WCHE, v.16, p.510)

On the morning of November 22, 1963, Oswald's co-worker Wesley Frazier gave him a ride to work and noticed that Oswald was carrying with him a heavy package wrapped in brown paper. Oswald was seen by several witnesses that morning working on the sixth floor of the TSBD. Several witnesses in Dealey Plaza waiting for the Presidential motorcade testified that they saw a man holding a rifle in an upper floor window of the TSBD shortly before the arrival of the motorcade. These witnesses include the mayor's wife, Elizabeth Cabell (WCHE, v.7, p.486), Malcolm Couch (WCHE, v.6, p.157), Amos Euins (WCHE, v.16, p.963); Arnold Rowland (WCHE, v.19, p.494), Carolyn Walther (WCHE, v.24, p.522a-b), James Worrell (WCHE, v.2, p.193-194) and Howard Brennan (WCHE, v.19, p.470). Brennan later identified Lee Oswald as the man he saw firing a rifle from the window. (WCHE, v.3, p.148)

After the shooting, Deputy Sheriff Eugene Boone found a rifle hidden among some boxes on the sixth floor of the Texas School Book Depository. (WCHE, v.3, p.293) Lt. J. C. Day of the Dallas Police Department Crime Lab identified the Italian rifle with serial number C2766 (CE139) as the rifle found on the sixth floor of the TSBD on November 22, 1963 – the same rifle ordered by Oswald from Klein's Sporting Goods. (WCHE, v.4, p.259) A palmprint which police took from the underside of the rifle barrel was identified by FBI fingerprint expert Sebastian

Latona as being "the right palmprint of Lee Harvey Oswald." (WCHE, v.4, p.24) Three cartridge cases said to have been found near the far right window on the sixth floor of the TSBD were determined by FBI expert Robert Frazier to have been fired from the Italian rifle bearing serial number C2766 (CE139). (WCHE, v.3, p.415) Frazier also determined that the bullet (CE399) said to have been found on a stretcher at Parkland Hospital had been fired in the C2766 rifle. (WCHE, v.3, p.429) Frazier also found that two bullet fragments said to have been found in the front seat of the Presidential car were fired in this same rifle. (WCHE, v.3, p.432, 435) In their summary report of the assassination, the FBI stated that "by actual tests it has been demonstrated by the FBI that a skilled person can fire three accurately aimed shots with this weapon in five seconds." (CD1, p.17)

Regarding the origin of the fatal head shot, Col. Pierre Finck, an experienced forensic pathologist who took part in the autopsy of Kennedy's body, testified that "President Kennedy was, in my opinion, shot from the rear. The bullet entered in the back of the head and went out on the right side of his skull, producing a large wound." Finck told the Warren Commission, "he was shot from above and behind" (WCHE, v.2, p.380) which would have been from the general direction of the Texas School Book Depository, where Oswald was working.

Within an hour after the assassination, Oswald was seen by several witnesses in the Dallas neighborhood of Oak Cliff. One of these witnesses, Helen Markham, said she saw Oswald shoot police officer J. D. Tippit, and then flee the scene (CD5, p.80), shedding empty cartridges from his revolver as he went. Several bystanders nearby also saw Oswald, or a man resembling Oswald, walking at a fast pace away from the scene, along a nearby street. The suspicion immediately arose that Oswald had been stopped by Officer Tippit, who was searching for suspects in the President's killing, and that Oswald shot Tippit in order to avoid being arrested for the assassination. Oswald was arrested a short time later in a nearby movie theater, after a brief scuffle, in which Oswald drew his gun on the arresting officer but was unable to fire it. (WCHE, v.24, p.241a) After his arrest, Oswald denied shooting anyone at all – not Kennedy, not Connally, not Tippit. (WCHE, v.24, p.234a)

With this evidence, a strong prima facie case can be made that Oswald did indeed assassinate President Kennedy and murder Officer Tippit. Based on this evidence alone, it is highly probable that any reasonable jury would have convicted Oswald for the President's murder. Many defendants have been sent to their death on less evidence than this.

Those who have defended the Warren Commission's conclusions have mostly done so using some variation of the argument presented in the foregoing paragraphs.

But as its name implies, a prima facie case may only stand up if we consider it superficially. Once we begin to dig underneath the surface and consider contrary evidence, the case against Oswald begins to fall apart and create many openings for reasonable doubt. The Warren Commission hearings were not conducted according to the normal rules of criminal procedure. There was no defense attorney to challenge the testimony of the government's witnesses or the validity of its evidence. There was no cross-examination of the government's expert witnesses and no presentation of defense experts to challenge the government's interpretation of the evidence. Many tactics which would have been ruled impermissible in a criminal trial were permitted in the commission's proceedings, such as leading questions, the assumption of facts not in evidence, acceptance of hearsay, and lack of foundation for admitted evidence. Many witnesses whose testimony was not consistent with the government's view of Oswald as lone assassin were either ignored or selectively quoted in the Warren Commission Report. In a real trial these witnesses would have been called by the defense and would have testified fully. The government's case against Oswald relied heavily on ad hominem arguments, presenting Oswald as a communist, a defector, a wife beater, and generally as an unpleasant character, without showing how these traits had any connection to whether he actually pulled the trigger on November 22, 1963. Even at the very end of its proceedings, the commission struggled to find a motive for Oswald's killing of the President, offering only speculations that Oswald wanted to be a big shot and carve out a place for himself in history. Yet the fact that Oswald denied shooting anyone on November 22 undercut this supposed motive, because a man who seeks notoriety for a criminal act does not disavow his act when caught.

For those who consider the charges against Oswald to be an open-and-shut case in the assassination of President Kennedy, it is instructive to compare the case against Oswald with the case against Jack Ruby, to see what an open-and-shut case really looks like. Ruby was captured with a revolver in his hand in the act of shooting Oswald in front of dozens of witnesses and with millions watching on live TV. Many of the officers present knew Ruby personally and recognized him immediately. He was arrested and put in jail within minutes after the shooting. Ruby readily admitted that he shot Oswald, although his stated reasons for doing so evolved over time. No one has ever suggested that anyone other than Ruby shot Oswald.

Oswald, on the other hand, was not captured in the act of shooting the President. He was arrested several miles away more than an hour after the shooting. He did not have a rifle with him when he was arrested. No one who knew him saw him shoot the President or even saw him with a rifle in his hands on that day. The one witness who supposedly identified him in a police lineup, Howard Brennan, was actually uncertain in his identification until much later. Brennan did not know Oswald personally and had never seen him before. Before viewing Oswald in the police lineup, Brennan had seen Oswald's picture on television. (CD205, p.15) And Oswald, who supposedly shot the President in order to achieve notoriety, denied having shot anybody on that day. It is obvious that compared to the case against Ruby, the case against Oswald has many gaps that need to be filled in. It is by no means an open-and-shut case.

In the following chapters we will present a much broader set of evidence than was presented in the Warren Commission Report. And yet almost all of the evidence to be cited here comes directly from the Warren Commission's own collection of hearings, exhibits, and documents. While it is true that since 1964 the work of congressional committees, as well as independent journalists, scholars, and researchers, has uncovered a great deal of additional evidence casting doubt on the commission's findings, it is also true that the commission itself had in its possession sufficient evidence to refute the theory that Oswald acting alone shot the President. A straightforward, common sense appraisal of the evidence presented to the Warren Commission in 1964 proves that President Kennedy was killed by at least three gunmen, with at least one shooter firing from the right front and at least two firing from the rear. Whether Oswald was one of those firing from the rear is less certain, but a preponderance of evidence indicates that he probably was not a shooter at all, but remained on the lower floors of the Texas School Book Depository during the shooting. Defenders of the single gunman theory have had to rely on speculative and fanciful inventions to preserve the semblance of logical consistency in their position, but in this they have done nothing more than pile more and more epicycles upon an already overloaded structure, rather than drawing the simple and obvious conclusions from the evidence.

THE INJURIES

KENNEDY'S HEAD WOUNDS PROVE A SECOND GUNMAN FIRING FROM THE FRONT

The conclusion reached by the Warren Commission Report was: "The detailed autopsy of President Kennedy performed on the night of November 22 at the Bethesda Naval Hospital led the three examining pathologists to conclude that the smaller hole in the rear of the President's skull was the point of entry and that the large opening on the right side of his head was the wound of exit." The report quotes one of the attending pathologists, Col. Pierre Finck: "President Kennedy was, in my opinion, shot from the rear. The bullet entered in the back of the head and went out on the right side of his skull. . . . He was shot from above and behind." (WCR, p.86) The commission concluded that "the shots which killed President Kennedy and wounded Governor Connally were fired from the sixth-floor window at the southeast corner of the Texas School Book Depository Building." (WCR, p.117) The evidence to be cited in this chapter refutes this conclusion.

The evidence will show that Kennedy was hit in the right side of the head from a position near the fence on the grassy slope on the north side of Elm Street. This shot could not possibly have come from the Texas School Book Depository, thus proving the existence of a second gunman firing from the front right of the motorcade. The evidence for this shot comes from eyewitnesses in the motorcade, spectators along the street in Dealey Plaza, witnesses who saw Kennedy's wounds at Parkland Hospital, and participants in the autopsy at Bethesda Medical Center, as well as from the Zapruder film. All these witnesses were known to the Warren Commission and available for questioning at the time of the commission's existence, but many were not called to testify, and their observations were ignored, dismissed or misinterpreted in the writing of the Warren Commission Report.

Numerous witnesses testified that Kennedy was shot in the right side of his head.

Witnesses in the motorcade:
* *George Hickey (Secret Service agent riding in the left rear seat of the Secret Service follow-up car directly behind the President's car):* In a typewritten statement written on the day of the assassination, Hickey wrote that after hearing an explosion, he turned to the rear, and then on turning back toward the President's car he heard two more shots "and it seemed as if the right side of his head was hit." (WCHE, v.18, p.765) In a later statement, dated more than a week after the assassination (11/30), Hickey wrote that "it looked to me as if the President was struck in the right upper rear of his head." (WCHE, v.18, p.762) This change in location for the head shot reflects a pattern that is seen in numerous witnesses, where their initial observations, shortly after or

contemporaneous with the assassination, tend to tell a story that conflicts with the conclusions of the Warren Report, while later testimony from the same witnesses evolves to conform to the commission's preferred scenario. Hickey was not called to testify before the commission, nor was his deposition taken.

- *Sam Kinney (Secret Service agent who drove the follow-up car directly behind the President's car):* In his report of 11/30/63, Kinney wrote that "I saw one shot strike the President in the right side of the head." (WCHE, v.18, p.731); Kinney was not called to testify in commission session, nor was his deposition taken.

- *Emory Roberts (Assistant to the Special Agent in Charge, riding in the front right passenger seat of the Secret Service follow-up car directly behind the President's car):* In his report of 11/22/63, Roberts wrote: "I could not determine from what direction the shots came, but felt they had come from the right side." (WCHE, v.18, p.739); In his 11/29 report, Roberts stated, "I do not know if it was the next shot or third shot that hit the President in the head, but I saw what appeared to be a small explosion on the right side of the President's head." (WCHE, v.18, p.734) Agent Roberts was not called to testify in commission session, nor was his deposition taken.

- *B. J. Martin (Motorcycle patrolman riding on the left rear of President Kennedy's car):* Martin describes his position in the motorcade at WCHE, v.6, p.289. In his deposition, taken by Joseph Ball on April 3, 1964, Martin described how after the assassination he noticed blood stains on his helmet and on the windshield of his motorcycle. (WCHE, v.6, p.292). The presence of blood and tissue being thrown to the left rear of the President's car refutes the suggestion by some that a "jet effect" caused by tissue being ejected toward the front right by a bullet entering from the rear was responsible for the violent head snap to the left rear.

- *Douglas Jackson (Motorcycle patrolman riding on the outside right rear of the Presidential car.* Jackson was not called to testify before the commission nor was his deposition taken. He was not even interviewed by the FBI until September 12, 1975. After hearing the first two shots, Jackson "turned to look at the Presidential car, [and] he heard a third shot and observed President Kennedy struck above the right ear and the top of his head exploded to the left of the Presidential car." Jackson told the FBI that on the night of November 22, 1963 "he prepared a detailed written account of the above incident for his personal retention, which he still possesses, and has never been interviewed by the FBI or the Warren Commission." (FBI 62-109060 JFK HQ File, Section 181, pp.93-95.)

Spectators in Dealey Plaza:

- *William Eugene Newman:* According to a statement that Newman gave to the Sheriff's Office on the afternoon of the assassination, he was watching the motorcade on the north curb of Elm Street, between the underpass and the

TSBD, when he heard a noise like a gunshot. He saw the President "jump up" in his seat, and then when the President was directly in front of Newman, "I was looking directly at him when he was hit in the side of the head. . . . I thought the shot had come from the garden directly behind me." (WCHE, v.19, p.490) In an interview with WFAA-TV immediately after the assassination, Newman told interviewer Jay Watson that a shot "hit the President in the side of the temple." ("Jay Watson Uncut Version Interview with Bill & Gayle Newman Immediately After the JFK Assassination" at youtube.com.); Neither Bill Newman nor his wife Gayle were called to testify before the commission, nor were their depositions taken.

- *Abraham Zapruder:* While viewing the assassination through his home movie camera, Zapruder testified in his deposition, when questioned by Wesley Liebeler, that he saw the President get hit on the right side of the head:

LIEBELER: As you stood here on the abutment and looked down into Elm Street, you saw the President hit on the right side of the head and you thought perhaps the shots had come from behind you?
ZAPRUDER: Well, yes.
LIEBELER: From the direction behind you?
ZAPRUDER: Yes. (WCHE, v.7, p.572)

- *Marilyn Sitzman (Zapruder's secretary):* Sitzman was not called to testify in commission session, nor was her deposition taken. In a 1966 interview, Sitzman told researcher Josiah Thompson that when she was standing with Zapruder, the President was almost directly in front of them when she saw the shot "that hit him on the side of his face. . . between the eye and the ear." (Thompson, *Six Seconds in Dallas,* p.102).

- *Emmett Hudson (groundskeeper for Dealey Plaza, employed by the Dallas Parks Department):* In his deposition taken July 22, 1964 by Wesley Liebeler, Hudson testified that he was "looking right at [Kennedy] when that bullet hit him, the second shot."

LIEBELER: That was when the bullet hit him in the head, is that correct?
HUDSON: Yes. It looked like it hit him somewhere along about a little bit behind the ear and a little bit above the ear".
LIEBELER: On the right-hand side or the left-hand side?
HUDSON: Right hand. (WCHE, v.7, p.560)

Witnesses at Parkland Hospital:
- *Hurchel Jacks (Texas State Highway Patrolman, driver of the vice-presidential car in which Lyndon Johnson was riding in the motorcade):* In a typewritten statement of November 28, 1963, Jacks states that he followed the Presidential car to the entrance of Parkland Hospital. When he walked past the President's

car he was able to see Kennedy lying in the back seat. Jacks wrote that "before the President's body was covered it appeared that the bullet had struck him above the right ear or near the temple." Jacks' typewritten statement is found in CE1024, which is an 80-page collection of eyewitness reports by Secret Service agents, sent by the Secret Service to the Warren Commission on June 11, 1964. (WCHE, v.18, p.801); Jacks was not called to testify in commission session, nor was his deposition taken.

- *Dr. Robert McClelland (Assistant Professor of Surgery at Parkland Hospital):* McClelland attended President Kennedy in the emergency room, and wrote in his notes on the day of the assassination that the "cause of death was due to massive head and brain injury from a gunshot wound of the left temple." (WCHE, v.17, p.12) (Since no one claims that Kennedy was shot in the left side of his head, McClelland's words can only refer to the left side as viewed from the front – Kennedy's right temple.) McClelland's comments about a wound in the temple are not mentioned in the Warren Report.

- *Seth Kantor, correspondent for Scripps Howard newspapers:* In his handwritten notes taken at Parkland Hospital on the afternoon of November 22, Kantor wrote "intered [sic] right temple". Kantor's notes do not indicate where he got this information. (WCHE, v.20, p.353)

Witnesses at the Bethesda autopsy:

- *Dr. John Ebersole (Acting Chief of Radiology at Bethesda Naval Hospital)* testified that based on the X-rays, the bullet would have come from the side. (ARRB, MD60, p.18) Dr. Ebersole was not called to testify in commission session, nor was his deposition taken.

- *Roy Kellerman (Secret Service Agent),* who was present during the autopsy, testified to the Warren Commission that the entry wound in the head appeared to be in the hairline immediately to the right of the ear, about the lower third of the ear. The wound was about the size of Kellerman's little finger. (WCHE, v.2, p.81)

- *Thomas Robinson (embalmer who prepared Kennedy's body for burial)* noticed a small wound "in the temples in the hairline." Robinson remembers that this wound was on the right side of Kennedy's head, "somewhere around the temples." He describes this wound as about a quarter inch in diameter. (ARRB, MD63, p.2-3) Robinson was not called to testify in commission session, nor was his deposition taken.

Witnesses at Parkland Hospital and at Bethesda described a large head wound in the back of the head, not on the right side of the head where the Warren Commission claimed the bullet exited.

The dispute over the appearance of the head wounds is often characterized as a dispute between those who saw Kennedy's wounds at Parkland and those who saw

9

them at Bethesda. But this is a false dichotomy. There were several witnesses at the Bethesda autopsy who saw the same large, gaping wound in the back of Kennedy's head that the Parkland doctors saw.

- *Dr. Charles Carrico (Surgical resident at Parkland Hospital)* described "a large gaping wound, located in the right occipitoparietal area." (WCHE, v.6, p.6)
- *Dr. Kemp Clark (Director of Neurological Surgery at Parkland)* saw a "large wound in the right occipito-parietal region" (WCHE, v.17, p.3) and further described it as a "large gaping wound in the posterior part." (WCHE, v.6, p.20)
- *Dr. Ronald C. Jones (Chief Resident of Surgery at Parkland Hospital)* saw a "large wound in the right posterior side of the head", a "large defect in the back side of the head." (WCHE, v.6, p.53)
- *Dr. Robert McClelland (Assistant Professor of Surgery at Parkland Hospital)* testified that "the right posterior portion of the skull had been extremely blasted." (WCHE, v.6, p.33)
- *Dr. Malcolm Perry (Assistant Professor of Surgery at Parkland Hospital)* wrote that "a large wound of the right posterior cranium was noted." (WCHE, v.17, p.6), and testified in his deposition that he saw "a large avulsive injury of the right occipitoparietal area." (WCHE, v.6, p.11); But when Perry testified in commission session, "occipitoparietal" had become "parietal occipital area", putting more emphasis on the bones toward the side of the head. (WCHE, v.3, p.372)
- *Secret Service agent Clint Hill* noted at Parkland Hospital that "the right rear portion of his head was missing." (WCHE, v.2, p.141)
- *Secret Service agent Roy Kellerman* saw a large circular wound about 5 inches in diameter in the rear portion of the head when he observed Kennedy's body in the morgue at Bethesda. (WCHE, v.2, p.80)
- *John Ebersole (Radiologist at Bethesda)*, noted that "the back of the head was missing." (ARRB, MD60, p.3)
- *Floyd Riebe (Bethesda autopsy photographer)* told David Lifton in a recorded interview that when the autopsy doctors sat Kennedy's body up, "nothing was left there, back of his head".

   LIFTON: Well, what did the back of the head look like?
   RIEBE: Nothing. . . . There was nothing there.
   LIFTON: What was there? . . .
   RIEBE: A big hole, right in the occipital region of the head. (Reproduced in the deposition of John T. Stringer, ARRB Testimony of John T. Stringer, July 16, 1996, p.99)

- *John Stringer (Photographer at the Bethesda autopsy)* When interviewed by Davis Lifton, Stringer said that the main damage to Kennedy's head was "in the back [of the skull] . . . in the occipital . . . up above the neck." (Lifton, *Best Evidence* (1988), p.516) In Stringer's deposition before the Assassination Records Review Board, he testified that Captain Stover, head of the Naval Medical School at Bethesda, ordered him to sign a document (ARRB, MD 78) containing a count of photographs taken during the autopsy, and stating that "to my personal knowledge this is the total amount of film exposed on this occasion." Even though Stringer told Stover he disagreed with this statement, Stover told him, "Sign it," and he did. (ARRB Testimony of John T. Stringer, July 16, 1996, p.137)

None of the Parkland doctors observed a small bullet entrance hole in the rear of Kennedy's head, which the Warren Report concluded was the entry point of the fatal shot.

The Warren Report stated that the autopsy doctors concluded that "the smaller hole in the rear of the President's skull was the point of entry and that the large opening on the right side of his head was the wound of exit." (WCR, p.86) However, the medical personnel at Parkland saw no small hole in the rear of Kennedy's head:

Dr. Kemp Clark, the Parkland neurosurgeon, was questioned by commission attorney Arlen Specter:

> SPECTER: Now, you described the massive wound at the top [sic] of the President's head. . . . Did you observe any other hole or wound on the President's head?
> CLARK: No, sir, I did not.
> SPECTER: Did you observe . . . a bullet hole or what appeared to be a bullet hole in the posterior scalp, approximately 2.5 cm laterally to the right, slightly above the external occipital protuberant, measuring 15 by 6 mm?
> CLARK: No, sir, I did not. (WCHE, v.6, p.25)

Dr. Malcolm Perry, who treated Kennedy in the emergency room, saw no bullet hole matching the description of the Warren Commission's entry hole:

> SPECTER: What did you observe as to the President's head, specifically?
> PERRY: I saw no injuries other than the one which I noted to you, which was a large avulsive injury of the right occipitoparietal area, but I did not do a minute examination of his head.
> SPECTER: Did you notice a bullet hole below the large avulsed area?
> PERRY: No, I did not. (WCHE, v.6, p.11)

Specter had no better luck with Dr. Charles Baxter:

SPECTER: Did you notice any bullet hole below that large opening at the top of the head?
BAXTER: No, I personally did not. (WCHE, v.6, p.42)

Emergency room nurse Diana Bowron didn't see the Warren Report's bullet entry hole either:

SPECTER: How many holes did you see?
BOWRON: I just saw one large hole.
SPECTER: Did you see a small bullet hole beneath that one large hole?
BOWRON: No, sir. (WCHE, v.6, p.136)

Dr. Adolph Giesecke didn't see a small hole either:

SPECTER: Did you observe any other wound or bullet hole below the large area of missing skull?
GIESECKE: No. (WCHE, v.6, p.74)

Dr. Robert McClelland was asked about his observation of the head wound:

SPECTER: You saw a large opening which you have already described?
MCCLELLAND: I saw the large opening which I have described.
SPECTER: Did you observe any other wound on the back of the head?
MCCLELLAND: No. (WCHE, v.6, p.35)

Dr. Charles Carrico described the large wound in the back of Kennedy's head, and was then asked by Specter:

SPECTER: Did you notice any other opening in the head besides the one you have just described?
CARRICO: No, sir. I did not. (WCHE, v.6, p.6)

Several observers at the Bethesda autopsy confirmed the observations of the Parkland doctors:

James Jenkins, lab technician during the autopsy at Bethesda, did "not recall a small hole in the head as drawn on the autopsy descriptive sheet. He said that the big hole would have covered the area where the little hole was drawn on the sheet." (Jenkins-Purdy HSCA Interview 8/29/1977, ARRB, MD65, p.12)

Paul O'Connor, another lab technician at the autopsy, told HSCA interviewers that there was a "massive hole, no little hole" in the back of Kennedy's head. The head wound led O'Connor to believe that "the bullet came in from the front right and blew out the top." (O'Connor-Purdy HSCA Interview 8/29/1977, ARRB, MD64, p.6)

From these responses it is clear that the key point which the commission sought to establish from the autopsy report, namely that a small bullet wound in the back of Kennedy's skull indicated he had been shot in the head from behind, received no support at all from the Parkland doctors and nurses who treated him. Not a single one of them reported seeing any hole in the back of his head except for the massive gaping wound which measured approximately 5 inches in diameter. The two lab technicians at the Bethesda autopsy also failed to see any small wound in the back of the head. They both confirmed the large hole described by the Parkland doctors.

At least 30 witnesses perceived shots coming from the grassy slope, the concrete pergola or the railroad tracks west of the TSBD:

(Directions used in these statements assume that Elm Street runs east and west, with the underpass and the railroad tracks on the west end, and the TSBD on the east end at the corner of Elm and Houston. The north curb of Elm Street is then the same side of the street as the TSBD and the Stemmons Freeway sign, and the south curb is the opposite side where the park or plaza is located. The grassy knoll is on the north side of Elm Street, sloping upward from the street.)

- Spectator William Eugene Newman thought that shots came "from the garden directly behind me." (WCHE, v.19, p.490) Newman was not called to testify before the commission, nor was his deposition taken.
- TSBD employee Victoria Adams, watching the motorcade from a 4th floor window, thought the shots came from her right, which would be in the direction of the grassy slope and the railroad tracks. (WCHE, v.6, p.388)
- TSBD employee Danny Arce heard shots coming from the railroad tracks to the west of the TSBD. (WCHE, v.6, p.366)
- TSBD employee Virgie Baker thought the shots came from the area near the underpass. (WCHE, v.7, p.510)
- TSBD vice-president O. V. Campbell believed the shots had come from the grassy area away from the TSBD. (As quoted by Mrs. Robert Reid at WCHE, v.3, p.274)
- TSBD supervisor William Shelley testified in his deposition that the sounds of the shots seemed to come from the west of the TSBD. (WCHE, v.6, p.329)
- TSBD building superintendent Roy Truly thought the shots came from west of the TSBD (WCHE, v.3, p.221), i.e., "from the vicinity of the railroad or the WPA project, behind the WPA project west of the building". (WCHE, v.3, p.227)
- Richard Carr, viewing the motorcade from the sixth floor level of the new courthouse on Houston Street, thought the shots came from the direction of the triple underpass. (CD385, pp.24-25)

- John Chism heard shots coming from behind while he was standing on the north side of Elm Street just east of the underpass, in front of the freeway sign. (CD205, p.38)
- M. Faye Chism (wife of John Chism) said the shots came from "behind us". (WCHE, v.19, p.472)
- Deputy Sheriff Harold Elkins submitted a report to the Sheriff's office stating that the shots sounded like they came from the "area between the railroads and the TSBD". (WCHE, v.19, p.540) Elkins was not called to testify in commission session, nor was his deposition taken.
- Deputy Sheriff Jack Faulkner rushed to the scene of the shooting and was told by a woman that the President had been shot through the head, and when Faulkner asked her where the shots had come from the woman pointed toward the concrete arcade." (WCHE, v.19, p.511)
- Police officer Joe Marshall Smith heard the shots and "thought they were coming from the bushes of the overpass." (WCHE, v.22, p.600a); In his deposition taken July 23, 1964, commission attorney Wesley Liebeler marks the spot indicated by Smith as being "there at the corner here behind this concrete structure where the bushes were down toward the railroad tracks." Smith agrees that this was the area where he thought the shots came from. (WCHE, v.7, p.536); As Smith was proceeding toward the scene of the shooting a woman told him, "They are shooting the President from the bushes." (WCHE, v.7, p.535)
- Motorcycle officer Bobby Hargis, riding on the left rear of the Presidential car, said "it sounded like the shots were right next to me." (WCHE, v.6, p.294)
- Jean Hill, who watched the motorcade from the south curb of Elm Street, told commission counsel Arlen Specter that she thought the shots were "coming from the knoll". (WCHE, v.6, p.212); She also saw a man running in the area near the top of the knoll, west of the TSBD. (WCHE, v.6, p.210); She saw him going toward the tracks, toward the west. (WCHE, v.6, p.211) Shortly thereafter, she heard someone yell, "It looks like he got away." (WCHE, v.6, p.213)
- Jesse Price also "saw a man run towards the passenger cars on the railroad siding." (WCHE, v.19, p.492) Price was not called to testify in commission session, nor was his deposition taken.
- In a statement to the Dallas County Sheriff's office, A. J. Millican wrote that he was "standing on the north side of Elm Street, about halfway between Houston and the underpass" and heard "three shots come from up toward Houston and Elm right by the Book Depository Building, and then immediately I heard two more shots come from the Arcade between the Book Store and the underpass, and then three more shots came from the same direction only sounded further back." (WCHE, v.19, p.486) Millican was not called to testify in commission session, nor was his deposition taken.

- Jean Newman heard shots coming from her right as she stood on the north side of Elm Street, just west of the Stemmons freeway sign. (WCHE, v.19, p.489) Newman was not called to testify before the commission, nor was her deposition taken.
- Railroad employee Frank Reilly thought the shots came from the trees west of the TSBD. (CD205, p.29); He repeated this at his deposition which was taken on April 8, 1964. (WCHE, v.6, p.230)
- Secret Service agent Emory Roberts, riding in the front seat of the follow-up car directly behind the President's car, wrote in his same-day report that "I could not determine from what direction the shots came, but felt they had come from the right side." (WCHE, v.18, p.739) Roberts was not called to testify before the commission, nor was his deposition taken.
- Secret Service agent Forrest Sorrels said in his typewritten statement of November 28, 1963 that he "looked towards the top of the terrace to my right as the sound of the shots seemed to come from that direction". (WCHE, v.21, p.548); In his deposition of May 7, 1964, Sorrels testified that "the noise from the shots sounded like they may have come back up on the terrace there." (WCHE, v.7, p.346)
- Secret Service agent Paul Landis, riding in the follow-up car behind the Presidential limousine, had the impression that the second shot "came from somewhere towards the front, right-hand side of the road". (WCHE, v.18, p.755) Landis was not called to testify before the commission, nor was his deposition taken.
- Presidential aide Kenneth O'Donnell, riding in the Secret Service follow-up car, testified in his deposition on May 18, 1964 that in his opinion, which was based in part on "reconstruction" the shots "came from the right rear." (WCHE, v.7, p.448) However, some years later O'Donnell told Congressman Tip O'Neill that he had heard two shots from behind the fence on the grassy knoll. (Quoted in David Talbot, *Brothers* (2007), p.293-294, citing Tip O'Neill's memoirs, *Man of the House: The Life and Political Memoirs of Speaker Tip O'Neill.*)
- Presidential aide David Powers, riding next to O'Donnell in the follow-up car, submitted an affidavit in which he stated that he "had a fleeting impression that the noise appeared to come from the front in the area of the triple overpass." (WCHE, v.7, p.473) Powers was not called to testify before the commission, nor was his deposition taken.
- Spectator James Tague, standing near the triple underpass, told commission attorney Wesley Liebeler that his impression was that the shots came from the concrete monument. Liebeler reminds him that "now we have other evidence that would indicate that the shots did come from the Texas School Book Depository". Liebeler then asks the leading question:

LIEBELER: Do you think that it is consistent with what you heard and saw that day, that the shots could have come from the sixth floor of the Texas School Book Depository?
TAGUE: Yes. (WCHE, v.7, p.557)

- Dallas police detective F. M. Turner interviewed several TSBD employees after the shooting, and said "they thought [the shots] all came from west of the building". (WCHE, v.7, p.219)
- Deputy Sheriff Harry Weatherford, in his report dated November 23, 1963, wrote that "it sounded as if [the first shot] came from the railroad yard." After hearing two more shots, he says "I was running towards the railroad yards where the sound seemed to come from." (WCHE, v.19, p.502)
- Officer Seymour Weitzman told the FBI that "he believed these sounds to have come from a northwesterly direction from where he was standing [at the corner of Main and Houston]. He heard someone say that the shots had come from behind a wooden fence which is located west and a little north of the intersection of Houston and Elm Streets." (CD5, p.124); Weitzman talked to a railroad yardman who "thought he saw somebody throw something through a bush." Indicating the source of the shots, this yardman "pointed out the wall section where there was a bunch of shrubbery." (WCHE, v.7, p.109)
- Standing near the base of the grassy slope, Mary Woodward stated in an interview with the FBI that her first reaction was that the shots had been fired from above her head and from possibly behind her. (WCHE, v.24, p.520a)
- Abraham Zapruder, who filmed the assassination from a concrete pillar on the north side of Elm Street, was asked in his deposition where he thought the shots came from:

LIEBELER: Did you have any impression as to the direction from which these shots came?
ZAPRUDER: No, I also thought it came from back of me. [based on his view of the President getting hit in the right side of the head, not from the sound of the shots] (WCHE, v.7, p.572)

Several witnesses saw smoke and/or smelled gunpowder in the area of the trees on the grassy slope.

Employees of the Union Terminal railroad company viewing the motorcade from the top of the overpass were well placed to observe the area around the fence and trees at the top of the grassy slope between the overpass and the TSBD. Several of these employees saw smoke in the area of the trees, or smelled gunpowder, when the shots were fired.

- Railroad employee S. M. Holland told the Dallas County Sheriff's Department that as President Kennedy slumped over, Holland "looked over toward the arcade and trees and saw a puff of smoke come from the trees." (WCHE, v.19, p.480)

- Another railroad employee, Austin Miller, in a statement to the Dallas County Sheriff's Department, said he "saw something which I thought was smoke or steam coming from a group of trees north of Elm off the railroad tracks." (WCHE, v.19, p.485)
- Clemon Johnson, a machinist for the Union Terminal Company, told the FBI that he observed white smoke near the pavilion at the top of the slope. Johnson "felt that this smoke came from a motorcycle abandoned near the spot by a Dallas policeman" but he does not claim that he actually saw smoke coming from the motorcycle. (WCHE, v.22, p.836a) Johnson was not called to testify before the commission, nor was his deposition taken.
- Patrolman Joe Marshall Smith told the FBI on December 9, 1963 that he smelled "what he thought was gunpowder" in the parking lot by the TSBD. (CD205, p.39)
- Patrolman E. V. Brown, who was stationed on the railroad overpass during the motorcade, told the FBI on December 9, 1963 that "he believed he could smell gunpowder in the air on the overpass." (CD205, p.40)
- Senator Ralph Yarborough, riding in the vice-presidential car two cars behind the President, smelled gunpowder and concluded from this that there had been shots fired from the front of the motorcade. "You don't smell gunpowder unless . . . it blows in your face," Yarborough was quoted as saying. Yarborough said "he could not have smelled the gunpowder if the shots had been fired from behind the motorcade." (Quoted in "JFK autopsy termed 'incompetent'", Dallas Times Herald, March 28, 1975, p.1B, reproduced in FBI 62-109060 JFK HQ File, Section 179, p.148)

The Zapruder film shows the impact of a bullet from the right front, as Kennedy's head is thrown backwards and to the left.

Probably the single most important piece of evidence in the Kennedy assassination is the movie film taken by Abraham Zapruder as he stood on the north side of Elm Street and watched through his viewfinder as the motorcade passed. Zapruder's film shows that at frame 313 Kennedy's head explodes in a halo of reddish-white blood and tissue, and the next several frames show his head reacting with a rapid acceleration toward the left rear of the car. This fact by itself proves that Kennedy's head was hit by a bullet coming from the right front. The science behind this conclusion is meticulously explained by physicist G. Paul Chambers in his book *Head Shot (2012)*, but we can briefly summarize the essential scientific points here.

The operative scientific principle in this case is the law of conservation of momentum, where the momentum of an object is equal to its mass times its velocity. In any physical system, the total momentum is constant. If we consider the head and the speeding bullet as our relevant physical system, and if we consider the head to be initially motionless, the total initial momentum in the system is that of the bullet. When the bullet hits the head, there are two extreme possibilities: (1) either the bullet goes through the head and out the other side, retaining most of its momentum, or (2) the bullet is stopped by the bone and brain tissue and thus transmits all of its momentum to the head. In the first case, very little movement of the head is to be expected, since the bullet retains most of its initial momentum as it passes through the head. In the second case the head accelerates in the direction that the bullet was traveling with a velocity such that the head's momentum (mass times velocity) is equal to that of the entering bullet. Between these two extremes the possibility exists that fragments of the bullet come to rest in the head, transmitting their momentum to the head, while other fragments exit the head and retain most of their momentum. If any tissue is ejected during this process then the momentum of that tissue must be taken into account in the conservation of total momentum in the system. The bottom line is that if the head stops the bullet, then the head itself must accelerate in the direction in which the bullet was travelling, in order to conserve the initial momentum. Or, to cite a different example, if you get punched in the face your head will recoil in the same direction as the punch. Your head will not jerk into the punch.

To apply this principle to the Kennedy head shot, we need to determine whether the bullet, or fragments of the bullet, came to rest in Kennedy's head, or whether it passed right through. Witnesses testified that bullet fragments were indeed recovered from Kennedy's head and there were numerous other fragments which were observed on X-rays but were not removed. These fragments coming to rest inside the head would have imparted their momentum to the head, causing a movement seen in the Zapruder film. Secret Service agent Kellerman, who was present at the Bethesda autopsy, described the recovered fragments to the commission:

SPECTER: Now, did you observe, during the course of the autopsy, bullet fragments which you might describe as little stars?
KELLERMAN: Yes, of the numerous X-rays that were taken mainly of the skull, the head. . . . From the X-rays, when you placed the X-ray up against the light the whole head looked like a little mass of stars; there must have been 30, 40 lights where these pieces were so minute that they couldn't be reached. . . . However, all through this series of X-rays this was the one that they found, through X-ray that was above the right eye, and they removed that.
SPECTER: How big a piece was that above the right eye, would you say?
KELLERMAN: The tip of a matchhead, a little larger." (WCHE, v.2, p.100)

The report by FBI agents James Sibert and Francis O'Neill, who attended the autopsy, recorded that "two fragments of metal were removed by Dr. Humes, namely, one fragment measuring 7x2 mm, which was removed from the right side of the brain. An additional fragment of metal measuring 1x3 mm was also removed from this area." (Sibert O'Neill report, CD7, p.284)

Dr. Humes, who conducted the autopsy, said that the X-rays disclosed "multiple minute fragments of radio opaque material . . . with a rather sizable fragment visible by X-ray just above the right eye." [and] "between 30 or 40 tiny dustlike particle fragments of radio opaque material." These were "less than 1 mm in size for the most part." (WCHE, v.2, p.353)

Dr. Kemp Clark, the director of neurological surgery at Parkland, observed Kennedy's head wound and concluded that the head wound was a tangential wound, i.e., a wound caused by the bullet "striking the object obliquely, not squarely or head on." Dr. Clark explained the effects of such a tangential wound:

> SPECTER: Will you describe at this time in somewhat greater detail the consequences of a tangential wound as contrasted with another type of a striking? . . .
> CLARK: The effects of any missile striking an organ [is] a function of the energy which is shed by the missile in passing through this organ. When a bullet strikes the head, if it is able to pass through rapidly without shedding any energy into the brain, little damage results, other than that part of the brain which is directly penetrated by the missile. However, if it strikes the skull at an angle, it must then penetrate much more bone than normal, [and] therefore is likely to shed more energy, striking the brain a more powerful blow." (WCHE, v.6, p.21)

Dr. Humes, in his handwritten autopsy report, originally wrote that the entry wound in the back of the head was "tangential to the surface of the scalp" (WCHE, v.17, p.36) but these words are crossed out and do not appear in his typewritten autopsy report.

This evidence shows that the fatal head shot did not penetrate as a whole bullet passing through Kennedy's head from the rear, but that the bullet fragmented, leaving many particles inside the skull and imparting much of its momentum to the head as it made a tangential hit on the right side of the President's skull. As we will see later, questions remain as to whether additional bullet fragments were removed from the head, but not described in official reports. The straightforward conclusion to be drawn from the evidence presented in this chapter, based on both scientific principle and on common sense interpretation of the testimony, is that a shot was fired at Kennedy from the front right side. Despite this evidence, most of which was ignored by the Warren Commission, the commission's report concluded that "*there is no evidence* that any shots were fired at the President from anywhere other than the Texas School Book Depository Building." (WCR, p.639-640)

Refuting the pseudoscientific rebuttals from the lone gunman theorists.

Various speculative theories have been put forth to explain the physical evidence by those who claim that Oswald alone fired the shots that struck Kennedy and Connally. These theories can only be maintained by ignoring the evidence presented above, and by misapplying basic scientific principles. We will deal briefly here with two of these theories: the so-called "jet effect" and the "neuromuscular reaction".

The "jet effect" is a popular name for Newton's third law of motion, which states that "for every action there is an equal and opposite reaction". The claim is that tissue ejected toward the front right by a bullet striking the back of the head would cause the head to jerk backward and to the left, as shown in the film. But the film and the witnesses testify that there was no "jet" of tissue flying out of the right front of Kennedy's head. Instead, the film and the witnesses testify to an "explosion" of Kennedy's head, with blood and tissue flying in multiple directions resembling a "halo". (WCHE, v.7, p.496) The large "jet" of matter flying upward would therefore contribute nothing to any recoiling of the head toward the left rear. Because only a small portion of the ejected tissue is seen to be exiting horizontally from the side of the head, physicist Paul Chambers calculates that this matter would have to be traveling at supersonic speed in order to produce the required momentum to propel the head backward as shown in the film. (Chambers, *Head* Shot, p.164) Moreover, if this tissue were traveling supersonically, we would not be able to see it, anymore than we can see a bullet traveling supersonically.

Some witnesses even reported tissue being ejected from the *left rear* of Kennedy's head, just the opposite from what the "jet" theory would require. Associated Press photographer James Altgens was standing on the south curb of Elm Street when Kennedy was hit in the head. Altgens testified that "there was flesh particles that flew out of the side of his head in my direction from where I was standing, so much so that it indicated to me that the shot came out of the left side of his head." (WCHE, v.7, 518) Motorcycle patrolman Bobby Hargis, who was riding on the outside *left rear* of the Presidential car, told the commission: "I was splattered with blood and brain". (WCHE, v.6, p.294)

Finally, the "jet effect" theory fails because a presumed jet of tissue ejected to the front right, propelling the head rearward and to the left, would require a shot to enter the head from the left rear. No such shot location is claimed by any witnesses and no such shot is seen on the Zapruder film.

There are videos to be found on youtube.com where a rifleman shoots at a cantaloupe (or other suitable produce) which rests on a stool or platform. The bullet goes right through the center of the cantaloupe and out the other side, while the cantaloupe itself rolls lazily backwards off the platform toward the shooter. This is supposed to prove that a shot from behind could have hit the back of Kennedy's head and resulted in the backward thrust seen in the Zapruder film. First of all, the slow roll does not mimic the violent head thrust seen in the film. Another flaw in this reasoning is that the experiment does not reproduce the exact nature of the head shot, which was, according to Dr. Clark, a tangential strike. As Dr. Clark testified, such a hit would impart much more energy to the head than would a shot which goes right through the center of the head and out the other side, striking less bone. From the standpoint of scientific theory, these amateur experiments are fundamentally flawed because they consider only the ejected tissue and do not include the momentum of the bullet in the total momentum of the entire system, where some of the bullet's momentum is transferred to the head. Thus, the fruit experiments are not relevant to explaining the rapid acceleration of the head toward the back and left.

Newton's third law derives from the more fundamental principle of conservation of momentum. The reason that a rocket is thrust forward by a jet of gases expelled from the rear is that the momentum of the rocket system must be conserved. Since the rocket on the launch pad had a momentum of zero, the rocket system in flight must also have a momentum of zero. The forward momentum of the rocket is negated by the backward momentum of the gases, resulting in a net momentum of zero, and the initial momentum is thereby conserved. Thus, the "jet effect" theory is simply a crude application of the law of conservation of momentum, which has already been discussed above. It is also worth pointing out that the conservation laws are among the most basic and fundamental of all physical principles. Most of the laws of basic physics derive directly or indirectly from the conservation laws.

Finally, the jet effect argument is only an argument for the *possibility* that ejected tissue propelled the head backward. It cannot conclusively establish that this scenario actually occurred. The experiments with cantaloupes can, at best, only show that it is *possible* to produce a backward reaction with a shot from behind. But the overwhelming testimony from many witnesses that a shot was in fact fired from the fence area atop the grassy slope, and the testimony of medical personnel and others that Kennedy sustained a bullet wound in the right temple, overcome any alternative scenario based only on possibility. The jet effect theory is inconsistent with the weight of the evidence, besides being scientifically flawed.

The argument that Kennedy's head movement resulted from a "neuromuscular reaction" is no more convincing than the jet effect argument. The neuromuscular theory was not invented by the Warren Commission. It was put forth years later by Larry Sturdivan, who was a research scientist for the U. S. Army's Aberdeen Proving Ground. Sturdivan testified before the House Select Committee on Assassinations (HSCA) on September 8, 1978. The gist of his argument may be briefly summarized as follows. Sturdivan calculates that the kinetic energy possessed by a 6.5 mm Mannlicher-Carcano bullet would not be sufficient to create the rapid head movement to the left rear shown in the Zapruder film. "The deposit of momentum from the bullet is not sufficient to cause any dramatic movement in any direction." (HSCA, v.1, p.414) Therefore, he says, the source of the head movement must be sought elsewhere. Sturdivan interprets the head movement as a "neuromuscular reaction". Sturdivan describes his theory: "Now, the extreme radial velocity imparted to the matter in the President's head, the brain tissue, caused mechanical movement of essentially everything inside the skull, including where the cord went through the foramen magnum, that is, the hole that leads out of the skull down the spinal cord. Motion there, *I believe,* caused mechanical stimulation of the motor nerves of the President, and since all motor nerves were stimulated at the same time, then every muscle in the body would be activated at the same time. . . . The muscles in the back of the trunk are much stronger than the abdominals and, therefore, the body would arch backward." (HSCA, v.1, p.415) In other words, he allows the bullet to impart "extreme radial velocity" to "everything inside the skull", but he maintains that the bullet imparts no acceleration to the skull itself. The material inside the skull supposedly presses upon the foramen magnum, but exerts no pressure on the skull and does not cause the skull to move. This is a bizarre concept where the momentum of the bullet is transferred entirely to the tissue inside the skull, but none of the momentum is transferred to the skull itself. There is no scientific basis for this targeted application of the bullet's momentum.

In support of his curious theory, Sturdivan shows the committee members a 1948 film of an experiment in which a live goat is shot between the eyes. The goat film shows that "the back legs go out, under the influence of the powerful muscles of the back legs, the front legs go upward and outward, that back arches, as the powerful back muscles overcome those of the abdomen." (HSCA, v.1, p.417) Anecdotal testimony is given by Sturdivan and by Rep. Floyd Fithian of the committee that if a jack rabbit is shot in the head it has a neuromuscular reaction which causes its powerful leg muscles to contract, launching the rabbit into the air. Rep. Fithian corroborates Sturdivan's assertion by saying "I have many years ago hunted these animals and what Mr. Sturdivan has testified to is not at all unusual." (HSCA, v.1, p.416)

The neuromuscular theory fails on multiple grounds. First of all, in calculating that a shot from the knoll would not have sufficient energy to produce the abrupt head movement seen in the film, Sturdivan mistakenly assumes that this gunman would have been using the same kind of Italian rifle which was allegedly found on the sixth floor of the TSBD. There is no justification for this assumption. A grassy knoll gunman would not necessarily have used a Mannlicher-Carcano rifle. Sturdivan correctly states the equation for kinetic energy as $E = \frac{1}{2} mv^2$. That is, the kinetic energy of the bullet (or any other moving object) is equal to $\frac{1}{2}$ times the mass of the bullet times the square of the bullet's velocity. Now, Sturdivan does not tell the committee what figure he used for the velocity of a Mannlicher-Carcano bullet, but testimony before the Warren Commission by FBI firearms expert Robert Frazier tells us that the rifle in evidence as Commission Exhibit 139 had an average muzzle velocity of 2165 feet per second. (WCHE, v.3, p.400) Frazier described this as "very low velocity". (WCHE, v.3, p.414) At 200 feet downrange, the velocity of the speeding bullet is approximately 2000 feet per second. (Testimony of Ronald Simmons, WCHE, v.3, p.443). Sturdivan does not trace out his calculations step-by-step, but given that these calculations are based on the assumption of a Mannlicher-Carcano bullet, and given that this velocity is approximately 2000 feet per second, it is not surprising that he obtained a relatively low figure for the energy that would have been imparted to the head and that he would have concluded that this impact was insufficient to produce the observed head movement. But in *Head Shot,* physicist Paul Chambers calculates the effect of a shot from the knoll using a Winchester .220 Swift rifle, which has a muzzle velocity of approximately 4000 feet per second, or almost twice the velocity of the Mannlicher-Carcano bullet. Since energy increases proportionally to the *square* of the velocity, this doubling of the velocity would cause the kinetic energy of the bullet to be quadrupled, as compared to the result obtained by Sturdivan using the Mannlicher-Carcano data. Chambers calculates that this energy would have been quite sufficient to produce the head movement recorded by Zapruder's film. (Chambers, *Head Shot,* p.208-209)

Sturdivan tells the House committee that the neuromuscular reaction would have activated *all the muscles* in the body at the same time. Specifically, he claims that "in an arm, for instance, this would have activated the biceps muscle but it would have also activated the triceps muscle, which being more powerful, would have straightened the arm out." (HSCA, v.1, p.415) Anyone viewing the Zapruder film can plainly see that after the head shot in frame 313, Kennedy's right arm does not straighten out, as Sturdivan's theory predicts, but instead flops limply in the air as the head and shoulders fly backwards. This is a direct refutation of Sturdivan's neuromuscular theory.

Sturdivan offers no experimental or theoretical support for his neuromuscular theory except for the goat film and the anecdotal jack rabbit tales. Even the lukewarm support offered by the experiences of Rep. Fithian turns out to refute his theory. Fithian says that in hunting jack rabbits he has found that the reaction postulated by Sturdivan is "not at all unusual". He does not say that it happens all the time, or even that it happens most of the time. He only says it is "not unusual". Depending on his definition of "unusual" the neuromuscular reaction might not be considered unusual even if it occurred only 10% or 20% of the time. In order for the neuromuscular reaction to be valid as an operative principle it must either occur in every situation where a person or animal is shot in the head, or it must be shown what factors influence its occurrence or non-occurrence, and then it must be shown that those factors which produce the reaction were present in the specific case of President Kennedy. As it stands, there is no experimental evidence that shows with what frequency this neuromuscular reaction occurs in real life scenarios, or what factors determine its presence or absence.

Sturdivan's qualifications to serve as an expert in the effect of bullet wounds on living humans is questionable. He describes himself as an "expert" in wound ballistics (HSCA, v.1, p.385), but then admits that in his work he typically works with simulated tissue made from gelatin, and occasionally with animal tissue. (HSCA, v.1, p.388) Although simulated gelatin tissue might be adequate for studying the deformation characteristics of bullets, Sturdivan admits that the gel and the animal tissue are not ideal for assessing the effects of bullet wounds on human tissue.

> REP. MATHEWS: You indicate you also use animal tissue, is that correct?
> STURDIVAN: Yes, sir.
> MATHEWS: Is that as good as human tissue for experimentation purposes?
> STURDIVAN: For the effects on human beings, no, of course not. But then we don't get that many volunteers. [Laughter.] (HSCA, v.1, p.388)

Acknowledging Sturdivan's expertise in physics, Rep. Dodd asks Sturdivan about his background in anatomy and physiology, and finds that it is mostly confined to academic coursework:

> DODD: Are you qualified to talk about anatomical responses and so forth, and, if so, what is your background in that area?
> STURDIVAN: Yes, sir, I did take a considerable amount of biology in high school and college. I took some graduate courses in physiology, and then, of course, I continued that biological training on the job, because it is a necessary part of wound ballistics." (HSCA, v.1, p.418)

Sturdivan's lack of experience with actual bullet wounds on human victims is displayed in an exchange with Rep. Fithian. Fithian notes that the entry wound on Gov. Connally's back was elliptical and not circular. He then asks:

> FITHIAN: So, is it your judgment, then, that the bullet had to have struck something else and was tumbling when it hit Governor Connally?
> STURDIVAN: If it indeed had the shape that was described, then it would have to have been yawed and having been yawed, it would require that it struck something else before it struck the Governor. (HSCA, v.1, p.423)

But it is not necessary for a bullet to have struck another object in order to produce an elliptical wound. An elliptical entry wound can also be produced by a bullet that strikes on a tangent, as Dr. Robert Shaw testified to the Warren Commission. Shaw, a practicing surgeon, had experience treating actual gunshot victims. He told the Warren Commission that the shape of the entrance wound in Connally's back "was long enough so that there might have been some tumbling. . . . It was not a spherical puncture wound. . . . The wound entrance was an elliptical wound. In other words, it had a long diameter and a short diameter. . . . Now, you have to also take into consideration, however, whether the bullet enters at a right angle or at a tangent. If it enters at a tangent there will be some length to the wound of entrance." (WCHE, v.6, 95)

The fact that Sturdivan did not mention the possibility of an oblique angle of contact causing an elliptical entry hole shows that his answer to this question was incomplete. We cannot say whether this was definitely due to his lack of experience in studying and treating actual gunshot wounds in real life. But it does make us wonder how many of Sturdivan's other answers to the House committee were incomplete or misleading. None of the committee members apparently had the scientific background to submit Sturdivan to effective cross-examination, so any weaknesses in his testimony may well have gone undetected during his appearance before the HSCA.

The foregoing evidence shows that the "neuromuscular reaction" is not scientifically based, is not consistent with the facts of the case, and that Sturdivan does not have the experience with gunshot wounds in live patients to serve as an expert in this area.

Conclusion:

The evidence presented in this section shows beyond a reasonable doubt that Kennedy was struck in the head by a bullet fired from the right front. Since this is not consistent with a shot from the TSBD sixth floor window, the existence of a second gunman is proven. The legal implications of this conclusion are significant. The Warren Report concluded that "President Kennedy could have survived the neck injury, but the head wound was fatal." (WCR, p.55) If the fatal head shot was fired from the right side, from somewhere behind the fence at the top of the grassy slope, then this suggests that whatever shots were fired from behind were not fatal, and any shooters firing from the TSBD were not guilty of murder, but only of attempted murder or conspiracy to commit murder. Thus, even if Oswald was the one firing from the TSBD, the evidence shows that he may not have been the one who killed the President. A shot from the TSBD may have wounded Kennedy in the back, or may have wounded Connally, but the fatal head shot came from elsewhere. (There is a possible exception, however. If Kennedy was hit simultaneously with two shots to the head, there could have been fatal shots fired from both front and rear.)

This combination of evidence gains strength by coming from many different witnesses, in multiple locations, with different perspectives. Some of the witnesses were in the motorcade. Others were spectators in the streets and on the overpass in Dealey Plaza. Some observed the President's wounds as he was being treated at Parkland Hospital. Others were witnesses to the autopsy at Bethesda. The testimony of all these witnesses, along with the medical evidence and the Zapruder film, points to a gunshot wound on the right side of the head and to a gunman on the grassy slope firing the fatal head shot.

THE SHOTS FROM BEHIND PROVE TWO GUNMEN FIRING FROM THE REAR

The Warren Commission Report stated that a "bullet wound was observed near the base of the back of President Kennedy's neck, slightly to the right of his spine." (WCR, p.87) Other evidence shows this location to be incorrect, but the commission used this presumed entry wound in the back of the neck to deduce that the wound observed in the front of Kennedy's neck was an exit wound and that a bullet had thus traversed his neck from back to front, and so had "confirmed the Bethesda surgeons' conclusion that the bullet had exited from the front part of the neck." (WCR, p.89) Furthermore, the commission asserted that "there is very persuasive evidence from the experts to indicate that the same bullet which pierced the President's throat also caused Governor Connally's wounds." There was not unanimous agreement among the commission members on this "single bullet theory". Senator Russell in particular had strong doubts that one bullet struck both men. The commission's report tries to accommodate these doubts by noting that "Governor Connally's testimony and certain other factors have given rise to some difference of opinion as to this probability but there is no question in the mind of any member of the Commission that all the shots which caused the President's and Governor Connally's wounds were fired from the sixth floor window of the Texas School Book Depository." (WCR, p.19)

But here the commission falls into a logical trap. Because of certain constraints imposed by the evidence, in particular the timeframe established by the Zapruder film, Kennedy and Connally must have been struck by a single bullet if all the shots were fired by the same bolt-action rifle located in the sixth-floor window of the TSBD. If they were not, and instead were struck by consecutive bullets, then there is no way three shots could have been fired by a single gunman from the TSBD within the required time limit, using the Italian rifle in evidence as CE139. Either the first shot passed through Kennedy and then caused all of Connally's wounds, or there were two shooters firing from behind the car. But the overwhelming weight of the evidence shows that Kennedy and Connally were hit too far apart for a single bullet to have inflicted all their injuries, and too close together for two shots to have been fired from the Italian bolt-action rifle. Therefore, the evidence shows that there must have been two gunmen firing from behind the Presidential car.

Establishing the timeframe

The Warren Commission Report states that "it is probable that the President was not shot before frame 210 [of the Zapruder film], since it is unlikely that the assassin would deliberately have shot at him with a view obstructed by the oak tree when he was about to have a clear opportunity." (WCR, p.98) This assessment is consistent with the fact that Kennedy is seen going behind the Stemmons Freeway sign around frame 200 with his right arm up waving to the crowd. He is seen emerging from behind the sign at frame 225 with his hands up near his throat in a distressed pose indicating that he has already been hit. Thus, the commission concluded that "the President was not hit until at least frame 210 and that he was probably hit by frame 225." (WCR, p.105) Kennedy was shot in the head at frame 313 of the Zapruder film, and the overwhelming consensus among eyewitnesses is that no more shots were fired after the head shot. Thus, if three shots were fired using the Italian rifle (CE139), they all would have had to be fired within the interval of frames 210 to 313. FBI photographic expert Lyndal Shaneyfelt determined that Zapruder's movie camera ran at 18.3 frames per second (WCHE, v.5, p.153). Thus, 103 frames running at 18.3 frames per second covers a time span of 5.6 seconds. If the timing is started at the time of the first shot, then the three shots must have been no more than 2.8 seconds apart. In order to fit three shots into the 5.6 second interval, a shooter would have to be able to fire the first shot, operate the bolt and re-aim in 2.8 seconds, fire the second shot, operate the bolt and re-aim again in 2.8 seconds, and then fire the third shot. The Warren Report uses 2.3 seconds as the minimum time required between shots of the rifle, which fits within the maximum 5.6 second interval. (We will examine later whether this estimate is realistic or probable.)

But this scenario requires that the shots be evenly spaced. If the shots were not evenly spaced, then either the time between shots 2 and 3, or between 1 and 2, must be reduced below the minimum time required to operate the bolt, or the minimum time to fire three shots must be increased beyond the allowed 5.6 seconds. Secret Service Agent Forrest Sorrels estimated the interval between shots 1 and 2 as double the interval between shots 2 and 3. (WCHE, v.7, p.345) Dallas Mayor Earle Cabell also estimated a 2:1 ratio between the first interval and the second. (WCHE, v.7, p.478). This would give a minimum firing time for 3 shots of 6.9 seconds (2x2.3 = 4.6 seconds between shots 1 and 2, and 2.3 seconds between 2 and 3), which is well beyond the time limit of 5.6 seconds imposed by the Zapruder film. As we shall see later, many other witnesses also reported the same uneven shot pattern.

With these time constraints established, we now turn to the facts of the matter, to determine whether Kennedy and Connally were indeed struck by a single bullet, causing all their wounds (except for the Kennedy head injuries).

Kennedy's wound was in the back, not in the back of the neck.

It is absolutely critical to the single bullet theory that Kennedy's back wound be high above the back in the region of the lower neck in order to be traveling downward at the proper angle when exiting the front of Kennedy's neck and striking Connally in the back. The evidence shows that the bullet did not strike the base of the back of the neck, but struck lower down on the back and did not penetrate his body, so did not exit from the front of his throat. Thus, the physical and eyewitness evidence disproves the single bullet theory. This means that Kennedy and Connally were hit with two separate bullets, within a timeframe which was too short to accommodate two separate shots with the Italian bolt-action rifle. Therefore, there were at least two gunmen firing at the car from behind.

The back wound was on the back, not at the base of the neck:

- Dr. Humes, the autopsy surgeon, wrote in his autopsy report that this wound was "in the upper right posterior thorax." (CE387, WCHE, v.16, p.981) ("Thorax" is the medical term for the upper body *below* the neck, i.e., the chest.)

- Secret Service Agent Glen Bennett, riding in the follow-up car directly behind the Presidential limousine, saw the first shot hit Kennedy in the back. In a report written the day after the assassination, Bennett wrote that he "saw the shot hit the President about four inches down from the right shoulder." (CE1024, WCHE, v.18, p.760) Bennett was well-placed to have a good view of the President, since the follow-up car was following closely, only a few feet behind the President's car according to driver Will Greer (WCHE, v.2, p.116)

- Agent Clint Hill, who was present at Bethesda late Friday night when the autopsy was taking place, was asked by Roy Kellerman to come into the morgue to view Kennedy's body after the autopsy. In his report of November 30, 1963, Hill wrote that "I observed a wound about six inches down from the neckline on the back just to the right of the spinal column." (CE1024, WCHE, v.18, p.744) In testimony before the commission, Hill testified that "I saw an opening in the back, about 6 inches below the neckline to the right-hand side of the spinal column." (WCHE, v.2, p.143)

- The President's personal physician, Admiral George Burkley, wrote on Kennedy's White House death certificate, dated November 23, 1963, that a "wound occurred in the posterior back at about the level of the third thoracic vertebra." (ARRB, MD6, p.2) [The thoracic vertebrae are below the cervical vertebrae, which are the bones of the neck.]

- In an Executive Session of the Warren Commission on January 27, 1964, General Counsel Lee Rankin told the commission members that "the bullet entered below the shoulder blade to the right of the backbone, which is below the place where the picture shows the bullet came out in the neckband of the shirt in front." (Warren Commission Executive Session of January 27, 1964, p.193) [Thus, the bullet would have had to travel upward in order to reach the spot in the front of the neck where it supposedly exited and headed for Gov. Connally.]

- The Autopsy Descriptive Sheet (face sheet) contains an illustration which shows the back wound down in the area of the right shoulder blade (CE397, WCHE, v.17, p.45), and not at the base of the back of the neck as shown in the cartoon drawing CE385 (WCHE, v.16, p.977)

- Even Arlen Specter, the architect of the single bullet theory, referred to the wounds in the President's *"back* and head", not "neck and head", in a memo to General Counsel Lee Rankin dated April 30, 1964. (HSCA, v.11, p.92)

Despite this evidence, autopsy doctor James Humes identified the back wound as "a wound in the low posterior neck of the President." (WCHE, v.2, p.361)

Kennedy's clothing confirms the location of the back wound:
The coat and shirt worn by Kennedy at the time of the shooting provide corroboration for the location of the back wound being 5 to 6 inches down from the collar, and not at the base of the back of the neck, as stated in the autopsy report.

- FBI expert Robert Frazier testified that "there was located on the rear of the coat 5-3/8 inches below the top of the collar, a hole, further located as 1-3/4 inches to the right of the midline or the seam down the center of the coat." (WCHE, v.5, p.59)
- On the back of Kennedy's shirt, Frazier found "a hole, 5-3/4 inches below the top of the collar, and as you look at the back of the shirt 1-1/8 inch to the right of the midline of the shirt." The holes in the coat and shirt are positioned such that Frazier concludes that both holes were made by the same bullet. (WCHE, v.5, p.60)
- The FBI's Supplemental Investigation Report states: "There was a small hole in the back of his coat and shirt approximately six inches below the top of the collar and two inches to the right of the middle seam of the coat." (CD107, p.2)
- In questioning Dr. Humes, Arlen Specter acknowledges that the coat has an entry hole "approximately 6 inches below the top of the collar, and 2 inches to the right of the middle seam of the coat." (WCHE, v.2, p.365)

A bullet entering 5 or 6 inches below the collar would have to turn upward in order to be able to exit Kennedy's body at the location of the frontal neck wound, then would have to turn downward again in order to hit Connally at the correct angle. This creates a severe inconvenience for the single bullet theory. In order to restore the wound location to the base of the neck and maintain a straight line of flight for the bullet, Dr. Humes speculated that Kennedy's "well developed set of muscles" in his upper body "would have a tendency to push the portions of the coat which show the defects here somewhat higher on the back of the President than on a man of less muscular development." Humes notes the action of waving to the crowd shown in the Zapruder film and adds, "I believe that this action would further accentuate the elevation of the coat and the shirt with respect to the back of the President." Specter accepts this explanation and moves on (WCHE, v.2, p.366)

Humes offers no explanation for how a man's musculature would have any effect on the height of his coat and shirt. It is also unclear how a tucked-in shirt with a buttoned collar, and an untucked coat with no front collar, would move up on the back by exactly the same amount so that the holes occurred in roughly the same position on both the shirt and coat. No experiments were conducted by the commission to test whether in fact the shirt and coat would ride up 6 inches on the back of a man with Kennedy's body type. Anyone can test this theory for himself by putting on a coat and tie with the shirt collar buttoned and waving his hand, as Kennedy did in the car, to see whether the coat and the tucked-in shirt move 6 inches from his back up to his neck. (The films show that when Kennedy was waving, his elbow was roughly at the level of his ear. His hand was not extended high above his head.) Clearly, Humes' speculative theory is mere fantasy and contrary to experience. In any case, it is debatable whether Kennedy's physique was exceptionally muscular. He certainly was not bulky in his physique. In fact, he was rather slender. The White House death certificate signed by Dr. Burkley lists Kennedy's height as 72 inches (6 feet) and his weight as 172 pounds. (ARRB MD6, p.1) This puts him physically in a class with major league second basemen, though he is a little bit on the low end in his weight, even for second basemen. (See mlb chart at "Here's the Ideal Body Type for Every Sport," at www.businessinsider.com/average-height-weight-nfl-nba-players-2014-8.)

Specter was on his guard to correct witnesses who spoke of the back wound as a back wound or shoulder wound. When Secret Service agent Thomas Kelley spoke of "the wound in the shoulder", Specter interrupted him to ask "By 'the wound in the shoulder' do you mean 'the wound in the back of the President's neck', the base of his neck?" Kelley agreed that that was what he had meant. (WCHE, v.5, p.175)

The bullet which wounded Kennedy in the back did not pass through his body:

- The FBI's Sibert-O'Neill report on the autopsy described the examination of the back wound: "Dr. Humes located an opening which appeared to be a bullet hole which was below the shoulders and two inches to the right of the middle line of the spinal column. This opening was probed by Dr. Humes with the finger, at which time it was determined that the trajectory of the missile entering at this point had entered at a downward position of 45 to 60 degrees. Further probing determined that the distance travelled by this missile was a short distance, inasmuch as the end of the opening could be felt with the finger." (Sibert-O'Neill report, CD7, p.284)
- Dr. Humes wrote in his autopsy report: "The missile path through the fascia and musculature cannot be easily probed." (WCHE, v.16, p.981)
- In his testimony before the commission, Humes testified that "attempts to probe in the vicinity of this wound were unsuccessful without fear of making a false passage. . . . We were unable . . . to take probes and have them satisfactorily fall through any definite path." (WCHE, v.2, p.361)
- In view of his inability to discover a passage from the back bullet hole to the front neck wound, Humes can only speculate that the front neck wound is "presumably" an exit wound, where the word "presumably" was inserted as an afterthought into his handwritten autopsy draft. (WCHE, v.17, p.39)
- Secret Service Agent Roy Kellerman, who attended the autopsy, testified that when he asked Col. Pierre Finck where the bullet went that hit the back, Finck replied: "There are no lanes for an outlet of this entry in this man's shoulder." (WCHE, v.2, p.93)

- Secret Service driver Will Greer, who also attended the autopsy, said that the doctors probed the back wound to see if they could find a bullet, but he heard no one say anything about a path being traced through from the back to the front of the neck. (WCHE, v.2, p.127)

- James Curtis Jenkins, a lab technician who assisted at the autopsy, told researcher David Lifton in 1979 that "the civilians who seemed to be in charge [at the autopsy] seemed to be trying to get Humes to conclude that a bullet passed from back to front through the body. Jenkins had a clear recollection that that wasn't possible. He remembered very clearly Humes' probing the back wound with his little finger. 'What sticks out in my mind,' Jenkins told [Lifton] 'is the fact that Commander Humes put his little finger in it, and, you know, said that . . . he could probe the bottom of it with his finger, which would mean to me [it was] very shallow." (David Lifton, *Best Evidence,* 1988 ed., p.612)

- Presidential aide Kenneth O'Donnell, riding in the Secret Service follow-up car, testified that the first shot hit Kennedy "and threw him to the left." (WCHE, v.7, p.449) This bullet could not have thrown Kennedy to the left if it had passed through his body hitting no bony structures and retaining nearly all of its momentum. It could only throw him to the left if it transmitted most of its momentum to Kennedy's body by coming to rest in his back. But in this case it would not have any momentum left to traverse the body and exit from the front of the neck.

- Secret Service agent Clint Hill, riding on the left running board of the Presidential follow-up car, also saw Kennedy "lurch forward and to the left" with the first shot, indicating a transfer of momentum from the bullet to the body, and implying that this bullet did not transit Kennedy's body while hitting only soft tissue. (WCHE, v.2, p.138)

Conclusion:

The Warren Report's claim that "the doctors traced the course of the bullet through the body" is contrary to the evidence. (WCR, p.60) Dr. Humes' opinion that the bullet entered the back of Kennedy's neck and exited through the front was not based on any anatomical examination. It was an inference, a deduction based on the premises that a bullet entered the back, no bullet was found in the body, and there was a wound ("presumably" of exit, as Humes wrote in his report) in the front of the neck. There was some bruising of soft tissue in Kennedy's neck. Ergo, there must have been a bullet passing through from the back and exiting out the front of the neck. But no actual bullet path was ever traced by dissecting the neck. The transiting of the neck by the bullet is not an observation, it is merely an exercise in logic.

Eyewitness testimony disproves the single bullet theory, showing that Kennedy and Connally were hit with two separate shots.

- Gov. Connally testified that he was sure that he and Kennedy were hit with separate shots. After hearing the first shot, Connally turned to his right, toward the President, did not see him out of the corner of his eye, and started to turn back to the left when he felt the second shot hit him in the back. (WCHE, v.4, p.132-133) Connally noted that the first shot could not have been the one that hit him, because he heard this shot before he himself was hit. Since bullets travel faster than sound, Connally knew that when he heard the first shot the bullet had already reached its target, so the first bullet could not be the one that struck Connally himself. When he felt the second shot hit him, he knew that this had to be a different bullet than the first one which he had heard being fired. (WCHE, v.4, p.135-136)

- Nellie Connally the Governor's wife, testified that when she heard the first shot, "I turned over my right shoulder and looked back, and saw the President as he had both hands at his neck. . . . Then very soon there was the second shot that hit John. . . . [and he] just crumpled like a wounded animal to the right." (WCHE, v.4, p.147)

- Witness Jean Hill, standing on the south curb of Elm Street, testified that as the limousine passed directly in front of her the President was hit with the first shot, and Connally with the second. She says that's "just the way it looked." (WCHE, v.6, p.209)

- Witness Gayle Newman, who was standing on the north side of Elm Street, told the Sheriff's Department in a statement dated 11/22/63 that she saw Connally get hit with the second shot. "When President Kennedy's car was about ten feet from us, I heard a noise that sounded like a firecracker going off. President Kennedy kind of jumped like he was startled and covered his head with his hands and then raised up. After I heard the first shot, another shot sounded and Governor Connally kind of grabbed his chest and lay back on the seat of the car." (WCHE, v.19, p.488)

- Presidential Assistant David Powers, who rode in the follow-up car, stated in an affidavit dated May 18, 1964, that Gov. Connally fell over with the second shot. "The first shot went off and it sounded to me as if it were a firecracker. I noticed then that the President moved quite far to his left after the shot from the extreme right hand side where he had been sitting. There was a second shot, and Governor Connally disappeared from sight and then there was a third shot which took off the top of the President's head." (WCHE, v.7, p.473)

- Motorcycle officer Douglas L. Jackson, who was riding on the outside right rear of the Presidential limousine, heard a loud noise like a backfire. Then he looked toward the car and at the same time heard a second loud report, which he recognized as gunfire. Jackson observed Connally jerk to the right simultaneously with this second shot. (*FBI 62-109060 JFK HQ File, Section*

181, pp.93) Jackson was interviewed by the FBI in 1975. He was never interviewed by the Warren Commission or the FBI before his 1975 interview.

Both the Secret Service and the FBI determined that Kennedy and Connally were hit by separate bullets.

- The Secret Service determined "from the movies that President Kennedy was struck with the first and third shots fired by the assassin, while Gov. Connally was struck with the second shot." (FBI report of interview with Secret Service agent John Joe Howlett at CD5, p.117)
- The FBI Summary Report on the assassination found that "three shots rang out. Two bullets struck President Kennedy, and one wounded Governor Connally." (CD1, p.1)

The Zapruder film shows two separate hits for Kennedy and Connally, within a timeframe in which it is impossible to fire two shots from the Italian rifle.

- The Warren Commission itself agreed that Kennedy was "probably shot through the neck between frames 210 and 225." (WCR, p.105)
- Governor Connally thought he himself was hit between frames 231 and 234. (WCHE, v.4, p.145)
- Connally's surgeon, Dr. Robert Shaw, concluded that Connally was hit around frame 236, "give or take 1 or 2 frames." (WCHE, v.4, p.114)
- In *Six Seconds in Dallas,* researcher Josiah Thompson noted the collapse of Connally's shoulder in frame 238, which would be consistent with a bullet striking at that point and pushing the shoulder downward due to transference of momentum. Thompson thus fixes the striking of Connally in the interval of frames 234 to 238. (Thompson, *Six Seconds in Dallas,* pp.74-76.) Note that Dr. Shaw's choice of frame 236, based on viewing the film, falls exactly in the middle of this range.

If Kennedy was hit in frame 210 at the earliest, and Connally was not hit until around frame 238, then the Zapruder film, running at 18.3 frames per second, gives us a maximum of roughly 1.6 seconds between the first and second shots, even if we extend Connally's shot to frame 240. This is below the absolute minimum time of 2.3 seconds (42 frames) required to operate the bolt of the Italian rifle (CE139), and proves that two gunmen were firing from the behind the car. Edward J. Epstein, in *Inquest* (1966) demonstrated the link between the single-bullet theory and the timeframe established by Zapruder's film. He noted that the Commission established that Kennedy could not have been hit before frame 207. [The difference between using frame 207 versus 210 as the starting point is the difference between "could have been hit" and "probably was hit".] The Commission also agreed with medical experts that Connally was not in a position to be hit after frame 240. Epstein continues: "Thus, the maximum time that could have elapsed between the times both men were first shot was 33 film frames, or about 1.8 seconds. Thus, according to the established facts, it was physically impossible for the assassination rifle to have been fired twice during the time period when the President and Governor Connally were first wounded. Either both men were hit by the same bullet, or there were two assassins." (Epstein, *Inquest,* p.45). As we have already seen from the evidence presented above, both men were *not* hit by the same bullet, since the bullet which struck Kennedy in the back did not exit the front of his body. And Connally felt the second bullet hit him after the sound of the first shot. Therefore there were at least two assassins firing from behind. With the shooter from the fence on the grassy slope, this gives us a minimum of three assassins firing in Dealey Plaza on November 22, 1963. It is unlikely that Connally was a target of the assassins. The second shooter had probably targeted Kennedy, but because the first shot shoved Kennedy to the left, when the second bullet arrived at the car, Connally was exposed and was hit with this bullet.

The "delayed reaction" theory has no basis in fact and is contradicted by the evidence.

Recognizing the problem of squeezing two shots within too small a timeframe, the commission speculates that Connally was in fact struck with the same bullet as Kennedy, but that he did not realize it at first, experiencing a "delayed reaction" a short time after the hit. According to this scenario, Connally was hit earlier than is shown on the film, but this is not evident because he did not "react" right away. No evidence is presented to support the existence of such a scenario, and the "delayed reaction" theory suffers from the further problem that it is purely a psychological theory, which ignores the visible physical impact of the striking bullet. As noted above in the citation from Josiah Thompson, the impact of the bullet is a physical one. The bullet imparts some of its momentum to the body part which is hit and the physical effect of this is seen in frame 238 with the collapse of Connally's shoulder. Being hit with a bullet from a high-powered rifle has physical consequences for the body being struck, regardless of whether the victim is psychologically aware of the hit at the time it occurs. In any case, Connally himself has a very clear memory of *being hit*, not just of realizing that he *had been hit*.

None of the experts examined by Arlen Specter were willing to support the "delayed reaction" theory. In questioning Army ballistics expert Dr. Arthur Dziemian, Specter had this exchange:

SPECTER: Dr. Dziemian, Governor Connally testified that he experienced the sensation of a striking blow on his back which he described as being similar to a hard punch received from a doubled-up fist. Do you have an opinion as to whether that sensation would necessarily occur immediately upon impact of a wound such as that received by Governor Connally, or could there be a delayed reaction in sensing that feeling?

DZIEMIAN: I don't have too much of an opinion on that. All I can say is that some people are struck by bullets and do not even know they are hit. This happens in wartime. But I don't know about that.
SPECTER: So that it is possible in some situations there is some delay in reaction?
DZIEMIAN: I couldn't say.
SPECTER: Is it a highly individual matter as to the reaction of an individual on that subject?
DZIEMIAN: I don't know. (WCHE, v.5, p.93-94)

Dr. Humes is the only one to support the *possibility* of a delayed reaction, but even his answer is expressed only in general terms and is based only on anecdotal reports and not his own personal experience with gunshot patients.

SPECTER: Could that missile have traversed Governor Connally's chest without having him know it immediately or instantaneously?
HUMES: I believe so. I have heard reports, and have been told by my professional associates of any number of instances where people received penetrating wounds in various portions of the body and have only the sensation of a slight discomfort or slight slap or some other minor difficulty from such a missile wound. (WCHE, v.2, p.376)

But this *possibility* is not consistent with the other evidence already cited which points to the two men being hit with separate shots. Nevertheless, the Warren Report asserted that "a victim of a bullet wound may not react immediately and, in some situations, according to experts, the victim may not even know where he has been hit, or when." (WCR, p.97) To support this claim, the Warren Report's footnote cites the testimony of Dr. Dziemian, whose tepid response is quoted above. The claim that delayed reactions can occur is true enough as a general statement, but the commission's rhetorical objective here is obviously to make the reader think that this statement refers to Governor Connally in particular – not just "*a victim* of a bullet wound" but *this victim,* and that this victim *did not* (instead of "may not") react immediately upon being hit. The report is not willing to claim definitely that Connally experienced such a delayed reaction, but only seeks to establish the *possibility* of such a reaction in the mind of the reader, in order to salvage some semblance of plausibility for the single bullet theory, even though other evidence contradicts such a phenomenon in this particular case. Similarly ambiguous language is used elsewhere in the Warren Report, showing the commission's reluctance to take a definite stand on the existence of a delayed reaction in the case of Connally's shot. The report states that "there was, *conceivably,* a delayed reaction between the time the bullet struck him and the time he realized that he was hit." (WCR, p.112). Again, there is a "possibility" that Connally "did not immediately feel the penetration of the bullet, and then felt the delayed reaction of the impact on his back." (WCR, p.112, 115) The delayed reaction remains only a theoretical possibility, and not an established fact in the particular case of Connally's injury.

Commission Exhibit 385: A cartoon masquerading as evidence

Humes presented to the commission a set of drawings, including Commission Exhibit 385 (WCHE, v.16, p.977), to illustrate the presumed location of the back wound and its presumed path through the neck and out the front. But this drawing is not evidence. It was not prepared from photographs or from eyewitness recollection by someone having first hand knowledge of the location of the wounds. Humes told the commission that this drawing and others like it were prepared by a medical illustrator in the Naval Medical School. Humes' testimony indicates that the illustrator did not see the actual wounds. Instead, Humes provided him with physical measurements regarding the position of the wounds. Humes told the commission that he had checked the drawings to verify their accuracy but does not say whether his examination found them to actually *be* accurate. Humes himself admits that "these drawings are in part schematic. The artist had but a brief period of some 2 days to prepare these. He had no photographs from which to work, and had to work under our description, verbal description, of what we had observed. . . . If it were necessary to have them absolutely true to scale, I think it would be virtually impossible for him to do this without the photographs." (WCHE, v.2, p.350)

COMMISSION EXHIBIT 385

Humes explains the difficulty in transmitting to the artist the exact location of the wounds: "When we attempt to give a description of these findings, it is the bony prominences . . . which we used as points of references, I cannot transmit completely to the illustrator where they were situated." (WCHE, v.2, p.350) By "bony prominences" Humes is referring to the mastoid process and the acromion process, which he used as reference points in describing the location of Kennedy's back wound. Humes explains: "We attempted to locate such wounds in soft tissue by making reference to bony structures which do not move and are, therefore, good reference points for this type of investigation. . . . We chose the two bony points of reference – we chose to locate this wound, where the mastoid process, which is just behind the ear, the top [sic – tip?] of the mastoid process, and the acromion which is the tip of the shoulder joint. We ascertained physical measurement at the time of autopsy that this wound was 14 cm. from the tip of the mastoid process and 14 cm. from the acromion was its central point." [14 cm is 5.5 inches] (WCHE, v.2, p.361) Thus Humes measured the vertical location of the wound in the back by its distance from a point near the ear, which even his experienced medical illustrator had trouble envisioning. Thus Humes chose as "good reference points" anatomical structures whose location he cannot explain to the illustrator.

There is an additional uncertainty involved in this selection of the right mastoid process as a reference point for the back wound. The mastoid process, as any anatomy textbook will confirm, is part of the temporal bone of the skull. Humes acknowledged that the large wound on the right side of the head extended "somewhat" into the temporal region. (WCHE, v.16, p.980) The Parkland doctors saw more extensive damage to the temporal bone. Dr. Baxter wrote in his handwritten notes that the "temporal and occipital bones were missing." (WCHE, v.17, p.8) And in his deposition Dr. Baxter testified that "literally the right side of his head had been blown off." (WCHE, v.6, p.41) Dr. Jenkins described "a great laceration on the right side of the head (temporal and occipital), causing a great defect in the skull plate." (WCHE, v.17, p.15) Dr. Crenshaw observed a head wound "behind the right ear, in the occipital-parietal region, in right rear quadrant of the head, and was baseball-sized. Brain matter was oozing out. . . . There was a complete absence of bone, hair and scalp at the wound site." (ARRB, MD 183, In-Person Interview 3/19/1997 with Dr. Charles Crenshaw, p.2) Given the extensive damage to the right temporal bone, of which the mastoid process is a part, we must ask whether Kennedy's right mastoid process was sufficiently whole and stable to serve as a fixed reference point for measurement of the back wound's location. If it was not, then the measurements for the back wound given by Humes and his team are meaningless.

You can find your own mastoid process as a bony projection of the temporal bone just behind your ear lobe. I challenge you to try to measure 5-1/2 inches below it. If you keep the measuring stick straight, your shoulder will get in the way (unless you have a very long neck). You cannot easily measure from this reference point to a point on your back. But it is undisputed that the mastoid process is higher than the collar, and therefore, 5.5 inches from the mastoid process must give a higher result than 5.5 inches down from the collar, which the eyewitnesses and the holes in the clothing attest to as the approximate location of the back wound. There is a real difference between the location of the back wound as given in the autopsy report and that given by the witnesses and the physical evidence – about 3 to 4 inches difference as I measure it.

As Humes himself admitted, it is very difficult to describe the location of the wound in relation to the reference points that he gave. But the ambiguity serves Specter well, because he is able to repeat these measurements over and over again, stating them as assumptions when he questions the doctors and other experts as to the possibility that a bullet could have penetrated Kennedy's neck and exited through the front. The obscurity of the measurement reference points allows Specter to use Humes' measurements as authoritative autopsy findings without it being obvious that the real wound was much farther down the back than his single bullet theory presupposes.

An example will illustrate how Specter made use of these obscure measurements in soliciting support for the single bullet theory. In questioning Dr. McClelland, Specter asked McClelland to "assume, if you will, that President Kennedy was shot on the upper right posterior thorax just above the upper border of the scapula at a point 14 cm. from the tip of the right acromion process and 14 cm. below a tip of the right mastoid process. Assume further that that wound of entry was caused by a 6.5 mm missile shot out of a rifle having a muzzle velocity of approximately 2000 feet per second, being located 160 to 250 feet away from President Kennedy, that the bullet entered on the point that I described on the President's back, passed between two strap muscles on the posterior aspect of the President's body and moved through the fascial channel without violating the pleura cavity, and exited in the midline lower third anterior position of the President's neck. Would the hole which Dr. Perry described to you on the front side of the President's neck be consistent with the hole which such a bullet might make in such a trajectory through the President's body? (WCHE, v.6, p.38) In other words, Specter is asking the doctor to assume that a bullet went through the neck and exited from the front of the neck. Given that assumption, could the hole in the front have been an exit wound? Since he is already assuming what he wishes to prove, the answer is invariably "yes", that it would be possible under those assumptions. The points of reference in the two bony structures help to obscure the actual location of the back wound when posing these questions. This line of questioning, with the same assumptions, was repeated again and again in Specter's questioning of the doctors, even though Humes' own medical illustrator was not sure what he meant when he gave these measurements.

Conclusion

To summarize, the hypothesized path of the bullet through the base of the back of the neck and out the front of the neck, as illustrated in the cartoon drawing CE385, is not supported by any actual evidence. The inscrutable points of reference in measuring the location of this wound play into Specter's strategy of distracting witnesses from the wound's true location between 5 and 6 inches down from the shoulder. This true location makes it obvious that the bullet which hit Kennedy in the back could not possibly have been positioned to also hit Connally, even if it had penetrated Kennedy's body. Based on the evidence presented above, we know that it did not penetrate Kennedy's body, and the single bullet theory is thus refuted, meaning that we must admit the existence of two shooters firing from behind the President's car.

THE HOLE IN THE FRONT OF KENNEDY'S NECK WAS PROBABLY A BULLET ENTRANCE WOUND

The evidence for the front neck wound being a bullet entrance is more ambiguous than the evidence for the head and back shots. However, testimony shows that this hole in the front of Kennedy's neck cannot be ruled out as an entry wound, and there is significant positive evidence that it is such a wound. The majority of the medical personnel at Parkland who saw the wound before it was obscured by a tracheotomy incision testified that they thought it was an entrance wound or that it looked like an entrance wound.

The neck wound looked like a bullet entrance wound.

- Dr. Charles Baxter said that the front neck wound resembled a bullet entry wound:

> SPECTER: Will you describe with as much particularity as you can the wound which you noticed on the President's neck?
> BAXTER: The wound on the neck was approximately an inch and a half above . . . the sternal notch. This wound was in my estimation 4 to 5 mm in widest diameter and was a spherical wound. . . . There was considerable contusion of the muscles of the anterior neck and a moderate amount of bleeding around the trachea. . . .
> SPECTER: Were the characteristics of the wound on the neck sufficient to enable you to form an opinion with reasonable medical certainty as to what was the cause of the hole?
> BAXTER: Well, the wound was, I think, compatible with a gunshot wound. It did not appear to be a jagged wound such as one would expect with a very high velocity rifle bullet. We could not determine, or did not determine at that time whether this represented an entry or an exit wound. Judging from the caliber of the rifle that we later found or became acquainted with, *this would more resemble a wound of entry*. However . . . depending upon what a bullet of such caliber would pass through, the tissues that it would pass through on the way to the neck, I think that the wound could well represent either exit or entry wound. (WCHE, v.6, p.42)

- Emergency room nurse Margaret Henchliffe also saw the neck wound and thought it was a bullet entry wound:

  HENCHLIFFE: It was just a little hole in the middle of his neck.
  SPECTER: About how big a hole was it?
  HENCHLIFFE: About as big around as the end of my little finger.
  SPECTER: Have you ever had any experience with bullet holes?
  HENCHLIFFE: Yes.
  SPECTER: And what did that appear to you to be?
  HENCHLIFFE: An entrance bullet hole – it looked to me like.
  SPECTER: Could it have been an exit bullet hole?
  HENCHLIFFE: . . . I don't remember seeing one that looked like that.
  (WCHE, v.6, p.141)

- Dr. Ronald Jones wrote in his handwritten notes on 11/23/63 that the "small hole in anterior midline of neck [was] thought to be a bullet entrance wound." (WCHE, v.20, p.333) He testified at his deposition that "the wound in the throat was probably no larger than a quarter of an inch in diameter." (WCHE, v.6, p.54) Dr. Jones explained the conditions that would have been required if this were an exit wound: "The hole was very small and relatively clean cut, as you would see in a bullet that is entering rather than exiting from a patient. If this were an exit wound, you would think that it exited at a *very low velocity* to produce no more damage than this had done, and if this were a missile of high velocity, you would expect more of an explosive type of exit wound, with more tissue destruction than this appeared to have." (WCHE, v.6, p.55) [This is a problem for Specter, because if the bullet exited Kennedy's neck at "very low velocity" it would not have had enough energy to penetrate Connally's chest and cause all his wounds.]

- Dr. Charles Crenshaw, interviewed by ARRB staff in 1997, told the interviewers that he had "observed what he interpreted as a classic bullet entrance wound in the anterior neck, the size of the tip of one's little finger, just prior to the performance of the tracheostomy by Dr. Perry." (ARRB, MD183, Summary of In-person interview 3/19/1997 with Dr. Charles Crenshaw., p.2)

- Dr. Malcolm Perry observed that the front neck wound was "not a punched-out wound . . . nor was it particularly ragged. It was rather clean cut." (WCHE, v.6, p.9) Rep. Boggs asked Perry if there was any indication that the neck wound had been inflicted from the front. Dr. Perry replied: "There is no way to tell, sir, for sure. . . . unless one were able to ascertain the trajectory." (WCHE, v.3, p.389) [As we have seen, the bullet trajectory in Kennedy's body was not discovered by Dr. Humes and his autopsy team.] During his press conference at Parkland Hospital on November 22, 1963, Dr. Perry had been more definite. At that time he stated unequivocally, "There was an entrance wound in the neck." When asked to elaborate, Dr. Perry answered, "The wound appeared to be an entrance wound in the front of the throat." (White House transcript of Perry press conference, quoted in David Lifton, *Best Evidence* (1988), p.61-62.)

At least three witnesses had recollections of a metallic object or fragment being found in Kennedy's chest

- Dr. Kemp Clark was quoted in the New York Times on 11/27/63 as saying that one bullet struck Kennedy at about the necktie knot. "It ranged downward in his chest and did not exit," said Dr. Clark. (New York Times, 11/27/63, p.20)
- Thomas Robinson, the embalmer who prepared Kennedy's body for autopsy, told HSCA interviewers on January 12, 1977 that he has a vague recollection of something metallic, "a piece of bullet", being found in Kennedy's chest at autopsy, but cannot provide specific details. (ARRB, MD63, p.10)
- Paul O'Connor, a lab technician who assisted at the autopsy, told HSCA staff that someone (he cannot remember clearly who) told him that the doctors had "found a fragment of a bullet lodged in the intercostal muscle on the right rear side" of the President's body". O'Connor was also told that "a lot of blood infiltrated the intercostal muscle". (ARRB, MD64, p.7) [The intercostal muscles run between the ribs and are used to move the chest wall during breathing.]

The size of the wound was roughly that of a 6.5 mm bullet

- Dr. Ronald Jones described the size of the wound as "no greater than a quarter of an inch in greatest diameter". (WCHE, v.6, p.53) [A quarter inch is equivalent to 6.5 mm.]
- Dr. Carrico estimated the front neck wound to be 5 to 8 mm in diameter. (WCHE, v.3, p.361)
- Dr. Perry's estimate of the neck wound was approximately 5 mm. (WCHE, v.3, p.372)

Was the front neck wound caused by a fragment of bullet or bone exiting from the head shot?

In *Six Seconds in Dallas,* author Josiah Thompson analyzed the characteristics of the front neck wound and concluded that it was made by a bone fragment which exited downward from the head shot. He noted that Dr. Perry described the hole as being too small for a bullet – between 3 and 5 mm in diameter. (from Dr. Humes' handwritten notes of a phone conversation with Dr. Perry at WCHE, v.17, p.29) However, Dr. Perry stated in his deposition that he "did not make a minute examination" of the throat wound, but only determined "the fact that there was a wound there, roughly 5 mm. in size or so." (WCHE, v.6, p.9) It isn't clear whether

Perry would consider a 6.5 mm bullet hole to be "roughly" 5 mm. Dr. Frederick Light, in his testimony before the commission, advised against putting too much stock into these emergency room measurements. He told the commission, "The measurements were not particularly precise as far as I could tell. You wouldn't expect them to be in an operating room." (WCHE, v.5, p.96) Thus, it would be premature to rule out the possibility that the throat wound was in fact large enough to be a bullet hole, based on Perry's emergency room estimate and his conversation with Dr. Humes.

We have noted above that Dr. Ronald Jones placed the size of the neck hole at around a quarter of an inch, i.e., 6.5 mm. Also, see Dr. Humes' theory of "elastic recoil", which he had used to explain why the alleged entry wound in the head was smaller than the 6.5 mm bullet. In that testimony, Humes testified that "it is not infrequent in missile wounds of this type that the measured wound is slightly smaller than the caliber of the missile that traversed it." (WCHE, v.2, p.360-361) If this elastic recoil theory has general application, and it not just an ad hoc invention to explain the small entry wound in the head, then it could easily explain a bullet entry hole in the neck being smaller than the caliber of the entering bullet.

The strongest evidence supporting Thompson's view that the hole in the neck was caused by an exiting bone fragment is the fact that the internal bruising of the tissues in the neck showed "a vertical channel of contusion (bruise), laceration, and hematoma . . . stretching above and below the tiny exit hole. . . . This channel stretched at least 4 to 6 inches up and down the President's neck." (Thompson, p.53-54) Pointing also to lacerations in the brain, Thompson concludes, "If we suppose that a bullet (or more likely a bone) fragment was driven downward on a slight right-to-left trajectory through the midbrain, we have a hypothesis that accords with all the known facts surrounding the throat wound." (Thompson, p.55) Support for this hypothesis comes from FBI expert Robert Frazier, who did not find any metallic residue on the hole through the button line in the front of Kennedy's shirt, whereas he did find traces of metal on the bullet hole in the back of the shirt. (WCHE, v.5, p.62) This alone, however, cannot be seen as proof that the front neck hole was not caused by a bullet, because no testimony exists to suggest that an entering bullet will always leave metallic traces. Also, as Thompson himself pointed out, "a well-defined path downward through the brain has not been found" leading to a front neck wound. (Thompson, p.55)

The hypothesis that the neck wound was caused by a bone fragment from the head shot is countered by the fact that witnesses described Kennedy as grabbing his neck at the sound of the *first* shot. Linda Kay Willis testified to the commission that when the first shot hit, "the President turned from waving to the people, and he grabbed his throat, and he kind of slumped forward." (WCHE, v.7, p.498) Riding in the Presidential car, Secret Service agent Kellerman saw Kennedy raise both arms to his neck, "in the collar section" after the first shot was heard. (WCHE, v.2, p.73-74) Secret Service agent Clint Hill saw the same movement. (WCHE, v.2, p.139) At the time of the first shot there were no bone fragments coming from the head, and so Kennedy's reaction to the first shot cannot plausibly be explained as a reaction to a bone fragment exiting the front of the neck after the head shot. It is more likely a reaction to being shot in the throat from the front.

Conclusion

The evidence is mixed as to the cause of the throat wound. However, testimony regarding the size and appearance of the hole and eyewitness testimony of Kennedy reaching for his neck after the first shot prevent us from ruling out a frontal shot as the cause of the hole in Kennedy's neck. The Parkland doctors and nurses who saw the neck wound before the tracheotomy was performed all said it looked like a bullet entry wound. The internal injuries in the neck region, mentioned by Josiah Thompson, may well have been caused by a bone fragment from the head shot, but it is not necessary to also suppose that these injuries are connected to the hole in the front of the neck, which could have arisen from a different source, namely, a bullet entering from the front.

THE AUTOPSY REPORT

The autopsy report written by Navy physician Dr. James Humes carried great weight with the commission members and with the general public after the publication of the Warren Report. The distinguished military men who conducted the autopsy commanded great confidence and respect because of their positions. Questioning the judgment and integrity of such illustrious gentlemen would have been considered unseemly and in poor taste. It just wasn't done. And so the autopsy results were accepted implicitly by the commission as a reliable guide to the description of Kennedy's wounds. We will therefore find it useful to examine the autopsy with a more skeptical eye than was done in 1964.

The WCHE contain both a handwritten draft, CE397 (WCHE, v.17, pp.29-44), and a typewritten version, CE387 (WCHE, v.16, pp.978-983), of Dr. Humes' autopsy report. Of course this handwritten draft is not the same one that Humes said he burned in his fireplace early on Sunday morning, November 24. (WCHE, v.2, p.373) The value of the handwritten draft of the autopsy report in volume 16 is that it shows some strikeouts and insertions that are not obvious in the typewritten copy, thus giving us some insight into Humes' state of mind as he wrote the report.

The commission, and staff counsel Arlen Specter in particular, used Dr. Humes' autopsy report to establish two critical "facts" about the Kennedy's wounds: 1) There was a shot that entered the base of the back of his neck and penetrated through to exit in the front of the neck; and 2) The fatal bullet struck Kennedy in the back of the head, leaving a small entry hole, and exited on the right side of the head, producing a large wound which removed a part of his skull in that region. We will be interested in finding out what evidence supports these conclusions.

Since the autopsy report contradicts the testimony of many other witnesses, we will have to consider what standard to use for evaluating conflicting testimony. If the FBI agents at the autopsy say that the back wound did not penetrate Kennedy's body and the autopsy report says it did, who do we believe? If the Parkland doctors and nurses saw no small bullet entry hole in the back of the head, while the autopsy doctors say they did see such a hole, do we believe the autopsy doctors simply because they are the autopsy doctors? It is obvious that in a case which is based on evidence, we cannot accept anyone's statement as truth simply by virtue of their title or position or the fact that they are experts in a subject. The argument from authority has long been recognized as a logical fallacy. Whether in a debate or in a real trial, the experts must present the evidence on which their opinions are based and must show how their conclusions derive from the facts of the case. It is never sufficient for them to simply render an opinion and command assent on the basis of their general expertise. This applies also when the expert opinions are numerous and even unanimous. It doesn't matter how many other experts agree with Humes' autopsy findings. Their conclusions must still be based on evidence, and they must be able to explain to us how their conclusions follow from the evidence. To say that four (or five or however many) government panels have looked at the autopsy results and that all are agreed that Kennedy was killed by one assassin firing from the rear, states no logical argument based on evidence. It is simply the old argument from authority. "Trust me, I'm a doctor."

We cannot overstate the importance of the autopsy findings to the commission's theory of the case. The commission members and staff viewed all the other medical and ballistic evidence through the lens of the autopsy results. Those who favor the lone gunman theory of the assassination can simply reject the evidence which points to three assassins on the grounds that it conflicts with the testimony of the autopsy doctors who, after all, had the closest look at Kennedy's wounds. The autopsy report must therefore be subjected to intense scrutiny in order to properly evaluate it in the context of the other evidence which conflicts with it.

BACKGROUND OF THE AUTOPSY DOCTORS

In the case of the Kennedy autopsy, it is not even certain that the autopsy doctors can be considered experts. Their lack of training and experience in forensic pathology has been pointed out by many commentators. (See, for example, Anthony Summers, *Not in Your Lifetime,* 2013, p.15.) Dr. Humes told the commission that he had once completed a course in forensic pathology at the Armed Forces Institute of Pathology, but one course does not make one an expert. Humes was the Director of Laboratories at the Naval Medical School at Bethesda, not a practicing forensic pathologist. Humes told the commission that he was board certified in anatomic pathology and in clinical pathology, but does not mention forensic pathology. Humes concedes that his own experience has been "more extensive in the field of natural disease than violence." He tells the commission that on "several occasions" he has had to "deal with" violent death, such as accidents and suicides. Humes does not state, and Specter does not ask, whether he has ever conducted a forensic autopsy on a gunshot victim, or indeed any type of autopsy at all. Humes says that he has supervisory responsibility over the laboratory operations at Bethesda Naval Medical Center, which comprises two broad areas: anatomic pathology, which includes post-mortem examinations, and clinical pathology. From this description it would appear that he has supervisory oversight of autopsies but there is no indication that he conducts them or has conducted them on his own. (WCHE, v.2, p.348) Based on his lack of training and experience in forensic pathology, Dr. Humes must be considered a novice when it comes to conducting autopsies on gunshot victims.

The second Navy doctor on the autopsy team was Commander J. Thornton Boswell. He was board certified in clinical and pathological anatomy (not forensic pathology). At the time of his testimony before the commission he was the Chief of Pathology at the National Naval Medical School. (WCHE, v.2, p.377) This is the only background information requested of Boswell by Specter. Dr. Boswell is not asked whether he has ever conducted a forensic autopsy or any autopsy at all.

Specter's subsequent questioning is limited to asking Boswell whether he agrees with the conclusions of Dr. Humes, as recorded in the autopsy report. Dr. Boswell's testimony comprises one page in the WCHE.

In these exchanges with Humes and Boswell about their backgrounds, Specter is the dog that doesn't bark. He does not ask either one of them how many autopsies they have performed and what types of autopsies they were. Nor do the doctors volunteer this information. Like any good attorney, Specter is not likely to ask a question without knowing beforehand what the answer is. If Humes and Boswell had performed hundreds of autopsies in gunshot cases Specter surely would have asked them about it, so as to get their experience on the record. The fact that he didn't tells us that he did not expect any advantage from asking that question, and may have feared that asking it would damage the perceived expertise and credibility of his witnesses.

Of the three autopsy doctors, only Lt. Col Pierre Finck of the U. S. Army was board certified in forensic pathology. (WCHE, v.2, p.378) And in 1967 when author Josiah Thompson checked into Finck's membership in the American Academy of Forensic Sciences, Thompson found that Finck was listed as only a "provisional member". (Thompson, *Six Seconds in Dallas,* p.198) Finck told the commission that between 1955 and 1958 he had performed "approximately 200 autopsies, many of them pertaining to trauma including missile wounds." Finck testifies that since 1958 his role has been more of a consultant and reviewer, rather than a practitioner of forensic autopsies. (WCHE, v.2, p.378) Thus Finck seems to be telling us that, at the time of his commission testimony, it had been at least five years since he performed an autopsy in a gunshot death case.

Based on their testimony before the commission, it is clear that the doctors at Parkland Hospital in Dallas had more experience with treating bullet wounds than did the autopsy doctors – certainly more than Humes and Boswell. Humes further notes that his own commanding officer, Captain John H. Stover of the Naval Medical School, was present during the autopsy, as was Admiral Galloway, the commanding officer of the National Naval Medical Center at Bethesda. (WCHE, v.2, p.349) Thus, it would be a stretch to say that Humes was "in charge" of the autopsy, given the presence of superior officers in the room. Any orders given to Humes by these higher-ranking officers would have to be obeyed, regardless of Humes' personal feelings toward such orders.

President Kennedy's personal physician, Admiral George Burkley, was also present at the autopsy, according to the FBI agents who were present. (Sibert-O'Neill Report, CD7, p.282) Dr. Burkley was the only doctor who was with Kennedy's body both in Dallas and at Bethesda. Yet he was not called to testify before the Warren Commission, nor was his deposition taken. In 1967 Dr. Burkley was interviewed for an oral history project for the JFK library. He was asked, "Do you agree with the Warren Report on the number of bullets that entered the President's body?" Burkley replied, "I would not care to be quoted on that".

(ARRB, MD67, p.18) Given Dr. Burkley's presence at the autopsy, his reluctance to endorse the conclusions of the autopsy report is remarkable.

Our task in this chapter will be to examine the autopsy report closely in order to discover the evidence on which the autopsy team's conclusions are based. Digging deeper into the claims of the autopsy report will require us to revisit all three wound locations – head, back, and neck – in order to judge the sufficiency of the autopsy doctors' findings and the Warren Commission's interpretation of those findings.

KENNEDY'S WOUNDS ACCORDING TO THE AUTOPSY REPORT

The Warren Report's description of the autopsy findings

The Warren Report tells us that the autopsy examination "revealed two wounds in the President's head. One wound, approximately one-fourth of an inch by five-eighths of an inch (6 by 15 millimeters), was located about an inch (2.5 centimeters) to the right and slightly above the large bony protrusion (external occipital protuberance) which juts out at the center of the lower part of the back of the skull. The second head wound measured approximately 5 inches (13 centimeters) in its greatest diameter, but it was difficult to measure accurately because multiple crisscross fractures radiated from the large defect. . . . The autopsy also disclosed a wound near the base of the back of President Kennedy's neck slightly to the right of his spine. The doctors traced the course of the bullet through the body and as information was received from Parkland Hospital, concluded that the bullet had emerged from the front portion of the President's neck that had been cut away by the tracheotomy at Parkland." (WCR, p.60) (As we have already seen, the autopsy doctors did *not* trace the course of the neck wound through the body.)

Elaborating on the back/neck wound, the Warren Report tells us that the autopsy examination found a hole "located approximately 5½ inches (14 centimeters) from the tip of the right shoulder joint and approximately the same distance below the tip of the right mastoid process, the bony point immediately behind the ear. The wound was approximately one-fourth by one-seventh of an inch (7 by 4 millimeters), had clean edges, was sharply delineated, and had margins similar in all respects to those of the entry wound in the skull. . . . The autopsy examination further disclosed that, after entering the President, the bullet passed between two large muscles, produced a contusion on the upper part of the pleural cavity (without penetrating that cavity), bruised the top portion of the right lung and ripped the windpipe (trachea) in its path through the President's neck. . . . No bone was struck by the bullet which passed through the President's body. By projecting from a point of entry on the rear of the neck and proceeding at a slight downward angle through the bruised interior portions, the doctors concluded that the bullet exited from the front portion of the President's neck that had been cut away by the tracheotomy. . . . The surgeons determined that the bullet had passed between two large strap muscles and bruised them without leaving any channel, since the bullet merely passed between them.

Commander Humes, who believed that a tracheotomy had been performed from his observations at the autopsy, talked by telephone with Dr. Perry early on the morning of November 23, and learned that his assumption was correct and that Dr. Perry had used the missile wound in the neck as the point to make the incision. This confirmed the Bethesda surgeons' conclusion that the bullet had exited from the front part of the neck." (WCR, p.87-89)

Identifying the small head wound as a bullet entry hole

Humes testified that the small head wound "was found in the right posterior portion of the scalp. This wound was situated approximately 2.5 centimeters to the right, and slightly above the external occipital protuberance which is a bony prominence situated in the posterior portion of everyone's skull." (WCHE, v.2, p.351) Humes testified that the dimensions of this wound were 15x6 mm. (WCHE, v.2, p.352) Humes' typewritten autopsy report adds: "In the underlying bone is a corresponding wound through the skull which exhibits beveling of the margins of the bone when viewed from the inner aspect of the skull." (WCHE, v.16, p.981) The handwritten autopsy report originally described this small wound as a "puncture" wound which was "tangential to the surface of the scalp" (WCHE, v.17, p.36), but these words have been crossed out and they are not included in the typewritten report.

"This [small, rear] wound had to us the characteristics of a wound of entrance for the following reason: The defect in the outer table [i.e., the outer layer of bone in the skull] was oval in outline, quite similar to the defect in the skin. . . . I am speaking here of the wound in the occiput. The wound on the inner table [of the skull], however, was larger and had what in the field of wound ballistics is described as a shelving or a coning effect. . . . [As when] a missile strikes a pane of glass . . . there will be a small, usually round to oval defect on the side of the glass from whence the missile came and a belled-out or coned-out surface on the opposite side of the glass from whence the missile came. . . . This wound then had the characteristics of wound of entrance from this direction [i.e., from the outside of the skull] through the two tables of the skull." (WCHE, v.2, p.352)

So Humes and his team concluded that this small bullet hole in the occipital bone was a point of entry because the corresponding point on the inner surface of the skull had the characteristic beveling of the surface associated with an entering projectile.

Identifying the large, right-side head wound as a wound of exit

In his testimony Humes describes this large head wound as "a huge defect over the right side of the skull. This defect involved both the scalp and the underlying skull, and from the brain substance was protruding. This wound measured approximately 13 centimeters [about 5 inches] in greatest diameter. It was difficult to measure accurately because radiating at various points from the large defect were multiple crisscrossing fractures of the skull which extended in several directions." (WCHE, v.2, p.351) The Humes typewritten report says that this wound involved "chiefly the parietal bone but extending somewhat into the temporal and occipital regions." (WCHE, v.16, p.980)

Having determined that the small rear (occipital) wound was the bullet entry hole, Humes concluded that "the large defect to the upper right side of the skull, in fact, would represent a wound of exit." (WCHE, v.2, p.352) But at first no evidence was found in the side of the head to confirm that a bullet actually exited at that point. Humes tells the commission that "a careful examination of the margins of the large bone defect at that point . . . failed to disclose a portion of the skull bearing . . . a point of impact on the skull of this fragment of the missile, remembering, of course, that this area was devoid of any scalp or skull at this present time. We did not have the bone." (WCHE, v.2, p.353)

But additional bones showed up later that night. Humes told the commission that "some time later on that evening or very early the next morning while we were all still engaged in continuing our examination, I was presented with three portions of bone which had been brought to Washington from Dallas by the agents of the FBI." Specter stops him here to ask if it might have been a Secret Service agent who delivered the extra bones. Humes says maybe – he doesn't know for sure who brought them or where they came from. "I do not recall specifically their statement as to where they had been recovered. It seems to me they felt it had been recovered either in the street or in the automobile, I don't recall specifically." Humes continued, "We were most interested in these fragments of bone, and found that the three pieces could be roughly put together to account for a portion of this defect. . . . I would estimate that approximately one-quarter of that defect was unaccounted for by adding these three fragments together and seeing what was left." Humes stated that on one of these pieces of late-arriving bone, the autopsy team saw a defect which they interpreted as an exit bullet wound, because there was enough of a curve for them to identify the inner and outer surfaces of the skull bone, and the characteristic beveling or shelving of an exit hole was detected on the outside surface. (WCHE, v.2, p.354) Humes concludes, "This would, to us, mean that a missile had made this wound from within the skull to the exterior." (WCHE, v.2, p.355) But neither in his autopsy report nor in his commission testimony does Humes identify what portion of the skull these new bones are from. He does not say that they are from the parietal bone. He says that their size approximates the size of the defect on the right side of the head. But he does not say that that's where they actually came from. So identifying a bullet passage from inside the skull to the outside on this bone does not mean that Humes has found an exit on the right side of the head. Indeed, we will hear later, from Dr. John Ebersole, that the late-arriving fragment was actually a piece of occipital bone.

In the typewritten report Humes describes the receipt of these additional skull fragments as follows: "Received as separate specimens from Dallas, Texas are three fragments of skull bone which in aggregate roughly approximate the dimensions of the large defect described above. At one angle of the largest of these fragments is a *portion of the perimeter* of a roughly circular wound presumably of exit which exhibits beveling of the outer aspect of the bone and is estimated to measure approximately 2.5 to 3.0 cm in diameter." (WCHE, v.16, p.981) It would appear from this description that this bone which displayed the characteristic beveling of an exit wound did not contain the complete hole, but only "a portion" of it. How big a portion is not stated in the autopsy report, but it was apparently enough for Humes to calculate the diameter of the entire hole.

FBI agents Sibert and O'Neill later (November 27) questioned Gerald Behn, who was the Secret Service agent in charge of the White House Detail, about the skull fragment which was delivered to Bethesda late Friday night/early Saturday morning while the autopsy was in progress. Behn advised that "this section . . . was found in the Presidential car on the floor between the front and rear seats." Behn provided no information as to who found this piece of bone or whose possession it was in between its discovery and its delivery to the Bethesda autopsy room. (Sibert-O'Neill Report, CD7, p.286) Note that the Sibert-O'Neill report speaks only of one skull fragment being delivered, while Humes says he received "three portions of bone". There is no explanation in the documents for this discrepancy.

Humes himself did not know where this additional bone came from, nor who had custody of it during the approximately 12 hours between the assassination its delivery. He had no way of knowing for sure that this bone was even from Kennedy's skull. He did not prove that the fragment was from the parietal bone, which would be necessary in order to support the autopsy finding that a bullet entering the back of the head made its exit through the right parietal bone. All of the concerns about faulty chain of possession apply to this evidence. Evidence is not admissible if it cannot be proven that it is what it purports to be. Humes cannot testify with certainty that the bone on which he based his conclusion of a side exit wound is actually from Kennedy's skull. If it is from Kennedy's skull, Humes cannot testify whether it has been tampered with or altered in some way during the time between the assassination and its delivery to Bethesda. Although the FBI interview with Gerald Behn indicates that the bone came from the Presidential limousine, there is no way to know whether he states this from his own knowledge or from hearsay. Nor does he say who found the bone or who had possession of the bone before it was delivered to Humes. These late-arriving bones would not have been admissible as evidence in a real criminal trial unless they could have been shown to be relevant to the assassination, by proving where they were found, that there was reason to believe they came from Kennedy's skull, and that the chain of possession was fully established in order to rule out substitution or tampering with the evidence before the bones were delivered to Bethesda. There is no way to know whether the beveling of the surface was caused by a gunshot wound or by some other mechanical means.

Without this additional piece of bone, there was no evidence discovered at the autopsy that would establish a bullet exit through the right side of Kennedy's skull.

Turning the back wound into a transiting neck wound

On initial examination at the autopsy, the front neck wound appeared to be only a tracheotomy incision. The wound in Kennedy's back was found to be shallow, not penetrating more than a couple of inches. As Sibert and O'Neill observed, "the individuals performing the autopsy were at a loss to explain why they could find no bullets." (Sibert-O'Neill Report, CD7, p.284) This assessment changed when Humes was informed that a bullet had been found on a stretcher at Parkland Hospital. (Sibert-O'Neill Report, CD7, p.284) This seemed to explain why no bullet could be found at Bethesda. Obviously (to Humes), the bullet had entered the back and made a shallow wound. "Since external cardiac massage had been performed at Parkland Hospital, it was entirely possible that through such movement the bullet had worked its way back out of the point of entry and had fallen on the stretcher." (Sibert-O'Neill report, CD7, p.285) Problem solved. But not for long.

On the Saturday morning following the autopsy, Dr. Humes phoned Dr. Perry in Dallas to confirm that the front neck wound was indeed a tracheotomy. Dr. Perry advised that it was, and then he volunteered that before he made the tracheotomy incision he had observed a small hole in the front of the neck "which he had interpreted as a missile wound". In fact, Dr. Perry used this wound as the starting point for his tracheotomy incision. (WCHE, v.2, p.361-362) New problem: How to account for a bullet wound in the front of the neck?

The Warren Report stated that "The doctors traced the course of the bullet through the body and, as information was received from Parkland Hospital, concluded that the bullet had emerged from the front portion of the President's neck that had been cut away by the tracheotomy at Parkland." (WCR, p.60) But this is manifestly untrue. Humes himself admitted that "attempts to probe in the vicinity of this wound [in the back] were unsuccessful without fear of making a false passage. . . . We were unable . . . to take probes and have them satisfactorily fall through any definite path at this point." (WCHE, v.2, p.361) Sibert and O'Neill, observing the autopsy proceedings, reported that "this opening [in the back] was probed by Dr. Humes with the finger. . . . Further probing determined that the distance travelled by this missile was a short distance inasmuch as the end of the opening could be felt with the finger." (Sibert-O'Neill Report, CD7, p.284) So the doctors did not trace the course of the bullet through the body. But Perry's information about the hole in the front of the neck did give Humes the opportunity to speculate on what might have happened: Humes told the commission: "We concluded that this missile . . . which entered the President's body traversed the President's body and made its exit through the wound observed by the physicians at Parkland Hospital and later extended as a tracheotomy wound. (WCHE, v.2, p.364) He concluded that the front neck wound was a "wound *presumably* of exit". (WCHE, v.16, p.981) [The handwritten report shows "presumably" was inserted here. (WCHE, v.17, p.39)] Dr. Humes did not conclude this based on any observations he made at the autopsy, but based on the Saturday morning conversation with Dr. Perry, and by putting two and two together. No path was traced through the neck. Instead, the presumption was made that if there's a hole in the back and a hole in the front, and no bullet to be found in the body, the bullet must have passed through from back to front. In order to help this theory along, Humes assumed that the bullet passing through hit no bone, but only passed through soft tissue, leaving no track which could be probed. Some would call it speculation. Humes might say he was just coming up with a hypothesis that fit the known evidence – at least the evidence as he knew it at the time. With this hypothesis, the single bullet theory was born. It is not yet fully mature, but further development by Arlen Specter will make this bullet go on to do amazing things in the body of Governor Connally.

How can a bullet hole be smaller than the bullet?

The Warren Report tells us that "the three examining pathologists . . . conclude[d] that the smaller hole in the rear of the President's skull was the point of entry and that the large opening on the right side of his head was the wound of exit. The smaller hole on the back of the President's head measured one-fourth of an inch by five-eighths of an inch (6 by 15 millimeters). The dimensions of that wound were consistent with having been caused by a 6.5 millimeter bullet fired from behind and above. . . . The dimension of 6 millimeters, somewhat smaller than the diameter of a 6.5-millimeter bullet, was caused by the elastic recoil *of the skull* which shrinks the size of an opening after a missile passes through it." (WCR, p.86) This "elastic recoil" theory is called upon to explain the awkward fact that a 6.5 mm bullet allegedly made a hole only 6 mm across in one of its dimensions. No evidence is given to explain the mechanism by which this "elastic recoil" process works,

Dr. Humes had introduced the "elastic recoil" theory in his testimony before the commission. Arlen Specter had asked Humes about the fact that the rear head wound was smaller than the diameter of a 6.5 mm bullet.

> SPECTER: Now, on one detail on your report, Dr. Humes, on page 4, on the third line down, you note that there is a lacerated wound measuring 15 by 6 mm, which on the smaller size is, of course, less than 6.5 mm?
> HUMES: Yes, sir.
> SPECTER: What would be the explanation for that variation?
> HUMES: This is in the scalp, sir, and I believe that this is explainable on the elastic recoil of the tissues of the skin, sir. It is not infrequent in missile wounds of this type that the measured wound is slightly smaller than the caliber of the missile that traversed it. (WCHE, v.2, p.360-361)

Here, Humes is obviously talking about a shrinking of the *scalp*, i.e., the skin covering the skull. The Warren Report extended the elastic recoil theory to the *bone of the skull*, which is not what Humes said. In fact, Humes denies that the elastic recoil theory can be applied to the bone of the skull, telling the commission that "the defect in the underlying bone is certainly not likely to get smaller than that of the missile which perforated it." (WCHE, v.2, p.359) The authors of the Warren Report have either misunderstood the proper application of the elastic recoil theory, or have deliberately misapplied it to explain away the fact that the alleged bullet entry hole in the back of Kennedy's skull is smaller than the bullet which was supposed to have made it.

In his autopsy report, Humes made it clear that the 6 mm hole in the scalp was accompanied by a similar hole in the skull as well. He described "a lacerated wound [in the scalp] measuring 15x6 mm. In the underlying bone is a *corresponding wound through the skull*." (WCHE, v.16, p.981) Here, the 15x6 measurement seems to apply to both the scalp and skull (i.e., skin and bone). So the hole in the skull is too small for a 6.5 mm bullet, and according to Humes, elastic recoil of the skull cannot be used to explain this anomaly.

With the wound in Kennedy's back we encounter another hole that is smaller than the bullet which is supposed to have made it. The Warren Report described the wound in Kennedy's back as "approximately one-fourth by one-seventh of an inch (7 by 4 millimeters), had clean edges, was sharply delineated, and had margins similar in all respects to those of the entry wound in the skull." (WCR, p.88) Once again we are faced with an oval bullet hole having one axis smaller (4 mm) than the diameter of the bullet which supposedly made the hole (6.5 mm). In contrast to their treatment of the small head wound, the commission does not call attention to this difference in the case of the back wound, and does not invoke the doctrine of "elastic recoil" to explain the anomalous dimensions of the back wound, nor does Dr. Humes mention the elastic recoil concept in his description of the wound, although it would seem to require some explanation – even more so than the head wound. (WCHE, v.2, p.361)

PRIOR SURGERY IN THE HEAD?

The missing bullet

In his book *Best Evidence,* assassination researcher David Lifton called attention to a portion of Humes' testimony which is laced with anatomical terminology that may seem cryptic to the layman but which potentially may lead to an answer for a question that conspiracists have been hard-pressed to answer: If Kennedy was shot in the head from the front, where's the bullet? The rear-shot hypothesis can claim the two bullet fragments CE567 and 569, which were allegedly found in the limousine and matched to the Italian rifle. But no bullet was found that could be associated with a head shot from the right front. Lifton points to a passage in the FBI's Sibert-O'Neill report, which mentioned "surgery" that was visible in "the head area, namely, in the top of the skull" at the time Kennedy's body arrived in the autopsy room. (Sibert-O'Neill Report, CD7, p.283) No surgery in the top of the head had been mentioned by any of the doctors at Parkland Hospital. Dr. Humes makes no direct mention of surgery in the top of the head, but some of his descriptive remarks may indicate that such surgery had been performed. If this is the case, it could only have been done after the body left Parkland, and before the official autopsy began in the Bethesda autopsy room. Lifton suggests that the purpose of this prior "surgery" may have been to locate and remove a bullet that contradicted the official story of a lone assassin firing from behind.

In fact, Lifton found an obscure newspaper article which seems to support this hypothesis. The Waukegan News Sun (suburban Chicago) published an article on May 1, 1975 which quoted a local man from Lake County, Illinois, who had contacted the newspaper in response to a series of articles the paper had run on the Kennedy assassination. The Lake County man, who requested anonymity, told the reporter that he had been present in the autopsy room at Bethesda on the night of Kennedy's autopsy. He stated that he doubted "that all the necessary information was forwarded to the commission or made available to experts." The paper reported that the Lake County man wrote a contemporaneous memo on orders from a Secret Service agent. "The memo for the official record of the autopsy stated that four large pieces of lead were removed from Kennedy. They were not separate bullets but had jagged edges like shrapnel. There was more material than would come from one bullet, but maybe not enough for two," he said. The man also told the News Sun reporter that "We were scared to death" by the situation. He said that Kennedy's body "was brought in through a back door in an unmarked ambulance. An official motorcade from the airport contained only an empty casket." (Quoted in Lifton, *Best Evidence,* 1988 ed., p.492)

Lifton later was able to track down and identify this Lake County man. His name was Dennis David. He had been an editor of training manuals for Hospital Corpsmen, affiliated with the U. S. Navy Medical School at Bethesda. On the night of November 22, 1963, David had been the Chief of the Day for the Medical School. (Lifton, p.571) In a 1979 conversation, Dennis David confirmed to Lifton that he typed up a memo on November 22, 1963, at about 10:00 p.m. in his Bethesda office, on orders from the Secret Service, stating that four pieces of lead had been removed from Kennedy's body, and specifying their sizes, which David no longer remembered in 1979. (Lifton, p.579) Lifton does not specifically quote David as saying that these fragments came from Kennedy's head, but that seems to be the implication. The Spartacus Education webpage for Dennis David does say that David "was asked to type a memorandum for an FBI agent, that said that four bullet fragments had been removed from Kennedy's head." (spartacus-educational.com/JFKdavidD.htm) These bullet fragments are not mentioned or accounted for in the Warren Commission Hearings and Exhibits.

The existence of these fragments provides support for at least one shot from the front. We can infer this without knowing the details of where they were found, simply because if the bullet fragments supported the government's theory they would certainly have been prominently featured in the Warren Commission's proceedings to support the lone gunman theory, especially if they could be matched ballistically with the Italian rifle. If the fragments exceeded the mass of a single bullet, this could imply two shots to the head, one from behind and another from the front. This possibility was already suggested in 1967 by Josiah Thompson, based on a slight forward movement of Kennedy's head in frame 312 of the Zapruder film (from a bullet impact to the back of the head), before the impact in frame 313 of the shot from the front right. (Thompson, *Six Seconds in Dallas,* p.111) In addition, Anthony and Robbyn Summers, writing in the December 1994 issue of Vanity Fair, identified five doctors who also found evidence of two head shots, based on analysis of X-rays taken at the autopsy. The doctors are Cyril Wecht, David Mantik, Randolph Robertson, Patrick Barnett, and Joseph Riley. ("JFK Case Re-opened," *Vanity Fair,* December 1994, p.97) Alternatively, one of the Dennis David fragments could have been from the shot that entered the front of Kennedy's neck, which also would be embarrassing the Warren Commission. In the absence of documentation confirming where in the body the fragments were found, both possibilities must be considered.

What Humes found in the brain

Humes' Supplementary Report of the autopsy (CE391 at WCHE, v.16, p.987-988), dated December 6, 1963, described what Humes found when he examined the brain. In his commission testimony, Humes summarized these findings for the commission. He described a "longitudinal laceration of the right hemisphere which was para-sagittal in position. . . . The sagittal plane, as you may know, is a plane in the midline which would divide the brain into right and left halves. This laceration was parasagittal [alongside the sagittal plane]. It was situated approximately 2.5 cm to the right of the midline, and extended from the tip of the occipital lobe, which is the posterior portion of the brain, to the tip of the frontal lobe which is the most anterior portion of the brain, and it extended from the top down to the substance of the brain a distance of approximately 5 or 6 cm. The base of the laceration was situated approximately 4.5 cm below the vertex in the white matter. By the vertex we mean the highest point on the skull. . . . The margins of this laceration at all points were jagged and irregular, with additional lacerations extending in varying directions and for varying distances from the main laceration." Then Humes described another laceration that he found in Kennedy's brain: "In addition, there was a laceration of the corpus callosum which is a body of fibers which connects the two hemispheres of the brain to each other, which extended from the posterior to the anterior portion of this structure, that is the corpus callosum. Exposed in this laceration were portions of the ventricular system in which the spinal fluid normally is disposed with the brain." But this was not all. There was yet another laceration discovered in JFK's brain: "When the brain was turned over and viewed from its basular or inferior aspect, there was found a longitudinal laceration of the mid-brain through the floor of the third ventricle, just behind the optic chiasma and the mammillary bodies. This laceration partially communicates with an oblique 1.5 cm tear through the left cerebral peduncle. This is a portion of the brain which connects the higher centers of the brain with the spinal cord, which is more concerned with reflex actions. There were irregular superficial lacerations over the basular or inferior aspects of the left temporal and frontal lobes. We *interpret* that these latter contusions were brought about when the disruptive force of the injury pushed that portion of the brain against the relative intact skull." Dr. Humes concludes by telling Specter that these "are the major points with regard to the President's head wound." In an amazing non sequitur, Specter asks no questions about these brain lacerations which Humes has been describing for the last several minutes. He does not ask Humes what can be inferred from these lacerations or how they might have been produced. Instead, Specter switches topics completely, to ask Humes whether he thinks that "dumdum" bullets were used in the shooting. (WCHE, v.2, p.356) Even to a layman, it is clear from Humes' description that these straight-line lacerations do not follow the alleged path of a bullet entering from the rear and exiting out the top right side of the head. If detailed discussion of these brain lacerations could have helped Specter's case, we can be sure he would have asked Humes to elaborate on them. The fact that he did not is another dog that didn't bark. What was Specter afraid of revealing if he probed further into the nature of these cuts?

When David Lifton read Humes' testimony to a friend of his, who happened to be a neurosurgeon, the neurosurgeon said without hesitation, "That brain's been sectioned." Lifton writes: "What I was reading to him did not sound like damage caused by a bullet." (Lifton, *Best Evidence,* (1988), p.200) Could these "lacerations" have been the "surgery" which was "apparent" to the FBI agents? If so, what would have been the purpose of this operation? Lifton concludes that the purpose was to locate and remove a bullet that would have confirmed a shot from the right front, thus demonstrating that Oswald did not fire the fatal head shot. Lifton's neurosurgeon friend continued to insist that he must be reading from a report written *after* the brain was sectioned, and indeed, Humes' Supplemental Report of December 6, 1963, on which his commission testimony about the brain examination is based, was derived not from the Friday night autopsy at Bethesda, but from an examination of the brain some days later, after it had been removed from Kennedy's skull and fixed in formaldehyde to make it firmer and more amenable to examination. The report of the Friday night autopsy tells us that "the brain is removed and preserved for further study following formalin fixation." (WCHE, v.16, p.981) As Humes told the commission, "the brain in its fresh state does not lend itself well to examination." (WCHE, v.2, p.355)

But even under these circumstances, it would make no sense for Humes to describe in such minute detail cuts which he himself had made in order to section the brain for examination. It is clear from the language of the report and from his testimony that in describing these lacerations Humes is describing what he *found*, not what he had *done*. In fact, the Supplemental Report describes how brain sections were taken from the already existing lacerations. (CE391 at WCHE, v.16, p.987) There is no support for the hypothesis that the lacerations described by Humes resulted from the routine anatomical sectioning of the brain in preparation for its examination. And their description suggests that they are not the paths of bullets or bullet fragments. They give the appearance of being lacerations made with a scalpel sometime after the body left Dallas and before the start of the autopsy at Bethesda.

Conclusions of the Bethesda autopsy team

The foregoing results from the autopsy allowed the Bethesda doctors to construct a scenario for how the assassination occurred. Humes told the commission that for the fatal head wound, "our interpretation is . . . that the missile struck the right occipital region, penetrated through the two tables of the skull, making the characteristic coning on the inner table which I have previously referred to. That one portion of the missile and judging by the size of the defect thus produced, the major portion of the missile, made its exit through this large defect. A second portion of the missile or multiple second portions were deflected, and traversed a distance as enumerated by this [dotted] line, with the major portion of that fragment coming to lodge in the position indicated [in CE388]." (WCHE, v.2, p.353-354)

As for the back/neck wound, Humes told the commission: "This missile, to the best of our ability to ascertain, struck no bone protuberances, no bony prominences, no bones as it traversed the President's body." X-rays disclosed no evidence of a bullet remaining in Kennedy's body. "We concluded that this missile depicted in CE385 . . . which entered the President's body traversed the President's body and made its exit through the wound observed by the physicians at Parkland Hospital and later extended as a tracheotomy wound." (WCHE, v.2, p.364)

The flies on the wall at Bethesda

In addition to the big names of Humes, Boswell, and Finck, and the even bigger names of Stover and Galloway, there were a number of other individuals in the autopsy room – doctors, assistants, photographers, and technicians, plus agents from the FBI and Secret Service – who witnessed or took part in the proceedings. Most of these were not heard in testimony by the Warren Commission. Why bother questioning a lab technician or a photographer or an FBI agent when you can hear from the men who actually performed the autopsy? What could these other "extras" have to offer the commission that could not be obtained more reliably from Dr. Humes and his team? We will answer that question by looking at information given by three of those in attendance, who were interviewed in 1977 by staffers of the House Select Committee on Assassinations. These Bethesda witnesses tell stories which are remarkably consistent with each other, and which contradict the major conclusions of the Warren Report.

Interview of James Curtis Jenkins (ARRB MD65)

Jenkins was attending lab technician school at Bethesda Medical Center in 1963 and worked as a student lab technician at the time of the assassination. His duties included assisting with autopsies. He was interviewed on August 29, 1977 by Andy Purdy and Jim Kelly of the HSCA staff.

Jenkins gave the interviewers his recollection of Kennedy's wounds as he observed them in the autopsy room. He remembered seeing "a throat wound which looked like a tracheotomy." He saw a head wound in the "middle temporal region back to the occipital". He described the back wound as being "just below the collar to the right of the midline". (ARRB, MD65, p.4)

Jenkins told the interviewers he believes that "Dr. Humes attempted to probe the back wound. He said he didn't believe the doctor found that the probe penetrated into the chest." "Mr. Jenkins was not clear as to who may have been giving the autopsy doctors their orders. He said 'a lot of people were making suggestions.'" (ARRB, MD65, p.5) Jenkins told the interviewers that numerous high-ranking officers were present. He said that Humes, Boswell, and the Captain of the Honor Guard were the only ones not of flag rank". Jenkins said "he was told subsequent to the autopsy by an admiral not to discuss the autopsy. He said he later learned this man was the Surgeon General." (ARRB, MD65, p.6)

According to Jenkins, the "visitors were so intense about finding the wound in the back of the head." He "recalls Humes trying to probe the [back] wound with his finger which enabled him to reach the end of the wound." (ARRB, MD65, p.8) Jenkins recalled "Humes discussing with someone the problem of finding the bullet. He said this discussion amounted to a 'disturbance'. Jenkins had the impression that everything 'seemed like it was predesignated . . . seemed they had an answer and wanted to prove it'". (ARRB, MD65, p.10)

In describing the wounds, Jenkins said the back wound was "very shallow" and did not enter the chest cavity. "He said the wound to the head entered the top rear quadrant from the front side." (ARRB, MD65, p.11) Jenkins did "not recall a small hole in the head as drawn on the descriptive sheet. He said the big hole would have covered the area where the little hole was drawn on the sheet." (ARRB, MD65, p.12) Jenkins turns again to the back wound recalling that "the doctors extensively attempted to probe the back wound. . . . He said Humes could probe the bottom of the wound with his little finger and said that the metal probe went in 2-4 inches. He said it was quite a 'fact of controversy' that the doctors 'couldn't prove the bullet came into the [chest] cavity'". (ARRB, MD65, p.13) Regarding the schematic drawing of the neck wound (CE385, WCHE, v.16, p.977), "Jenkins said he didn't see the possibility that it was accurate. . . . He added that he thought the entry wound in the back was lower than that shown in the drawing. . . . He said that according to his recollection of the location of the back wound the bullet would have been going upward through the body to have exited in the front of the neck. . . . Jenkins said he believed the autopsy face sheet was essentially accurate regarding the location of the wound in the back." (ARRB, MD65, p.14-15) [Autopsy face sheet is CE397 at WCHE, v.17, p.45]

Jenkins was interviewed in 1979 by assassination researcher David Lifton. He told Lifton that he remembered Humes probing the back wound and being able to touch the bottom of the wound with his finger. Jenkins said that there was "no way that that [bullet in the back] could have exited in the front because it was then low in the chest cavity . . . somewhere around the junction of the descending aorta or the bronchus in the lungs." Based on his observations at the autopsy, Jenkins had expected the autopsy report to conclude that Kennedy had been shot once in the back from behind, and once in the head from in front. According to Jenkins, "Humes was a 'super-military type of person' – not in the sense that he was authoritarian, but that he was concerned with his next promotion and his career in general. 'He was the type of individual that would do anything anybody above him told him to do. . . . my personal feeling is that he was probably directed to write the autopsy report.'" As for who might have directed Humes in writing the autopsy report, Lifton noted that Humes had a short chain of command. His direct superior was Capt. Stover, chief of the Bethesda medical school. Next was Admiral Galloway, head of the Bethesda Medical Center, and next the Surgeon General. After that, Lifton remarked, any orders would have had to come from either the Joint Chiefs, or the White House. To this suggestion, Jenkins replied, "I didn't say that, you did." (Lifton, *Best Evidence*, 1988 ed., p.612-613)

We see that this information from Jenkins challenges the views expressed in Humes' autopsy report:

1. Back wound was below the collar line.
2. Back wound was shallow and could not be probed.
3. Back wound was lower than the front neck wound.
4. No small bullet wound was found in the back of the head.
5. Big hole was found in the back of the head.
6. Head wound entered from the front side.

Interview of Paul O'Connor (ARRB MD64)

O'Connor's duties were similar to those of James Jenkins, and they often worked together on autopsies. He was interviewed on August 29, 1977 by Andy Purdy and Jim Kelly of the HSCA. O'Connor said that the body was brought in in a "pink shipping casket and it arrived approximately eight o'clock. He said the body was in a body bag and the head was wrapped in a sheet." (ARRB, MD64, p.2) O'Connor described the large head wound as being in the region from the "occipital around the temporal and parietal regions" He said there was a "massive hole, no little hole". The interview records that "O'Connor believes the bullet came in from the front right and blew out the top." Later, said O'Connor, the doctors found the wound in the back. He locates it "just above C-7". (ARRB, MD64, p.6) (i.e., the seventh cervical vertebra). This is slightly higher than Kennedy's personal physician Dr. Burkley identified it. When he filled out Kennedy's death certificate, Burkley placed the back wound at the third thoracic vertebra. (ARRB, MD6, p.2)

At one point during the autopsy, O'Connor was asked to wait outside the autopsy room. The HSCA interviewers recorded that later "Jenkins or someone else told him that the doctors had 'found a fragment of a bullet lodged in the intercostal muscle on the right rear side' of the President's body. O'Connor was also told that 'a lot of blood infiltrated the intercostal muscle.'" (ARRB, MD64, p.7) O'Connor did not recall that the autopsy doctors had discussed the possibility of a bullet exiting through the front of the neck. (ARRB, MD64, p.8-9)

O'Connor was asked about CE386 [WCHE, v.16, p.977], a drawing which is supposed to illustrate the head wounds. O'Connor told the interviewers that this drawing did "not reflect what I saw. The little head hole was not there." He thought CE385 looked "fairly accurate". He thought the back hole on the autopsy sheet was "too far down". (ARRB, MD64, p.9)

Again, we find in O'Connor's testimony information which challenges the views of Humes and the Warren Commission:

1. Large wound was in the back of the head.
2. No little wound was in the back of the head.
3. Looked like bullet entered head from front right.
4. Bullet fragment were found in the muscles of the chest.

HSCA testimony of Dr. John Ebersole (ARRB, MD60)

Dr. Ebersole was Acting Chief of Radiology at the Bethesda Naval Hospital. He was present during Kennedy's autopsy. Like Jenkins and O'Connor, Ebersole was not called to testify before the Warren Commission, nor was his deposition taken. He testified before the medical panel of the HSCA on March 11, 1978.

When Kennedy's body was removed from the coffin, Ebersole noted "a neatly *sutured* transverse surgical wound across the low neck (This is the first we have heard about the tracheotomy wound being sutured sometime prior to the autopsy. None of the Dallas doctors spoke of suturing the tracheotomy incision.) He also saw that "the back of the head was missing" (ARRB, MD60, p.3) Ebersole's task was to X-ray the body to determine whether a bullet was present.

Ebersole testified that "about 12:30 a large *fragment of the occipital bone* was received from Dallas and at Dr. Finck's request I X-rayed these. . . . The X-rays were taken by the Secret Service that evening. I did not see them again." (MD60, p.5) This statement of Ebersole's is highly significant. Humes had testified that the additional skull fragments brought in from Dallas contained evidence of a bullet exit hole, based on coning or shelving of the exterior surface of the skull. (WCHE, v.2, p.354-355) If, as Dr. Ebersole recalled, this skull fragment was actually part of the occipital bone, which is in the back of the head, it means that Humes discovered evidence that the bullet exited the *back* of the head, implying that it had entered from the front. Perhaps this is what Humes had in mind when he made his cryptic comment to the Warren Commission that "it is impossible for [the head shot] to have been fired from other than behind. Or to have exited from other than behind." (WCHE, v.2, p.360) Perhaps Humes simply misspoke. But Ebersole's identification of the late-arriving bone as part of the occipital lends significance to this perplexing remark from Humes. Recall that Humes did not actually identify which part of the skull the newly delivered skull fragment belonged to. The impression was given that it constituted part of the parietal bone, but this was not actually stated.

Ebersole was asked by Dr. Michael Baden what the X-rays indicated as to the direction of the head shot.

> BADEN: Do you on examination of these [X-ray] films have an opinion as to where the gunshot wound of entrance was in the head radiologically?
> EBERSOLE: In my opinion it would have come from the side on the basis of the films. (ARRB, MD60, p.18)

Again, we have discrepancies with respect to the official version of events:
1. Skull fragment delivered during the autopsy was from the occipital bone.
2. X-rays indicate bullet entry from the side of the head.

Parkland vs. Bethesda?

Clearly the observations and conclusions of the autopsy doctors are at variance with the observations made by the doctors at Parkland Hospital and with many of the eyewitnesses to the assassination. But it would be wrong to characterize this conflict as "Parkland vs. Bethesda". As we have just seen, there were several witnesses at Bethesda, not only Jenkins, O'Connor, and Ebersole, but also FBI agents Sibert and O'Neill, who saw things and drew conclusions at variance with what became the official version that appeared in the Warren Report. The presence of dissenting witnesses at Bethesda means that the government's version cannot be upheld by simply dismissing the Parkland doctors and the Dealey Plaza witnesses and accepting the testimony of Humes and his Bethesda autopsy team as the "best evidence".

Conclusion:

The official interpretations of the front neck wound and the side exit wound in the head were developed outside the actual autopsy itself. The explanation of the front neck wound as a bullet exit wound was an inference drawn by Dr. Humes after Dr. Perry told him about this wound on the morning after the autopsy. This inference was not based on anatomical observations from the autopsy itself, nor was this neck wound even discovered during the autopsy examination.

The interpretation of the side head wound as an exit wound was prompted by the late delivery of a skull bone late Friday night or early Saturday morning, which allegedly contained the characteristic beveling of a bullet exit. Until this last minute delivery occurred, the doctors were unable, based on examination of the body alone, to discover any physical evidence to demonstrate that a bullet exited through this large head wound on the right side. But there is no confirmed chain of possession for this skull fragment which was delivered to the autopsy room. Therefore, we cannot be sure that it was not artificially altered between the assassination and its arrival in Dallas, and there is no testimony that it even belonged to the parietal bone, as opposed to the occipital bone.

It might seem reasonable to simply assume by default that the side head wound was an exit wound because the rear head wound was an entry wound and the bullet had to exit somewhere, and we have a big hole on the right side of the head, so why isn't it obvious that the large wound was an exit wound? But we cannot conclude this, because there is an alternative explanation for the side wound: a tangential shot from the right front could have sheared through the bone and sliced off the large flap of bone seen in the autopsy pictures. This is precisely the scenario suggested by Dr. Kemp Clark, the Parkland Hospital neurosurgeon, who believed that the head wound was a tangential wound. (WCHE, v.6, p.21) So the determination that the side head wound represents a bullet exit hole does not automatically follow from the determination that the small rear hole (which no one at Parkland saw) was an entry wound. It must depend on concrete physical evidence showing that a bullet passed through this region of the skull. And any such evidence must have a solid chain of possession to ensure that the bone is what it is claimed to be. There is only one bone which displays the beveling on which Humes relied to infer an exit hole, and there were at least 12 hours between the assassination and the delivery of this bone to the autopsy room. This was plenty of time for someone to doctor the evidence to conform to the single gunman theory.

There was another skull fragment found which was not rushed to the autopsy doctors during the night. This piece of bone was found on Saturday, November 23 – after the autopsy was completed – by William "Billy" Harper, a student at Texas Christian University. According to an FBI report, while taking photographs on Elm Street at about 5:30 p.m. on Saturday, November 23, 1963, Harper found a piece of bone "in the area just south of the spot where President Kennedy was assassinated. . . . The bone was located approximately 25 feet south of the spot where President Kennedy was shot." (CD5, p.150) Harper's uncle, Dr. Jack Harper showed the bone to Dr. A. B. Cairns, Chief Pathologist at Methodist Hospital in Dallas, and Dr. Cairns "stated that the bone specimen looked like it came from the occipital region of the skull. He said he performed no tests on this piece of bone and evaluated it purely from its gross appearance." (FBI 105-82555 Oswald HQ File, Section 237, p.240) Billy Harper turned the bone over to Agent James Anderton of the Dallas FBI office "for whatever disposition the FBI desired". (CD5, p.150) The FBI turned the bone over to the President's personal physician, Dr. George Burkley. (CD5, p.151) We are not told whether the autopsy doctors were ever aware of it. When interviewed in 1977 by the Assassination Records Review Board, Dr. Harper said that "the skull fragment had relatively fresh blood on it." (AARB, MD19, p.1) The fact that this bone was found on the south curb of Elm Street, lends support to the presence of a shooter on the grassy slope, on the north side of Elm, firing from the right side, and a shot which would have blown this bone and other tissue to the left rear, toward the south curb of Elm Street.

THE EXPERTS

The Warren Commission relied on the opinions of numerous expert witnesses in the fields of pathology, ballistics, documents, fibers, and fingerprints in order to support their case against Oswald. As a general rule, in a real criminal trial, opinion testimony is not permitted. Witnesses must testify based on their knowledge, not on their opinions. Expert testimony is an exception to this rule, because experts in a field are deemed to have experience and training which makes their opinions more valuable and trustworthy than those of ordinary witnesses. In order to testify as an expert, a witness must be qualified, i.e., the witness must demonstrate that he or she has the necessary experience and background to justify confidence in their opinions. In addition, the witness's expertise must pertain to the subject matter upon which he or she is being asked to testify. For example, a ballistics expert could be asked for an opinion on bullet trajectories, but not on identification of fingerprints.

With few exceptions, the witnesses called as experts by the Warren Commission were legitimate experts. There is generally no objection to be raised against their qualifications to render expert testimony in their field. However, this does not mean that the expert witnesses always helped the commission's case. In some instances, the witnesses declined to give an opinion on the topic in question. In other instances, the witness testified the opposite of the point the attorney was trying to establish. Many of the experts testified to matters which had no bearing on the question of who shot the President. The multiplicity of expert witnesses testifying to irrelevant matters made for an impressive parade, but in the end did not strengthen the government's case against Oswald. When all is said and done, the expert witnesses failed to provide testimony sufficient to convict Oswald for the President's murder. This is in no small measure due to the inability to link up the physical evidence of the exhibits with the actual crime scene.

THE RIFLE – COMMISSION EXHIBIT 139

Commission Exhibit 139, the Italian rifle said to have been found on the sixth floor of the Texas School Book Depository, was the subject of numerous tests by various expert witnesses. A key question was whether it was possible to fire the rifle accurately within the minimum timeframe of 5.6 seconds established by the Zapruder film. As it turns out, tests conducted by both the FBI and the U. S. Army failed to confirm that such a feat was possible, or – if it was possible – that it actually happened on November 22, 1963 in Dallas.

How fast and how accurately could the Italian rifle be fired?

Tests were conducted by the FBI and the U. S. Army to determine how fast the rifle (CE139) could be fired with accuracy. None of these tests involved moving targets as was the case in the actual assassination. Yet *in none of these tests were the riflemen able to hit the aiming point with three shots within the 5.6 second interval imposed by the Zapruder film.*

For comparison, we note here that the distance from the sixth floor window to the point on the street corresponding to frame 210 of the Zapruder frame was calculated as approximately 177 feet, or 59 yards (CE894 at WCHE, v.18, p.89), and the distance to the point corresponding to frame 313 was approximately 265 feet, or 88 yards. (CE902 at WCHE, v.18, p.95) Secret Service agent John Joe Howlett had calculated the same distances as 170 feet and 260 feet on November 29, 1963. (CD5, p.117)

The FBI tests with the rifle

The FBI conducted three separate types of tests, under the supervision and direction of firearms and ballistics expert Robert Frazier. In Test 1, three different shooters – Charles Killion, Cortlandt Cunningham, and Robert Frazier – fired three shots at a stationary silhouette target 15 yards away (45 feet). (WCHE, v.3, p.402-403) Each man fired three shots. Killion fired his three shots in 9 seconds, Cunningham fired his in 8 seconds, and Frazier's time for firing three shots was 5.9 seconds. (WCHE, v.3, p.420); Thus, in this the simplest of all the rifle tests, *not one of the shooters was able to fire all three shots within the 5.6 seconds determined by the Zapruder film.* In this test, all the shots landed high and to the right of the aiming point, but were tightly bunched. (WCHE, v.3, p.404) This tight dispersion is what Frazier has in mind when he calls the rifle "a very accurate weapon". In calling it "accurate" he does not mean that the shooters actually hit the point aimed at, but simply that the hits were closely bunched. Frazier also told the committee that when the FBI received the rifle, the scope had been taken off in the search for fingerprints, and then put back on. So it was not possible to draw any conclusions about the condition and settings of the scope at the time of the assassination. (WCHE, v.3, p.411)

The second FBI test was performed by Frazier alone. (One wonders if this was because he achieved the fastest firing time in the first test. By "winning" the first round, Frazier effectively eliminated the two slower shooters from further participation.) In Test 2, Frazier fired two series of three shots each at a distance of 25 yards (75 feet) "to determine how fast the weapon could be fired primarily, with secondary purpose accuracy. . . . I did not attempt to maintain in that test an accurate rate of fire." These two series of shots were fired in 4.8 seconds and 4.6 seconds. (WCHE, v.3, p.404) The time of 4.6 seconds, the fastest of all the attempts, was later used as the basis for the claim that 2.3 seconds is the minimum time required between shots for the rifle (WCR, p.97), although at this rate of fire, the aiming point was not hit, and no time was allowed for re-aiming between shots, which would be essential in the case of a moving target at greater distances. Furthermore, at this point in the testing five series of shots have been fired, and only one of those series was able to achieve the 2.3 second minimum time per shot – even though all these tests were conducted by experienced FBI riflemen.

In his first series of the Test 2 firings, Frazier's three shots landed "from 4 to 5 inches high and from 1 to 2 inches to the right of the aiming point, and landed within a 2-inch circle." For his second series, one shot was "about one inch high, and the other two about 4 or 5 inches high, and the maximum spread was 5 inches" on the stationary target at 25 yards. (WCHE, v.3, p.404) Thus, the stationary target point *could not be accurately hit* using the CE139 rifle at a distance of 25 yards within the 5.6 second time limit. All the test shots landed high and to the right. The bias shown in these shots at 25 yards would have been even greater at 59 yards, which is the approximate distance from the TSBD sixth floor window to the spot where President Kennedy was hit with the first shot, and an even greater deviation from the target would be expected at 88 yards, which is the approximate distance from the window to the spot where Kennedy was hit in the head.

In FBI Test 3, Frazier himself fired four series of three shots each at four separate stationary targets from a distance of 100 yards. (WCHE, v.3, p.404) Once again, all of the hits were high and to the right of the aiming point. Frazier's times for these four series of shots were 5.9, 6.2, 5.6, and 6.5 seconds. In other words, when firing for accuracy, Frazier was not able to maintain the 4.6 second time achieved in Test 2. On Test 3, only one series of three shots fell within the 5.6 second timeframe established by the Zapruder film, with no margin to spare, and these shots "landed in a 3-inch circle located about 2-1/2 inches high and 2 inches to the right of the aiming point." (WCHE, v.3, p.405) In Test 3, the minimum time between shots is thus calculated to be 2.8 seconds, not the 2.3 seconds from Test 2. This adds a whole second to the total time required to fire 3 shots. If the minimum time between shots is 2.8 seconds, and the maximum time allowed for three shots is 5.6 seconds, then Oswald's shooting performance would have had to exceed that of the three FBI experts, since *none of Frazier's tests at 100 yards resulted in hitting the aiming point within a 5.6 second timeframe*. And these results are from a test involving a stationary target, not a moving target.

Thus, the FBI shooting tests do not establish that Oswald or anyone else was able to fire the Italian rifle three times within 5.6 seconds and achieve three hits even on a stationary target, much less a moving one. Therefore, the FBI Summary Report is wrong when it states that "by actual tests it has been demonstrated by the FBI that a skilled person can fire three accurately aimed shots with this weapon in five seconds." (CD1, p.17) The minimum time of 2.3 seconds per shot, which the Warren Report uses to establish the possibility of three shots in 5.6 seconds, is chosen as the minimum time to work the bolt of the rifle, with no time for aiming, even though all but one of the FBI tests took longer than the 2.3 second interval. Far from proving that Oswald could have accurately fired his Italian rifle three times in the 5.6 seconds established by the Zapruder film, the FBI succeeded in proving that this feat was most improbable, if not downright impossible. (The Warren Report's rationalization of these disappointing test results is on p.194 of the WCR.

But their explanation relies on assumptions about the scope settings, which, as we saw above, could not be determined due to prior removal and re-installation of the scope. See WCHE, v.3, p.411.)

Tests conducted by the U. S. Army

Another set of test firings with the CE139 rifle was conducted by the U. S. Army, under the supervision of Ronald Simmons, Chief of the Infantry Weapons Evaluation Branch of the Ballistics Research Laboratory of the Department of the Army. His expertise is in the evaluation of military rifles for accuracy, killing and wounding power, and tactical performance. (WCHE, v.3, p.441-442) In testing the Italian rifle, three riflemen were selected as the shooters. According to Simmons, all were rated as Master riflemen by the National Rifle Association. Simmons himself was not one of the test shooters. (WCHE, v.3, p.445)

Simmons' team conducted a test to determine the dispersion of shots fired. At 100 yards, the dispersion was equivalent to a little more than one inch. Note, however, that dispersion does not measure accuracy in hitting a target. It simply measures how far apart from each other the hits land when aimed at the same point. Simmons then conducted a test involving three stationary silhouette targets placed at distances equivalent to those which Oswald supposedly encountered in the actual assassination: 175 feet, 240 feet, and 265 feet. (These distances were given to Simmons by Warren Commission staff attorney Melvin Eisenberg – WCHE, v.3, p.444) The shooters fired at these stationary targets from a 30-foot tower, which is half the height of the sixth floor windowsill from which the shots were allegedly fired. (WCHE, v.3, p.408) The marksmen in this test were instructed to obtain hits on all three targets within as short a time interval as possible. Simmons reports that "the marksmen were instructed to take as much time as they desired at the first target, and then to fire at the first target – being at 175 feet – to then fire at the target emplaced at 240 feet, and then at the one at 265 feet." (WCHE, v.3, p.444)

This test conducted by the Army marksmen under Simmons' supervision deviates in several important respects from the actual assassination conditions:

- The targets in the test were stationary, not moving;
- The Army marksmen were able to take as much time as they wished to fire at the first target. Under the actual conditions of the assassination, the gunman would not have been able to do this because the oak tree would have obscured his vision until the target came out from under the tree at frame 207 in the Zapruder film, as shown in the re-enactment photo of CE892 (WCHE, v.18, p.88) After the car came out from under the tree, the time available to fire the first shot would have been limited to less than a second, if the first shot was fired between frames 210 and 225, as the Warren Report concludes. (WCR, p.105);
- The height of the tower from which the test shooters fired was only half the height of the actual sixth floor window (WCHE, v.3, p.408). The actual angle

of firing would thus have been greater in the actual assassination, requiring an assassin to make a greater adjustment between shots than in the test, in order to re-aim the rifle to the new target point below. Less adjustment in re-aiming between shots would have been required shooting from the 30-foot tower than from the 60-foot windowsill.

- In order to count as a hit, the test firers only had to hit the silhouette target anywhere on the target. They did not necessarily have to achieve at least one "fatal" hit – i.e., in the head of the silhouette. Simmons notes that it was not possible to tell what exact point in the target the shooters were aiming at. They were just told to aim at the target but not at any particular point on the target. In other words, the test shooters were firing at a bigger target (head and shoulders) than an actual assassin aiming for a fatal head shot. (WCHE, v.3, p.445)

Thus, the conditions under which the Army test shooters fired were easier in every respect than the conditions which were present in Dealey Plaza on November 22, 1963. Yet even with these advantages, the marksmen on Simmons' team were unable to achieve three hits within the 5.6 second time interval. Simmons' shooters "each fired two series of three rounds, using the telescopic sight. Then one of the firers repeated the exercise using the iron sight. . . . All firers hit the first target, and this was to be expected, because they had as much time as they desired to aim at the first target." (WCHE, v.3, p.445) On the first four attempts, all firers missed the second target. (WCHE, v.3, p.446) Two of the test shooters took 6.45 seconds or more to fire their shots. Each one of these shooters attempted the exercise twice, with elapsed time ranging from 6.45 seconds to 8.25 seconds. The third shooter, Specialist Miller, was able to fire his three shots within the 5.6 second time interval imposed by the Zapruder movie. In two attempts using the telescopic sight, Miller fired his three shots in 4.6 seconds and 5.15 seconds. But when using the telescope, he missed the second target on both attempts. In his attempt using the iron sight, he fired three shots in 4.45 seconds. (WCHE, v.3, p.446) When using the iron sight, Miller hit the second target, but with the third target he "missed the boards completely." Simmons tells the commission that each of the test shooters spent 2 or 3 minutes before the exercise practicing the operation of the bolt without ammunition. They did not pull the trigger during this practice, because they were concerned about breaking the firing pin. (WCHE, v.3, p.447)

Conclusion

In tests using the CE139 Italian rifle, *none of the test shooters were able to duplicate the assassination scenario of three hits within 5.6 seconds.* In every respect, the actual assassination conditions were more challenging for a lone sniper than were the test conditions. The commission speculated that perhaps one of the shots missed on November 22, 1963, which would allow a miss by the testers without contradicting the actual assassination results. But the commission is uncertain which shot missed, if any, and each missed shot scenario is contradicted by other evidence. A missed shot in a 3-shot scenario requires that Kennedy and Connally were hit by the same bullet. This single bullet theory has already been refuted above, so cannot be used to excuse the many missed shots by the test shooters.

The inevitable conclusion to be drawn from these test firings is that the success attributed to the lone gunman firing from the sixth floor window of the TSBD on November 22, 1963 could not be duplicated by any of the expert marksmen from the FBI and the U. S. Army. Oswald would have had a valid defense, if he had come to trial, that the shots attributed to him by the government version of events could not possibly have been fired by one shooter who scored three hits during the required timeframe established by the Zapruder film, while using the Italian rifle allegedly found on the sixth floor of the TSBD.

Warren Commission counsel Wesley Liebeler, in a memorandum to the commission, dated September 6, 1964, questioned whether the commission's use of 2.3 seconds as the minimum firing time between shots was the correct figure to use in evaluating the plausibility of Oswald's performance. Liebeler wrote: "As I read through the section on rifle capability it appears that 15 different sets of three shots were fired by supposedly expert riflemen of the FBI and other places. According to my calculations those 15 sets of shots took a total of 93.8 seconds to be fired. The average of all 15 is a little over 6.2 seconds. Assuming that time is calculated commencing with the firing of the first shot, that means the average time it took to fire the two remaining shots was about 6.2 seconds. That comes to about 3.1 seconds for each shot, not counting the time consumed by the actual firing, which would not be very much. I recall that chapter 3 [of the Warren Report draft] said that the minimum time that had to elapse between shots was 2.25 seconds, which is pretty close to the one set of fast shots fired by Frazier of the FBI. The conclusion indicates that Oswald had the capability to fire three shots with two hits in from 4.8 to 5.6 seconds. The conclusion at its most extreme states that Oswald could fire faster than the Commission experts fired in 12 of their 15 tries. . . . The figure of 2.25 as a minimum firing time for each shot is used throughout chapter 3. The present discussion of rifle capability shows that expert riflemen could not fire the assassination weapon that fast. Only one of the experts managed to do so, and his shots, like those of the other FBI experts, were high and to the right of the target. The fact is that most of the experts were much more proficient with a rifle than Oswald could ever be expected to be." (Wesley Liebeler memorandum to the Warren Commission dated 9/6/64. Reproduced in HSCA, v.11, p.231, JFK Exhibit No. 36)

The rifle was in poor condition, inaccurate, and the scope could not be properly sighted.

The experts who examined the rifle and conducted the test firings noted its poor condition, as well as its idiosyncrasies with regard to the trigger pull and bolt operation. They concluded that a shooter using this rifle would need considerable practice and familiarity with these specific characteristics of the rifle in order to fire it effectively.

Robert Frazier testified that "the stock is worn, scratched. The bolt is relatively smooth, as if it had been operated several times . . . The barrel . . . was not, when we first got it, in excellent condition. It was, I would say, in fair condition. In other words, it showed the effects of wear and corrosion." (WCHE, v.3, p.394); "The lands and the grooves were worn, the corners were worn, and the interior of the surface was roughened from corrosion or wear." (WCHE, v.3, p.395)

The muzzle velocity averaged 2165 feet per second in Frazier's tests. (WCHE, v.3, p.400) Frazier called it a "low velocity" weapon, and noted that it would have less "killing power" than higher velocity bullets from a more powerful weapon. But he allows nonetheless that the Italian Mannlicher-Carcano rifle "has very adequate killing power with reference to humans". (WCHE, v.3, p.414) In tests conducted by the U. S. Army, the muzzle velocity was approximately 2200 feet per second. (WCHE, v. 3, p.443) Frazier measured the overall length of the rifle as 40.2 inches. When disassembled, the longest component (the wooden stock) is 34.8 inches. (WCHE, v.3, p.395)

Frazier testified that his FBI team had difficulty using the telescopic sight on the rifle. "When we attempted to sight in this rifle at Quantico, we found that the elevation adjustment in the telescopic sight was not sufficient to bring the point of impact to the aiming point. In attempting to adjust and sight-in the rifle, every time we changed the adjusting screws to move the crosshairs in the telescopic sight in one direction it also affected the movement of the impact or the point of impact in the other direction. That is, if we moved the crosshairs in the telescope to the left it would also affect the elevation setting of the telescope. And when we had sighted-in the rifle approximately, we fired several shots and found that the shots were not all landing in the same place, but were gradually moving away from the point of impact. This was apparently due to the construction of the telescope, which apparently did not stabilize itself – that is, the spring mounting in the crosshair ring did not stabilize until we had fired five or six shots." (WCHE, v.3, p.405) Obviously Frazier was not considering the impact of these imperfections on a shooter's ability to fire the rifle accurately when he told the commission that "it requires no training at all to shoot a weapon with a telescopic sight once you know that you must put the crosshairs on the target and that is all that is necessary." (WCHE, v.3, p.413) In Liebeler's memo to the commission, he wrote that "there is a great deal of testimony in the record that a telescopic sight is a sensitive proposition. You can't leave a rifle and scope laying around in a garage underfoot for almost 3 months, just having brought it back from New Orleans in the back of a station wagon, and expect to hit anything with it, unless you take the trouble to fire it and sight the scope in." (Wesley Liebeler memorandum to the Warren Commission dated 9/6/64. Reproduced in HSCA, v.11, p.230, JFK Exhibit No. 36)

Ronald Simmons testified to the commission that his Army test shooters "could not sight the weapon in using the telescope. . . . We did adjust the telescopic sight by the addition of two shims. (WCHE, v.3, p.443) Simmons reports that his test firers encountered other difficulties in using the rifle. "There were several comments made particularly with respect to the amount of effort required to open the bolt. As a matter of fact, Mr. Staley had difficulty in opening the bolt in his first firing exercise. He thought it was completely up and it was not, and he had to retrace his steps as he attempted to open the bolt after the first round. There was also comment made about the trigger pull, which is different as far as these firers are concerned. It is in effect a two-stage operation where the first, in the first stage the trigger is relatively free, and it suddenly required a greater pull to actually fire the weapon." (WCHE, v.3, p.447) According to Simmons, in order to achieve maximum accuracy with this particular weapon, considerable experience with the rifle would be required, "because of the amount of effort required to work the bolt. . . . In our experiments, the pressure to open the bolt was so great that we tended to move the rifle off the target, whereas with greater proficiency this *might not* have occurred." (WCHE, v.3, p.449)

Conclusion

The Italian rifle said to have been recovered from the sixth floor of the TSBD was in such poor condition and its operation was so quirky that even expert riflemen from the FBI and the Army were not able to fire it and achieve the hits attributed to Oswald. The idiosyncrasies of the trigger pull and the bolt, plus the inability to sight in the scope, add to the difficulties an assassin would face if he had attempted to pull off the assassination using this weapon. These factors make it highly unlikely that the assassination was actually accomplished by a single gunman using this rifle.

THE BALLISTICS EVIDENCE AND THE CHAIN OF POSSESSION

The ballistics evidence consists of expert testimony regarding the bullets and shells found at or near the scene of the assassination, and their relationship to the rifle alleged to have fired them. The expert witnesses were able to state definitely that the following items were fired in the Italian rifle known as CE139: 1) three cartridge cases said to have been recovered from the sixth floor window of the Texas School Book Depository; 2) two bullet fragments which were said to have been found in the Presidential car; and 3) the bullet allegedly found on a stretcher at Parkland Hospital. The Warren Commission used this expert testimony to conclude that "the nearly whole bullet from the stretcher and the two larger bullet fragments found in the Presidential limousine [had been] fired in the [serial number] C2766 Mannlicher-Carcano rifle found in the Depository to the exclusion of all other weapons." The same conclusion was reached regarding the three cartridge cases from the TSBD. (WCR, p.85) Additional bullet fragments were found, but were too small to be positively connected to the rifle.

In analyzing this ballistic evidence, it is important to keep in mind the legal concept known as "foundation". In a criminal trial, "laying foundation" means providing authentication that the evidence you are about to present is really what you say it is. As expressed by Rule 901 of the Federal Rules of Evidence: "To satisfy the requirement of authenticating or identifying an item of evidence, the proponent must produce evidence sufficient to support a finding that the item is what the proponent claims it is."

For example, Commission Exhibit 399 is a bullet said to have been found on a stretcher at Parkland Hospital on the afternoon of November 22, 1963. How do we know that the bullet in evidence as CE399 is actually the bullet that was found at Parkland? Normally this would be established by maintaining a "chain of possession" for the evidence. The person who found the evidence might scratch his or her initials on the bullet at the time it is found, so that it can later be identified on the witness stand as the same bullet. If this foundation cannot be established, the purported evidence cannot be connected with the case and is therefore irrelevant and inadmissible, since the evidence in that case may have been falsified, substituted, or planted sometime after the fact.

An example from the testimony of FBI firearms expert Cortlandt Cunningham shows what lack of foundation looks like. Cunningham was examined before the Warren Commission by Melvin Eisenberg regarding the revolver which was in evidence as Commission Exhibit 143. During the questioning, it is alleged and assumed that this revolver is the one that was taken from Oswald at the time of his arrest. After Cunningham testifies that the cartridge cases presented by Eisenberg were definitely fired in the CE143 revolver, commission member Hale Boggs raises the question of foundation in the following exchange:

> BOGGS: What you are saying is that there is no doubt about the fact that the cartridges that you examined came from this revolver?
> CUNNINGHAM: That is correct.
> BOGGS: And, of course, there is no question about the fact that this was Mr. Oswald's revolver. Is that so?
> EISENBERG: That will be proved, I hope, before the end of the hearings. This witness cannot himself testify.
> BOGGS: I understand that. I am asking you.
> EISENBERG: There is no question, I don't think, about that. That will be the subject of testimony.
> BOGGS: I know. We are not following the exact rules of evidence around here. (WCHE, v.3, p.473)

Thus, at the time of this questioning, it has not been proven that the CE143 revolver belonged to Oswald. In a real criminal trial, the defense would have objected to Cunningham's testimony regarding the revolver until it had been proven that this revolver was what the prosecution claimed it to be – i.e., the revolver taken from Oswald when he was arrested. If this has not been proven, then the testimony linking the cartridge cases to the revolver is irrelevant and inadmissible. As Boggs correctly notes, failure to lay this foundation is a violation of the rules of evidence, which the commission was not obligated to follow and which they in fact did not follow. The commission admitted a great deal of evidence without establishing the necessary foundation, as we are about to see.

The question of foundation is not just a legal nicety which can be dispensed with as a technical nuisance. Especially in the case of Oswald, the prevailing conspiracist position is not simply that Oswald was innocent of Kennedy's murder, but that he was framed. Planting of evidence and substitution of evidence are two ways that a suspect can be framed. So if the items in evidence for ballistic analysis are not what they are claimed to be, then they may very well have been planted at the crime scene or substituted for the ones found at the crime scene, and in that case expert ballistic testimony is of no value in establishing Oswald's guilt.

In evaluating the ballistics evidence in the Kennedy assassination, we must first evaluate whether the necessary foundation has been laid for the physical items of evidence. Only then can we evaluate the probative value of that evidence.

To establish foundation for these items of evidence we must answer the following questions:

> 1) Is the Italian rifle – known as Commission Exhibit 139 – the same rifle that was found on the sixth floor of the TSBD on the afternoon of the assassination?
> 2) Were the three cartridge shells CE543, CE544, and CE545 the same ones that were discovered on the sixth floor of the TSBD?
> 3) Were the bullet fragments CE567 and CE569 actually found in the front seat of the Presidential car?
> 4) Was the bullet CE399 the actual bullet which was found on a stretcher at Parkland Hospital on the afternoon of November 22, 1963?

If the answer to these questions is "yes", then the physical evidence is relevant to the case, and the next step is to assess their probative value – i.e., their value in answering the factual questions at the heart of the case. If the answer to any one of these questions is "no", then that physical item cannot be linked with the assassination, and therefore is of no value in establishing the guilt of Oswald or anyone else.

Is the Italian rifle CE139 the same rifle that was found on the sixth floor of the TSBD on the afternoon of November 22, 1963?

The rifle is first offered in evidence by Lee Rankin in his interrogation of Marina Oswald on February 6, 1964. Rankin presents the rifle along with a series of other items shown to Marina Oswald for identification. Rankin does not actually ask her a foundational question for the rifle. Indeed, he does not ask her any question at all about the rifle. After showing her a camera flash attachment, Rankin produces the rifle and declares, "Exhibit 139." Marina responds, "This is the fateful rifle of Lee Oswald," after which Rankin requests that the rifle be received in evidence as Commission Exhibit 139. (WCHE, v.1, p.119) At the time of this questioning Marina had already told Rankin that she cannot tell the difference between a rifle and a shotgun. (WCHE, v.1, p.13) So she is not competent to testify as to whether the CE139 rifle was one that belonged to Oswald or not. On the afternoon of the assassination, when Captain Will Fritz showed Marina the rifle recovered from the TSBD, "she couldn't identify it positively but she said it looked like the rifle that he had, but she couldn't say for sure." (WCHE, v.4, p.211) More importantly for the evidential question is the fact that Marina Oswald is not competent to testify whether this rifle was the one found on the sixth floor of the TSBD, simply because she was not there when it was found. Thus, Marina's identification of the rifle, even if she were familiar enough with guns to identify it, would not establish the foundation necessary to admit the rifle into evidence as the assassination weapon.

CE139 makes its next appearance during a brief interrogation of FBI agent Cortlandt Cunningham in a commission session held on March 11, 1964. Cunningham appears before the commission for the sole purpose of demonstrating how fast the CE139 rifle can be assembled and disassembled. He assembled it before the commission in six minutes, although he has some difficulty getting the retaining screw and the top stock to engage correctly. (WCHE, v.2, p.252) During this brief appearance, in response to a question from Earl Warren, Cunningham asserts "This is the assassination weapon." And commission counsel Joseph Ball informs the commission, "This is the weapon found on the sixth floor of the Texas Book Depository." (WCHE, v.2, p.252) But Cunningham is not competent to testify where the rifle was found, and Ball is an attorney, not a witness, so also cannot testify from personal knowledge as to where the rifle came from. So with Cunningham's testimony at this time no foundation has been laid for accepting the CE139 rifle as having been found on the sixth floor of the TSBD.

At the interrogation of Michael Paine by Wesley Liebeler on March 18, 1964. Liebeler identifies CE139 as "a rifle that was found in the Texas School Book Depository Building." At this stage of the proceedings, no one has yet testified that CE139 was found in the Texas School Book Depository. Foundation has still not been established for identifying CE139 as having been found at the assassination scene. Liebeler asks Paine whether he ever saw the CE139 rifle prior to November 22, 1963, and Paine testifies that he had not. (WCHE, v.2, p.416)

The first witness to be questioned who could possibly identify the rifle as the one found on the sixth floor of the TSBD is Deputy Sheriff Eugene Boone. While searching the sixth floor shortly after the assassination, Boone "caught a glimpse of the rifle, stuffed down between two rows of boxes with another box or so pulled over the top of it. And I hollered that the rifle was there." (WCHE, v.3, p.293) Questioning Boone before the commission on March 25, 1964, commission counsel Joseph Ball tried to elicit the necessary foundation:

BALL: I show you a rifle which is Commission Exhibit 139. Can you tell us whether or not that *looks like* the rifle you saw on the floor that day?

BOONE: It looks like the same rifle. I have no way of being positive.

BALL: You never handled it?

BOONE: I did not touch the weapon at all. (WCHE, v.3, p.294)

Not only is Boone unable to positively identify CE139 as the rifle he found, Ball does not even ask him whether it is the same rifle. Ball only asks if CE139 *looks like* the rifle he found. Boone originally thought the rifle "appeared to be a 7.65 mm Mauser with a telescope sight on the rifle," and this is what he stated in his report dated November 22, 1963. (WCHE, v.19, p.507)

Deputy Seymour Weitzman, who was with Boone when the rifle was discovered, also reported that "this rifle was a 7.65 Mauser bolt action equipped with a 4/13 scope [and] a thick leather brownish-black sling on it." (WCHE, v.24, p.228a) Weitzman was not called to testify before a session of the commission. His deposition was taken by Joseph Ball on April 1, 1964, but during his deposition Weitzman was not shown the CE139 rifle for identification. (WCHE, v.7, pp.105-109) Weitzman does testify that "we made a man-tight barricade until the crime lab came up and removed the gun itself." (WCHE, v.7, p.107)

Deputy Luke Mooney, who was present on the sixth floor when the rifle was found, appeared in a commission session on March 25, 1964, and he, too, was interrogated by Joseph Ball, but Ball did not present the CE139 rifle to Mooney to ask for his identification. (WCHE, v.3, p.289-290)

Capt. Will Fritz appeared before the commission on April 22, 1964. He was the first person to handle the rifle after it was discovered. (WCHE, v.4, p.220) He ejected a live round from the chamber, but he did not initial this cartridge for identification. (WCHE, v.4, p.205); Nor did Fritz initial or mark the rifle for identification. Fritz says he thinks he gave the rifle to Lt. Day to bring to City Hall. "I don't believe I ever carried that rifle to city hall. I believe Lieutenant Day carried it to city hall. Anyway, if you will ask him he can be more positive than I." Ball does not show the CE139 rifle to Fritz during his testimony in order to get a positive identification as to whether CE139 is the same rifle he handled on the sixth floor of the TSBD. (WCHE, v.4, p.206)

Finally, Lt. J. C. Day of the Dallas police crime lab testifies to the Warren Commission on April 22, 1964 and is presented with the CE139 rifle and identifies it as "the rifle found on the sixth floor of the [TSBD]. (WCHE, v.4, p.259) He is able to make this identification because he had scratched his name on the stock. (WCHE, v.4, p.260) However, Lt. Day does not tell us when he scratched his name on the rifle. Did he do so after he got back to the police station? How long after? Was there any opportunity for the rifle to have been switched with another rifle before Day put his initials on it? These questions are not asked or answered in his testimony. However, he was not present when the rifle was discovered by Boone and Weitzman. And we know from his testimony on the three cartridge shells that he did not mark the shells themselves at the time they were recovered, but only marked the envelope in which they were placed. The shells were marked later. (WCHE, v.4, p.253) Thus, we see that Lt. Day was not always prompt in marking the evidence for identification, so that it would not be out of the question for him to have waited until he got back to the office to mark the rifle, too. Day testified that he released the rifle to the FBI at 11:45 p.m. on the night of November 22, but says it was sent back to Dallas on November 24 (the day Oswald was killed), only to be returned to the FBI on November 26. (WCHE, v.4, p.261-262)

So neither of the two officers who discovered the rifle on the sixth floor is able to identify CE139 as the rifle they found, and both of them originally stated that the rifle they found was a 7.65 mm Mauser, not a 6.5 mm Italian Mannlicher-Carcano. Capt. Fritz did not mark the rifle for identification, and he is not asked to identify CE139 as the rifle he handled at the TSBD. Lt. Day did mark the rifle with his name and identified CE139 as the rifle found at the TSBD, but he does not say when he marked it, and he is not the person who found it, so we cannot rule out substitution of a different rifle after Day (or Fritz) took the rifle back to the police station and before Day placed his name on it.

A Mauser was seen in the TSBD just two days before the assassination.

Early identification of the rifle as a Mauser is rendered more plausible by the fact that a Mauser was actually seen in the TSBD two days before the assassination, and there is no corroborated testimony that it ever left the building. It was Oswald himself who told Capt. Will Fritz about this incident, during his interrogation by Fritz. (WCHE, v.4, p.214; WCHE, v.24, p.265b) In a deposition taken by Joseph Ball on May 14, 1964, TSBD superintendent Roy Truly confirmed Oswald's statement:

BALL: Do you recall anytime that you saw any guns in the [TSBD]?
TRULY: Yes, I did.
BALL: Prior to November 22, 1963?
TRULY: Yes, I saw two guns on November 20.
BALL: Whose guns were they?
TRULY: They belonged to Mr. Warren Caster. (WCHE, v.7, p.381)

Warren Caster worked in the TSBD building but was employed as an assistant manager for Southwestern Publishing Co., which had offices in the building. Truly explains that Caster had shown Truly two rifles during the noon hour on Wednesday, November 20, just two days before the assassination. Caster told Truly that he had just bought a deer hunting rifle and a .22 rifle for his son. (WCHE, v.7, p.381) Truly examined the larger rifle, but not the .22. Truly said that TSBD manager William Shelley was also present when the rifles were shown. Truly testified that Caster then put the rifles back into the cartons and carried them out the lobby door. (WCHE, v.7, p.382) On the day of the assassination, Truly had told the FBI about the incident with Caster's rifles. (CD5, p.323), but it was not until the deposition of May 14, 1964 that the commission chose to question Truly about it.

Caster's deposition had already been taken just half an hour before Truly's. Caster confirmed the story of the two rifles. He identified the Remington single-shot .22 as a Christmas present for his son. He says he bought the other rifle, "a .30-06 sporterized Mauser" for deer hunting. Caster tells Joseph Ball: "I purchased the single-shot .22 . . . and at the same time was looking at some deer rifles. I had, oh, for several years been thinking about buying a deer rifle and they happened to have one that I liked and I purchased the .30-06 while I was there. . . . I picked both rifles up in cartons just like they were, this was during the noon hour, and as I entered the [TSBD] on my way up to the buying office, I stopped by Mr. Truly's office, and while I was there we examined the two rifles that I had purchased." (WCHE, v.7, p.387)

> BALL: What did you do with the guns after that?
> CASTER: I put them back in the carton and carried them up to my office.
> BALL: And what did you do with them after that?
> CASTER: I left at the end of the working day, oh, around 4 o'clock and took the guns in the cartons and carried them and put them in my car and carried them home.
> BALL: Did you ever have them back in the Texas School Book Depository Building thereafter?
> CASTER: They have never been back to the Texas School Book Depository Building since then.
> BALL: Where were those guns on November 22, 1963?
> CASTER: The guns were in my home, 3338 Merrell Road. (WCHE, v.7, p.388)

There is no record of any witnesses confirming that Caster did indeed remove the rifles from the TSBD at the end of the day on November 20. Caster's uncorroborated testimony is the only evidence we have that he took the rifles home with him on that day. Caster had told the FBI as early as November 24, 1963 that he had brought the rifles to the TSBD on November 20. At that time, he had stated to the FBI that originally "he had intended to hide the two rifles in his office because he was going to give the .22 rifle to his son for Christmas. On second thought, he was afraid that the guns might be stolen, so he took them to his home on November 20, 1963." (CD205, p.278) So even though Caster says he took the rifles home with him on November 20, he admitted that he at least considered leaving them hidden in the office. His November 24 statement to the FBI raises some suspicion, as he told the agents that he at first intended to hide the guns in his office until Christmas, yet he bought the Mauser for deer hunting, and deer hunting season was just getting started in November. Why would a person buy a rifle for deer hunting and then plan to hide it in his office for several weeks during deer hunting season?

William Shelley, who was present at Caster's demonstration of the rifles, confirmed to Ball that it was not customary to have guns displayed in the TSBD. In fact, Shelley told Ball that he had never seen any guns in the building before November 20, 1963, when Caster brought his two rifles into the building. During his deposition, Shelley further described Caster's Mauser as "a foreign make converted to a .30-06." (WCHE, v.7, p.390)

The removal of Caster's Mauser from the TSBD on November 20 is attested only by Caster's own testimony. The story of Caster's rifles provides a more plausible alternative for how the assassination rifle was brought into the building, given that the "curtain rod" package favored by the commission was not the right size to have contained the Italian rifle (CE139). The package which Wesley Frazier and his sister saw Oswald carrying on the morning of November 22 was no more than 28 inches long. (WCHE, v.2, p.250; WCHE, v.24, p.409a) As we have seen, FBI expert Robert Frazier testified that the longest part of the Mannlicher-Carcano rifle, when unassembled, was 34.8 inches. (WCHE, v.3, p.395) Captain Fritz testified that the rifle when broken down would have been about the right size for the package that Wesley Frazier described, but as we now see, Fritz was mistaken. Even when disassembled, the rifle would have still been too long to be transported in the "curtain rod" package.

Conclusion:

Lt. Day's identification of the CE139 rifle would probably be sufficient to pass the foundation test in a criminal trial. Based on his testimony, the rifle would most likely have been admitted, under the rules of evidence, as the one found on the sixth floor of the TSBD. But this is only the first step in evaluating the rifle's connection to the assassination. The fact the rifle was originally identified as a Mauser, the fact that a Mauser was known to have been in the building just two days earlier, the fact that no one saw Caster removing his Mauser from the building, and the fact that neither Boone, nor Weitzman, nor Mooney, nor Fritz identified CE139 as the rifle they found on the sixth floor must be weighed against Day's testimony in deciding whether the Italian rifle CE139 is really the assassination weapon, or whether it was substituted for another rifle, perhaps a Mauser – perhaps even Caster's Mauser – before Lt. Day placed his mark on it.

Were the three cartridge shells CE543, CE544, and CE545 really discovered on the sixth floor of the TSBD?

The rifle shells CE543, CE544, and CE545 were determined in expert testimony to have been fired in the Italian rifle, CE139. (Testimony of Robert Frazier, WCHE, v.3, p.415) But this finding has no probative value unless it is proven that these shells were actually found on the sixth floor of the TSBD during the police search on the afternoon of November 22, 1963.

According to Deputy Sheriff Luke Mooney, Capt. Will Fritz was the first person to pick up the ejected cartridge shells. (WCHE, v.3, p.286)

Lt. L. C. Day of the Crime Lab testified that the photo CE716 (WCHE, v.17, p.500) shows the position of the three empty rifle shells "before anything was moved, to the best of my knowledge." But it turns out that Day does not have any first-hand knowledge of whether the shells had been moved before he arrived on the scene and before the photo was taken. He explains, "I was advised when I got there nothing had been moved." David Belin, conducting the examination, asks him, "Who so advised you?" Day replies, "I believe it was Detective Sims standing there, but I could be wrong about that." (WCHE, v.4, p.251)

Belin asks Day if he marked these shells for identification at the time they were collected:

BELIN: You have mentioned these three hulls. Did you put any initials on those at all, any means of identification?
DAY: At that time they were placed in an envelope and the envelope marked. The three hulls were not marked at that time. Mr. Sims took possession of them.
BELIN: Well, did you at any time put any mark on the shells?
DAY: Yes, sir.

Belin hands Day an envelope (CE717), which Belin says is part of CE543-544 and asks if he can identify it:

DAY: This is the envelope the shells were placed in.
BELIN: How many shells were placed in that envelope?
DAY: Three.
BELIN: It says here that, it is written on here, "Two of the three spent hulls under window on sixth floor."
DAY: Yes, sir.
BELIN: Did you put all three there?
DAY: Three were in there when they were turned over to Detective Sims at that time. The only writing on it was, "Lieut. J. C. Day". Down here at the bottom. . . .
BELIN: In other words, you didn't put the writing in that says, "Two of the three spent hulls."
DAY: Not then. About 10 o'clock in the evening this envelope came back to me with two hulls in it. . . . I don't know who brought them back. . . . At that time there were two hulls inside. I was advised the homicide division was retaining the third for their use. At that time I marked the two hulls inside of this, still inside this envelope. . . . I put the additional marking on at that time. . . .

BELIN: Now, at what time did you put any initials, if you did put any such initials, on the hull itself?

DAY: At about 10 o'clock when I noticed it back in the identification bureau in this envelope.

BELIN: Had the envelope been opened yet or not?

DAY: Yes, sir. It had been opened.

BELIN: Had the shells been out of your possession then?

DAY: Mr. Sims had the shells from the time they were moved from the building or he took them from me at that time, and the shells I did not see again until around 10 o'clock.

BELIN: Who gave them to you at 10 o'clock?

DAY: They were in this group of evidence being collected to turn over to the FBI. I don't know who brought them back.

BELIN: Was the envelope sealed?

DAY: No, sir.

BELIN: Had it been sealed when you gave it to Mr. Sims?

DAY: No, sir. No. (WCHE, v.4, p.253-254)

Day explains that he originally told Belin he had marked the empty shells at the scene of the TSBD, but later, upon reflection, realized he had not.

DAY: I told you in our conversation in Dallas that I marked those at the scene. After reviewing my records, I didn't think I was on all three of those hulls that you have, indicating I did not mark them at the scene. Then I remembered putting them in the envelope, and Sims taking them. It was further confirmed today when I noticed that the third hull, which I did not give you, or come to me through you, does not have my mark on it. . . . I remember you asking me if I marked them.

BELIN: Yes.

DAY: I remember I told you I did. . . . I got to reviewing this, and I got to wondering about whether I did mark those at the scene.

BELIN: Your testimony now is that you did not mark any of the hulls at the scene?

DAY: Those three, no, sir. . . .

BELIN: Now, I am going to ask you to state if you know what Commission Exhibit 543 is?

DAY: That is a hull that does not have my marking on it.

BELIN: Do you know whether or not this was one of the hulls that was found at the School Book Depository Building?

DAY: I think it is. . . . That was retained. That is the hull that was retained by homicide division when the other two were originally sent in with the gun.

BELIN: You are referring now to Commission Exhibit 543 as being the one that was retained in your possession for a while?
DAY: It is the one that I did not see again. (WCHE, v.4, p.254-255)

This remarkable exchange between Day and Belin shows that there is no assurance that the three rifle shells labelled CE543, CE544, and CE545 were the same three shells allegedly found near the sixth floor window of the TSBD on November 22, 1963. Day did not mark the shells themselves when he first collected them at the TSBD, even though he at first told Belin that he had marked them. The envelope containing the three shells was not sealed, and was out of Day's possession for several hours, before two shells were returned to him late Friday night in the unsealed envelope. There is no way to know whether these two shells were among the three shells originally placed in the envelope or whether they were substituted for two of the original shells. The third shell, which was retained by the homicide division, may or may not be the same shell which later turned up as CE543, without Day's initials. CE544 and 545 would be the shells which came back to Day in the open envelope around 10 p.m. Friday night, and which he then marked with his initials. It was not until nearly a week later that Capt. Fritz turned over a third shell (CE543) to agent Vincent Drain of the FBI (WCHE, v.7, p.404), a delay which provided the opportunity for further tampering.

Especially important is Day's admission that he was being untruthful when he first told Belin that he had marked the three shells at the scene in the TSBD. This lack of candor (to put it politely) must lead us to question Day's truthfulness throughout all his testimony. It does not mean that all his testimony is false, but it does mean we cannot blindly accept what he tells us without additional corroboration.

The question of foundation for the shells came up during the testimony of Robert Frazier when commission counsel Melvin Eisenberg introduced CE543, CE544, and CE545 into evidence during a commission session chaired by John McCloy, presiding in place of Earl Warren. In accepting the shells into evidence McCloy asked Eisenberg:

MCCLOY: Will you introduce evidence to show where they [the shells] came from?
EISENBERG: Well, sir, the record will show at the conclusion of the hearings where they came from. This witness is able to identify them only as to his examination.
MCCLOY: I understand that. I understand that witness cannot identify them. But I simply asked for the record whether you have evidence to show where they did come from.
EISENBERG: Yes, for the record, these cartridges were found on the sixth floor of the School Book Depository Building. They were found

near the southeast corner window – that is the easternmost window on the southern face of the sixth floor of that building. (WCHE, v.3, p.399)

Eisenberg cannot testify from his own personal knowledge where the shells came from, because he was not present when they were found. As we have seen, there is no chain of possession proving that CE543, CE544, and CE545 were ever found on the sixth floor of the TSBD. McCloy is asking the right questions, but Eisenberg's inability to provide a satisfactory answer illustrates a major weakness in the government's case.

In *Six Seconds in Dallas,* author Josiah Thompson reproduces a photograph showing that CE543 has a noticeable dent on the lip of the open end. He says that this dent "resembles what happens when an empty case is 'dry loaded' in the breech and strikes some sharp metal projection." This interpretation is confirmed by Joseph Nicol, Superintendent of the Bureau of Criminal Identification and Investigation for the State of Illinois, who testified before the commission that the markings on CE543 lead him to the opinion that this shell "had been introduced into a chamber at least three times prior to its final firing. So that this would represent, you might say, a practice or dry-run loading the gun and unloading it." (WCHE, v.3, p.509)

Thompson notes that "in its present condition [CE543] could not have been fired in any rifle – its lip will not receive a projectile. The possibility suggests itself that CE543 was never fired on November 22 but was dropped by one of the assassins, either inadvertently or as a means of throwing the subsequent investigation off the track." (Thompson, p. 144) As we have seen, it cannot even be positively established that CE543 was ever on the sixth floor of the TSBD, because of the broken chain of possession. But given the dented lip, it is almost certain that no bullet was fired in this shell from the sixth floor window. So this constitutes evidence that at least one, and perhaps all three shells were planted or substituted for those actually found at the TSBD. Because of the faulty chain of possession, it is not only the assassins who may have planted CE543 at the scene. There was ample opportunity for the police themselves to have substituted three different shells from the CE139 rifle in place of whatever shells were actually found at the TSBD – if any.

Conclusion

The chain of possession for these shells has many missing links. The expert ballistic testimony on the rifle shells has no probative value because we cannot possibly know that the shells in evidence were the ones found at the scene. Even if it is proven that these shells were fired in the CE139 rifle, this does not prove that they were fired from the TSBD window on November 22, 1963. They could have been fired from the rifle either before or after the assassination. Furthermore, Day's sloppy handling of the rifle shells, and his uncertain memory of when, where, and whether they were marked with his initials, must be taken into consideration as we evaluate his credibility concerning the identification of the CE139 rifle and whether CE139 is really the rifle which was found on the sixth floor after the assassination.

There is a very curious exchange between commission members John McCloy and Allen Dulles during Robert Frazier's testimony which seems to suggest that Dulles may be privy to information indicating that only two shells were found at the TSBD window, or at least that the number of shells found is uncertain:

> MCCLOY: At least three shots were fired and probably three shots were fired because of the three shells that were found.
> DULLES: Three shells?
> MCCLOY: Yes.
> DULLES: We probably won't settle that today. (WCHE, v.5, p.174)

Were the bullet fragments CE567 and CE569 actually found in the front seat of the Presidential car?

Commission Exhibits 567 and 569 are two bullet fragments said to have been recovered from the front seat of the Presidential car. The FBI's internal designation for these two fragments are Q-2 and Q-3. FBI ballistics expert Robert Frazier determined definitely, by analysis of microscopic markings on the fragments and on the rifle barrel, that both fragments were fired in the CE139 rifle. (WCHE, v.3, p.432, 435) Of these two fragments, "one can't tell whether they come from a single bullet or from two separate projectiles. One is a nose portion and the other is a base." (WCHE, v.3, p.435) So these two fragments could easily represent only one fired bullet. (Testimony of Joseph Nicol, WCHE, v.3, p.497) FBI agent Vincent Drain reported on 11/26/63 that the FBI Laboratory received Q-2 and Q-3 on 11/22/63 from FBI agent Orin Bartlett. (CD5, p.162)

These bullet fragments were introduced into evidence during Frazier's testimony before the commission on March 31, 1964. In questioning Frazier, commission counsel Melvin Eisenberg remarked: "For the record, this was found – this bullet fragment [CE567] was found – in the front portion of the car in which the President was riding." (WCHE, v.3, p.432) As the examining attorney, Eisenberg has no personal knowledge of where the fragment was found, and neither does Frazier. A couple of pages later in the transcript, commission member John McCloy again asks an awkward question:

> MCCLOY: Do we have any proof in the record thus far as to where the fragment referred to a moment ago came from?
> EISENBERG: Honestly, I am not sure. I know it will be in the record eventually, but I have not taken that up as part of this testimony.
> MCCLOY: That will be subject to further proof.
> EISENBERG: Yes. (WCHE, v.3, p.434)

Arlen Specter tries to remedy this gap in the chain of possession when Frazier was again called before the commission on May 13, 1964. He questions Frazier about the origin of bullet fragment CE567:

> SPECTER: Now, where, according to information provided to you then, was the fragment designated Commission Exhibit 567 found?
>
> FRAZIER: That was found by the Secret Service upon their examination of the limousine here in Washington when it first arrived from Dallas, and Commission No. 567 was delivered by Deputy Chief Paul Paterni and by a White House detail chief, Floyd M. Boring, to a liaison agent of the FBI, Orrin Bartlett, who delivered them to me in the laboratory at 11:50 p.m. on November 22, 1963."
>
> SPECTER: Does that constitute the total chain of possession then from the finder with the Secret Service into your hands, as reflected on the records of the FBI?
>
> FRAZIER: Yes, sir. (WCHE, v.5, p.67)

Specter then tries to establish the chain of possession for the other fragment, CE569:

> SPECTER: Would you state what the chain of possession was from the time of discovery of Exhibit 569 until the time it came into your possession, based on the records of the FBI, please, if you have those records available?
>
> FRAZIER: Yes, sir. It was delivered by Secret Service Deputy Chief Paul Paterni, and SAC of the White House detail Floyd M. Boring of the Secret Service again, to Special Agent Orrin Bartlett of the FBI who delivered it to me at 11:50 p.m. on November 22, 1963.
>
> SPECTER: Are the records which you have just referred to relating to the chain of possession of Exhibits 567 and 569 maintained by you in the normal course of your duties as an examiner of those items?
>
> FRAZIER: Yes, sir. (WCHE, v.5, p.67-68)

This is a valiant attempt by Specter, but it fails to prove that the fragments CE567 and 569 were in fact found in the Presidential automobile. First, Frazier does not testify from personal knowledge when he says the "Secret Service" found the fragments. The "Secret Service" is not a person, and attributing the discovery to the agency rather than to an individual simply emphasizes the fact that Frazier has no direct knowledge as to who found the fragments. His impression is that the fragments were discovered after the limousine was returned to Washington, and there is no way to tell who may have had access to the car during the hours between the assassination and their discovery, as the limousine made its way back to Washington. Furthermore, there is no indication in Frazier's testimony how many times the fragments changed hands before arriving in the possession of Paul Paterni. Thus, Frazier's testimony does not and cannot constitute the "total chain of possession" for the fragments because his knowledge is lacking and records do not identify the finder nor whether there were intermediaries in the chain between the finder and Paterni.

Specter obviously recognizes the fact that Frazier has no personal knowledge of the complete chain of possession, since he resorts to a different legal principle in attempting to establish Frazier's competence to testify on this issue. He gets Frazier to say that the FBI records he relies on are "maintained in the normal course" of Frazier's duties with the FBI. The records of a business or organization would ordinarily come under the hearsay exclusion, but there is an exception which allows such records to be introduced if they are kept "in the normal course of regularly conducted business activity." In the case of the bullet fragments, the FBI records themselves are not introduced. Frazier simply testifies that there are such records and that they constitute normal business practice. But even if Frazier's testimony is allowed as an exception to the hearsay rule, it is substantially inadequate to establish the chain of possession for this evidence. He still doesn't know who actually found the fragments and he covers up this lack of knowledge by attributing the discovery to the "Secret Service". In the end, the chain of possession cannot be established for CE567 and 569. We do not know, and the commission does not know, who found these fragments, and how they were maintained, and whose hands they passed through, before Paul Paterni received them. Thus, it cannot be stated with certainty that the fragments in evidence as CE567 and 569 were actually discovered in the Presidential car after the assassination.

Two months after Frazier's testimony cited above, on July 7, 1964, the FBI provided the commission with a report tracing various items of physical evidence, including the two bullet fragments (CE567 and CE569) said to have been found in the limousine. Referring to them under the FBI's own designators C2 and C3, the FBI report states that C2 was shown on June 2, 1964 to Thomas G. Mills of the U. S. Navy, who was assigned to the White House medical office. The report asserts that "Mills identified the fragment as the one he recovered from the space between the right front seat and the door panel of the right front door on the President's car." The second fragment, C3, was shown on June 2, 1964 to Paul Paterni, Deputy Chief of the Secret Service. "Paterni identified this fragment as the one he recovered from the middle of the front seat of the President's car." (WCHE, v.24, p.413)

Note that neither Mills nor Paterni offer any details as to how they are able to identify these two amorphous clumps of metal as the same fragments they found on the night of November 22, 1963, now that more than six months have passed since their discovery. The fragments are pictured at WCHE, v.17, p.256-257.

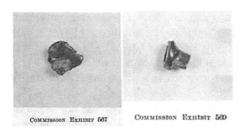

COMMISSION EXHIBIT 567   COMMISSION EXHIBIT 569

The FBI letter of July 7, 1964 is, to all appearances, a desperate attempt to plug holes in the chain of possession of the evidence. But without any hint as to how Mills and Paterni are able to identify these fragments we cannot be confident in their identification. They do not say that they put any identifying mark on them when they were discovered, and they do not mention any unique features of these fragments which would enable them to identify them. Neither Mills nor Paterni were called to testify before the commission as to what facts enable them to identify these fragments as the ones found in the limousine on November 22, 1963.

Was the bullet CE399 the actual bullet which was found on a stretcher at Parkland Hospital on the afternoon of November 22, 1963, and did it come from Governor Connally's stretcher?

The 6.5 mm bullet known as Commission Exhibit 399 plays a critical role in the government's case against Oswald as the lone assassin. The Warren Report asserts that "Commission Exhibit No. 399 [was] found on Governor Connally's stretcher and [is] believed to have been the bullet which caused his chest wound." (WCR, p.583) The report also states that "there is very persuasive evidence from the experts to indicate that the same bullet which pierced the President's throat also caused Governor Connally's wounds. (WCR, p.19) But the report waffles a bit on this point, noting that there is some "difference of opinion as to this probability". Realizing that the single bullet theory suffers from a lack of persuasive evidence, the commission tries to claim that "it is not necessary to any essential findings of the Commission to determine just which shot hit Governor Connally." (WCR, p.19) But it is absolutely necessary to prove that Kennedy and Connally were hit with the same bullet in order to fit all the shots into the timeframe necessary for firing the rifle. As Edward Jay Epstein observed: "Either both men were hit by the same bullet, or there were two assassins." (Epstein, *Inquest*, p.45)

Commission Exhibit 399

85

But before we can evaluate whether CE399 supports the single bullet theory, we must first answer two foundational questions: 1) Was a bullet really found on the stretcher used in treating Governor Connally in the emergency room? 2) Is CE399 really the bullet found at Parkland Hospital on the afternoon of November 22, 1963? In order to support the government's single bullet theory, CE399 must be associated with Connally's stretcher, because the theory holds that the single bullet came to rest after hitting Connally's thigh. Since it was not found in the car, it must have been on or in Connally and must have fallen out while he was on the stretcher from which it was later recovered.

It cannot be determined which stretcher the bullet was found on.

A bullet was found during the afternoon of November 22 at Parkland Hospital by Darrell Tomlinson, senior engineer in charge of the hospital's power plant. (WCHE, v.6, p.130) Tomlinson, in turn, gave the bullet to O. P. Wright, the Personnel Director of Security for Dallas hospitals. (WCHE, v.24, p.412a) In taking Tomlinson's deposition, commission counsel Arlen Specter tried to establish that the stretcher on which the bullet was found was the one used to treat Connally in the emergency room. But he does not establish this essential point. The commission concluded anyway that "the bullet came from the Governor's stretcher." (WCR, p.81) But it based this conclusion on a faulty deduction, reasoning that the stretcher could not have been Kennedy's, so it therefore must have been Connally's.

Allen Dulles, during the questioning of Dr. Humes, was under the impression that the "stretcher bullet" (CE399) was found on President Kennedy's stretcher, and asked what evidence exists regarding the location of this bullet. Specter assures him that there will be evidence forthcoming that shows the CE399 bullet was actually recovered from Connally's stretcher. He tells Dulles: "The thought preliminarily was that [CE399] was from President Kennedy's stretcher, and that is what led to the hypothesis which we have been exploring about [that the bullet fell out of Kennedy's back onto his stretcher during cardiac massage in the emergency room], but which has since been rejected." [Rejected by whom? At this point the commission has made no determinations of fact.] Specter continues: "But at any rate the evidence will show that it was from Governor Connally's stretcher that the bullet was found." (WCHE, v.2, p.368) Unfortunately for Specter's theory, no persuasive evidence is ever introduced showing that the stretcher on which the bullet was found was that of Governor Connally.

Specter's questioning of Tomlinson shows that Tomlinson's memory of the bullet's discovery is vague, and that he is uncertain which of two stretchers the bullet rolled out of. When Tomlinson went to the emergency elevator after Connally had been taken up to the operating room, he noticed that there was one stretcher (stretcher A) on the elevator. There was another stretcher (B) already standing in the elevator lobby. Tomlinson took stretcher A off the elevator and placed it against the wall. Shortly thereafter, a man went to use the restroom and pushed stretcher B out of the way. After the man left the restroom, Tomlinson pushed stretcher B back so it would not block the elevator. In doing so, stretcher B bumped the wall and out rolled a bullet which "apparently had been lodged under the edge of the mat." (WCHE, v.6, p.130) Specter then tries to confirm which stretcher the bullet rolled off of:

> TOMLINSON: I bumped the wall and a spent cartridge or bullet rolled out that apparently had been lodged under the edge of the mat.
> SPECTER: And that was from which stretcher?
> TOMLINSON: I believe that it was B. . . .
> SPECTER: Now, Mr. Tomlinson, are you sure that it was stretcher A that you took out of the elevator and not stretcher B?
> TOMLINSON: Well, really, I can't be positive, just to be perfectly honest about it. I can't be positive, because I really didn't pay that much attention to it. (WCHE, v.6, p.130-131)

After reminding Tomlinson that he previously had told a Secret Service agent that the bullet was found on the stretcher that came out of the elevator, Specter continues:

> SPECTER: So would it be a fair summary to say that . . . you really can't be completely sure about which stretcher you took off of the elevator, because you didn't push the stretcher that you took off of the elevator right against the wall at first?
> TOMLINSON: That's right." (WCHE, v.6, p.133)
> SPECTER: Do you know where the stretcher came from that you found on the elevator?
> TOMLINSON: No, sir. I do not. It could have come from two, it could have come from three, it could have come from some other place. . . . It was on the elevator when I got there." (WCHE, v.6, p.134)

So Tomlinson does not know which stretcher the bullet came from, and does not know where either of the two stretchers came from. Unfortunately, the commission members do not get to hear Tomlinson testify about his discovery, since Tomlinson is not invited to appear in a commission session. His testimony was taken in a deposition with only Specter and a court reporter present. From Tomlinson's testimony there is no way to connect the bullet with Governor Connally's stretcher. The commission's assertion that "Commission Exhibit No. 399 [was] found on Governor Connally's stretcher" is not supported by the evidence.

The third patient

In *Six Seconds in Dallas*, author Josiah Thompson concluded, based on a comparison of all the testimony with hospital records, that the stretcher on which the bullet was found was in fact neither Connally's nor Kennedy's, but probably belonged to another patient, a little boy named Ronald Fuller, who had suffered a cut on his jaw and was admitted to the hospital shortly after Connally on November 22. (Thompson, *Six Seconds in Dallas* (1967), pp.154-165) The presence of a third patient demonstrates the flaw in the commission's reasoning. By ruling out the possibility that the bullet came from Kennedy's stretcher, the commission concluded by elimination that it must have come from Connally's. This reasoning requires that there be only two patients, but if there were three, then the alternatives have not all been eliminated. It is entirely possible, even likely, that the bullet rolled off the stretcher which was used in treating the little boy.

At first glance, this may seem to be an implausible option. Why would a bullet be found on the stretcher of a little boy with a cut on his jaw? But the plausibility is increased when we remember that the stretcher was standing unattended near the elevator, and that the alternative hypothesis to the lone gunman theory is a scenario in which evidence was planted for the express purpose of incriminating Oswald. Under this hypothesis, it is not so far-fetched that someone planted the bullet on the little boy's stretcher, so that it would be found and connected to Oswald's rifle via ballistic markings on the bullet. This unknown person had no way of knowing that one of the stretchers was unconnected with the victims of the assassination.

Jack Ruby emerges as a likely candidate for planting the bullet. Journalist Seth Kantor saw Ruby at Parkland around 1:30 p.m. (WCHE, v.15, p.78) Although Ruby denied being at Parkland that afternoon, and the commission chose to believe Ruby's denial over Kantor's testimony (WCR, p.336), the House Select Committee on Assassinations determined that Kantor was probably not mistaken in saying that he saw Ruby at Parkland. (HSCA Final Report, p.158) Burt Griffin, the Warren Commission counsel in charge of investigating Ruby, "told the [HSCA] committee he had come to believe, in light of evidence subsequently brought out, that the [Warren] Commission's conclusion about Kantor's testimony was wrong." (HSCA Final Report, p.159)

It cannot be shown that CE399 is the same bullet that Tomlinson found on a stretcher in the elevator lobby.

When the bullet marked CE399 (FBI C-1) was later shown to Tomlinson by FBI agent Bardwell Odum, Tomlinson told Odum that "it appears to be the same one he found on a hospital carriage at Parkland Hospital on November 22, 1963, but he cannot positively identify the bullet as the one he found and showed to Mr. O. P. Wright." When Odum showed CE399 to O. P. Wright, Wright stated that the bullet "looks like the slug found at Parkland Hospital on November 22, 1963, which he gave to Richard Johnsen, Special Agent of the Secret Service. . . . He advised he could not positively identify C1 as being the same bullet which was found on November 22, 1963." On 6/24/64, Secret Service Agent Johnsen was shown the bullet CE399 by FBI agent Elmer Todd. "Johnsen advised he could not identify this bullet as the one he obtained from O. P. Wright [at] Parkland Hospital . . . on November 22, 1963." (WCHE, v.24, p.412a); Agent Todd showed the bullet CE399 to James Rowley, Chief of the U.S. Secret Service on 6/24/64. "Rowley advised he could not identify this bullet as the one he received from Special Agent Richard E. Johnsen and gave to Special Agent Todd on November 22, 1963." Agent Todd himself identified CE399 (FBI C1) as being "the same one he received from James Rowley . . . on November 22, 1963. This identification was made from initials marked thereon by Special Agent Todd at the [FBI] laboratory upon receipt." (WCHE, v.24, p.412b)

Thus, none of the individuals who handled the hospital bullet on November 22 were able to positively identify CE399 as being that same bullet. Even the vague resemblance hinted at in the phrases "appears to be" and "looks like" may be exaggerated. In the book *Six Seconds in Dallas*, author Josiah Thompson reports an interview with O. P. Wright in November 1966, in which Wright told Thompson that the bullet that Tomlinson gave to Wright on November 22 had a pointed tip, not rounded like CE399. Of three sample bullet shapes (long and rounded, squat and rounded, or pointed) that Thompson presented to Wright, "Wright picked the pointed tip as the one that most resembled the bullet found on the stretcher." When Wright was shown photographs of CE399, CE572 (test firings from the Italian rifle) and CE606 (revolver bullets), Wright "rejected all of these as resembling the bullet found on the stretcher." Thompson notes that "as a professional law-enforcement officer, Wright has an educated eye for bullet shapes." (Thompson, *Six Seconds in Dallas* (1967), p.175, n.17)

However, we now have a problem in accounting for the presence of a pointed-tipped bullet on the hospital stretcher. Why would a conspirator plant a bullet that did not match the ammunition of Oswald's rifle? If CE399 had been switched for the actual bullet found by Tomlinson, that means that CE399 was not planted on the stretcher. So where did the pointed-tip bullet that Wright described come from? Thompson offers a plausible hypothesis which fits the evidence and the timeline. "In such a chaotic atmosphere as that which reigned at the hospital, is it beyond the realm of possibility that some hospital employee found bullet 399 [or the pointed-tip bullet] on the floor, in the President's clothes, or on his stretcher, and momentarily snatched it as a souvenir, only to recognize its importance and quickly secrete it on a stretcher where it might be found by someone else – no questions asked?" Thompson notes that as the emergency room personnel left the trauma room and headed downstairs on the elevator, they would have brushed past the stretcher in the elevator lobby and it would have been easy to deposit the temporarily purloined bullet discreetly on the stretcher. (Thompson, *Six Seconds in Dallas,* p.168-169) This explanation would comport perfectly with the first version of Humes' autopsy findings, as recorded by Sibert and O'Neill, that the bullet in Kennedy's back penetrated only a couple of inches and then fell out on his stretcher during cardiac massage. This would have been the bullet with a pointed tip, and would conform to the O. P. Wright's description. Later, CE399 could have been substituted for this bullet, in order to link Oswald's rifle to the shooting.

Warren Commission defenders often refer to this type of hypothesis generating as "speculation", but it is really just coming up with a model that fits the data. Often, more than one hypothesis is consistent with the known data. As more data is received, the hypotheses can be tested against it and rejected or modified as needed. This is how scientific knowledge progresses. It is not idle speculation by any means. It is a mistake to think that a hypothesis must be rejected simply because there currently is not enough evidence to confirm it, when it is consistent with all the known facts.

Conclusion:

The expert testimony is unanimous that the three shells (CE543, 544, 545), the two fragments (CE567, 569) and the intact bullet (CE399) were all fired in the Italian rifle (CE139). However, there is no testimony that conclusively links any of these items with the assassination. It would have been possible for anyone having access to the rifle to have fired several shots before the assassination, or even after the assassination, and then planted the shells, fragments, and whole bullet so as to frame Oswald. In the case of the shells and the whole bullet, there is persuasive evidence that such substitution has in fact occurred. In the case of the rifle, there are conceivably several hours unaccounted between its discovery and the time when Lt. Day carved his name on the rifle, allowing for the possibility of exchanging it for the actual rifle, possibly a Mauser, recovered from the sixth floor of the TSBD. Because evidence connecting these items to the assassination is lacking, the shells, fragments and whole bullet would be inadmissible as evidence. Therefore, these items of evidence do not support convicting Oswald for the murder of President Kennedy.

Was CE399 the magic bullet?

This is the substantive question regarding bullet CE399 and the single bullet theory. It is a necessary (but not sufficient) condition for proving that only one assassin was at work in Dealey Plaza on November 22, 1963. As we have already shown, the foundational threshold has not been met for the admissibility of CE399 as evidence. But even if we accept, for the sake of argument, that CE399 is the bullet which was found at Parkland and if we accept that it was found on Connally's stretcher, there is still no persuasive evidence that this bullet passed through the back of Kennedy's neck, out the front of his neck, into Connally's back, out his chest, through his wrist, and into his thigh. The single bullet theory cannot be proven. Indeed, the weight of the expert testimony is that it is a most unlikely scenario, if not downright impossible.

As we have already seen, the fact that no path was traced during the autopsy from the back wound to the opening in the front of the throat means that the existence of a bullet path between those two wounds is entirely speculative on the part of the commission. But the single bullet theory is Arlen Specter's only hope of pinning the assassination on a single gunman, so he plows ahead, asking the doctors and the ballistics experts whether it is *possible*, in their opinion, that CE399 could have passed through both Kennedy and Connally, causing all of Connally's wounds. Specter's theory depends on establishing the following facts: that CE399 could have caused all the wounds found in Kennedy's back and neck and in Connally's chest, wrist, and thigh, and could have done all its damage without suffering any deformity, since the bullet in evidence is virtually pristine, showing no obvious deformation, and furthermore that CE399 passed through Kennedy and into Connally in a straight line, without any deflection.

In a memo written to Warren Commission General Counsel Lee Rankin on April 30, 1964, Specter himself seemed to harbor doubts about the evidentiary support for the single bullet theory. In this memo, Specter called for the commission to examine directly the photographs and X-rays made at Kennedy's autopsy. He told Rankin, "Someone from the Commission should review the films to corroborate the autopsy surgeons' testimony that the holes on the President's back and head had the characteristics of points of entry." [Note that he says "back", not "neck".] Specter goes on to point out that "none of the doctors at Parkland Hospital in Dallas observed the hole in the President's back or the small hole in the lower portion of his head. With all of the outstanding controversy about the direction of the shots, there must be independent viewings of the [X-ray and still photo] films to verify the testimony which has come only from Government doctors. . . . The Commission should determine with certainty that there are no major variations between the films and the artist's drawings." (Specter memo reproduced in HSCA, v.11, p.92) Specter testified to the HSCA that "from my own personal point of view . . . the investigation should not have been closed and the conclusion should not have been reached and I did not want to come to final conclusions without seeing the X-rays and photographs." (HSCA, v.11, p.94) But the commission as a whole, and Specter in particular, had no opportunity to inspect the X-rays and photographs taken at the autopsy. Specter was therefore obliged to interview witnesses and write his report without the benefit of the photographic evidence of Kennedy's wounds. (HSCA, v.11, p.92)

Testimony of Robert Frazier:

Testifying in commission session on June 4, 1964, FBI firearms and ballistics expert Robert Frazier is questioned by Specter about the single bullet scenario:

> SPECTER: Mr. Frazier, assuming the factors which I have asked you to accept as true for the purposes of expressing an opinion before, as to the flight of the bullet and the straight line penetration through the President's body [Again, Specter assumes the facts that he wants to prove.], considering the point of entry and exit, do you have an opinion as to what probably happened during the interval between frames 207 and 225 [of the Zapruder film] as to whether the bullet which passed through the neck of the President entered the Governor's back?

FRAZIER: There are a lot of probables in that. First, we have to assume there is absolutely no deflection in the bullet from the time it left the barrel until the time it exited from the Governor's body. . . . However, I myself don't have any technical evidence which would permit me to say one way or the other . . . which would support it as far as my rendering an opinion as an expert. I would certainly say it was *possible*, but I don't say that it probably occurred because I don't have the evidence on which to base a statement like that. . . . We are dealing with the fact that we don't know . . . whether there was any deviation in the bullet which struck the President in the back, and exited from his front. If there were a few degrees deviation then it may affect my opinion as to whether or not it would have struck the Governor. We are dealing with an assumed fact that the Governor was in front of the President in such a position that he could have taken [the bullet]. So when you say would it probably have occurred, then you are asking me . . . to base my opinion on a whole series of hypothetical facts which I can't substantiate." (WCHE, v.5, p.172)

As for whether it is reasonable to assume a straight line path through the two men with no deflection, Frazier says: "I have seen bullets strike small twigs, small objects, and ricochet for no apparent reason except they hit and all the pressure is on one side and it turns the bullet and it goes off at an angle. If there was no deviation from the time the bullet left the rifle barrel until the time it exited from the Governor's body, then the physical setup exists for it to have gone through the President, and through the Governor. . . . If you have deviation anywhere along the line then you . . . affect the position at which the Governor could have been shot." (WCHE, v.5, p.172-173)

The WCR relies on Frazier's testimony in concluding: "The bullet that hit President Kennedy in the back and exited through his throat most likely could not have missed both the automobile and its occupants. Since it did not hit the automobile, Frazier testified that it probably struck Governor Connally." (WCR, p.105) But the full context of Frazier's testimony shows that his response is tightly constrained by the assumptions imposed on him by Specter. Frazier tells Specter: "You make these assumptions and I would say under those conditions only two shots hit the occupants or the car because the one through the President had to cause Connally's wounds, otherwise it would have struck somewhere else in the car and it did not strike somewhere else." (WCHE, v.5, p.174)

Testimony of Dr. Charles Gregory:

Dr. Charles Gregory, the surgeon who operated on Connally's wrist, was examined by Specter in a commission session on April 21, 1964. Specter fared no better with Dr. Gregory than he did with Robert Frazier. Specter asked Dr. Gregory whether a single bullet could have passed through Kennedy's neck, hitting only soft tissue, and then passed through Connally producing the wounds in his chest, wrist, and thigh. Gregory replied, "I believe one would have to concede the *possibility*, but I believe firmly that the probability is much diminished. . . . I think that to pass through the soft tissues of the President would certainly have decelerated the missile to some extent. Having then struck the Governor and shattered a rib, it is further decelerated, yet it has presumably retained sufficient energy to smash a radius. Moreover, it escaped the forearm to penetrate at least the skin and fascia of the thigh, and I am not persuaded that this is very probable. I would have to yield to possibility." (WCHE, v.4, p.127)

Testimony of Dr. Robert Shaw:

Dr. Shaw was the surgeon who operated on Connally to repair his chest wound. He has no firm opinion that Connally's wounds were even caused by a single bullet, much less that a single bullet passed through Kennedy's neck and then inflicted the wounds in Connally's chest, wrist, and thigh.

> MCCLOY: You have no firm opinion that all these three wounds were caused by one bullet?
> SHAW: I have no firm opinion. . . .
> MCCLOY: I gather that what the witness is saying is that it is possible that they might have been caused by one bullet, but that he has no firm opinion now that they were. . . .
> SHAW: That is correct. (WCHE, v.4, p.109) . . .
> SPECTER: What is your opinion as to whether bullet 399 could have inflicted all of the wounds on the Governor, then, without respect at this point to the wound of the President's neck?
> SHAW: I feel that there would be some difficulty in explaining all of the wounds as being inflicted by bullet Exhibit 399 without causing more in the way of loss of substance to the bullet or deformation of the bullet." (WCHE, v.4, p.114)

Testimony of Lt. Col. Pierre Finck:

Col. Finck was one of the attending pathologists at the Kennedy autopsy performed at Bethesda on the night of November 22, 1963. He is the only one of the three autopsy doctors to have received intensive training in forensic pathology. (WCHE, v.2, p.378) In his testimony before the commission on March 16, 1964, Dr. Finck rejected the notion that CE399 could have caused all of Connally's wounds, mentioning in particular the wound of the wrist. Dr. Finck finds that there were too many bullet fragments in the wrist and CE399 does not show sufficient loss of mass to be consistent with the fragments deposited in the wrist.

> SPECTER: Dr. Finck, have you had an opportunity to examine Commission's Exhibit 399?

FINCK: For the first time this afternoon, sir. . . .

SPECTER: And could it have been the bullet which inflicted the wound on Governor Connally's right wrist?

FINCK: No, for the reason that there are too many fragments described in that wrist. (WCHE, v.2, p.382)

Various firing tests were conducted by representatives of the U. S. Army to assess the impact of the Mannlicher-Carcano ammunition on animal tissue and on the fired bullets. From these experts, Specter received no more than lukewarm support for the *possibility* of CE399 penetrating both men and causing all of Connally's injuries:

Testimony of Dr. Alfred Olivier:

Olivier supervised a series of tests to simulate the wounds inflicted on Kennedy and Connally, using gelatin blocks and animal tissue, such as horsemeat and goatmeat. The ammunition used was 100 rounds of 6.5 mm ammunition manufactured by Remington and another 160 rounds from Winchester. (WCHE, v.5, p.75) From these tests, Olivier concludes that "the bullet that passed through the President's neck had lost very little of its wounding potential and was capable of doing a great deal of damage in penetrating. . . . This means that had the bullet that passed through the President's neck hit in the car or anywhere you would have seen evidence, a good deal of evidence." (WCHE, v.5, p.78) The conclusion drawn by the commission from this opinion, as well as from Frazier's opinion noted above, is that the bullet which hit Kennedy must have struck Connally, given the lack of any visible damage to the inside of the car. But in this reasoning the commission commits a logical error. It would be equally valid to conclude, since there is no evidence of the bullet striking inside the car, and very persuasive medical evidence that the bullet did not pass through Kennedy's neck, that Connally was wounded by a different bullet than the one which struck Kennedy's back. But this would immediately destroy the single bullet theory, leading to the unavoidable conclusion that there were two assassins firing from behind.

But even Dr. Olivier is unable to give enthusiastic support to Specter's single bullet theory, despite being favorably disposed to the government's case. Olivier told the commission:

OLIVIER: The question that it [the wrist experiments on human cadavers] brings up in my mind is if the same bullet that struck the wrist had passed through the Governor's chest, if the bullet that struck the Governor's chest had not hit anything else would it have been reduced low enough to do this, and I wonder, based on our work – it brings to mind the possibility the same bullet that struck the President striking the Governor would account for this more readily. I don't know. I don't think you can ever say this, but it is a very good possibility, I think more possible, more probable than not. (WCHE, v.5, p.84)

Specter tries to get a more definite answer:

SPECTER: Based on the nature of the wound inflicted on the Governor's wrist, and on the tests which you have conducted then, do you have an opinion as to which is more probable on whether the bullet passed through only the Governor's chest before striking his wrist, or passed through the President first and then the Governor's chest before striking the Governor's wrist? . . .
OLIVIER: You couldn't say exactly at all. My feeling is that it would be more probable that it passed through the President first. (WCHE, v.5, p.86-87)

Testimony of Dr Arthur Dziemian:
Dr. Dziemian was head of the Army's Biophysics Division at Edgewood Arsenal. He was Dr. Olivier's direct supervisor. He generally agrees with Dr. Olivier's description of the tests performed with the gelatin blocks and animal tissue. At the time of his commission testimony on May 13, 1964, Dr. Dziemian had not seen the Zapruder film, nor had he seen Connally's actual wounds.

SPECTER: "What is your opinion as to whether all of the wounds on Governor Connally were inflicted by one bullet?
DZIEMIAN: My opinion is that it is most probably so, that one bullet produced all the wounds on Governor Connally. [Recall that Dr. Shaw, who operated on Connally's actual wounds, was not willing to state such a firm opinion.]
SPECTER: And what is your opinion as to whether the wound through President Kennedy's neck and all of the wounds on Governor Connally were produced by one bullet?
DZIEMIAN: I think the probability is very good that it is, that all the wounds were caused by one bullet." (WCHE, v.5, p.92)

Dziemian's opinion is based solely on the velocities of the bullets, and on the fact that the bullet must have been slowed down somewhat before striking Connally's wrist; otherwise the wrist wound would have been more severe. (WCHE, v.5, p.92); He does not factor in any details of the angle of fire or the relative positions of the two men, saying that "I do not know enough details about that to make an opinion on that. This is just on the basis of the velocities of the bullets." (WCHE, v.5, p.93) His opinion then, is not based on any of the wound ballistic tests that his laboratory conducted, or on any other facts of the situation, but solely on the velocities of the bullets. Essentially, his opinion is that a bullet passing through Kennedy would not have lost enough of its velocity to be incapable of penetrating Connally's chest and inflicting all his wounds. But at the same time, he thinks that it *would* have been slowed down enough to reduce the severity of the wrist wound which it produced.

As we have seen above, Dr. Dziemian declined to support Specter's delayed reaction theory to explain Connally's visible reaction to being shot in the Zapruder film.

Testimony of Dr. Frederick Light

Dr. Light was Chief of the U. S. Army's Wound Assessment Branch at Edgewood Arsenal and assistant chief of the Biophysics Division. His branch is under Dr. Dziemian's division. Dr. Light testifies that he is unable to agree fully with the opinions expressed by Drs. Olivier and Dziemian. In general, he takes a more skeptical and hesitant tone in his testimony. Testifying after the other two Army experts, Dr. Light is asked by Specter to explain his differences with Dr. Olivier.

> LIGHT: I am not quite as sure in my mind as I believe he is that the bullet that struck the Governor was almost certainly one which had hit something else first. I believe it could have produced that [chest] wound even though it hadn't hit the President or any other person or object first. . . . I don't believe that in passing through the tissue which was simulated by what Dr. Olivier described first, 13 or 14 centimeters of gelatin, I don't believe that the change in velocity introduced by the passage through that much tissue can be relied upon to make such a definite difference in the effect.
> SPECTER: Do you believe that if the Governor had been struck by a pristine bullet which had gone through his chest, that it would have caused no more damage than which appeared on the Governor's chest [sic – wrist?].
> LIGHT: I think that is possible, yes. (WCHE, v.5, p.95)

Light states that the belief that both men were hit by the same bullet is best supported by the fact of their relative sitting positions in the car, but that the simulated tissue gelatin experiments alone cannot establish this scenario. Throughout his testimony, Dr. Light accepts Specter's assumptions as facts, i.e., that a bullet penetrated Kennedy's neck from back to front, exiting from the front of his throat.

Light emphasizes the difficulty in drawing firm conclusions from uncertain measurements, such as those postulated in Specter's scenario.

> LIGHT: I didn't see, of course, none of us saw the wounds in the Governor in the fresh state or any other time, and I am not too convinced

from the measurements and the descriptions that were given in the surgical reports and so on that the actual holes through the skin were unusually large. [indicating an unstable bullet which had passed through another object] (WCHE, v.5, p.96)

After confirming that Dr. Light has reviewed the autopsy records, the surgery reports and the Zapruder film, Specter continues:

SPECTER: Do you believe that there would have been the same amount of damage done to the Governor's wrist had the pristine bullet only passed through the Governor's body without striking the President first? LIGHT: I think that is possible, yes. It won't happen the same way twice in any case, so you have got a fairly wide range of things that can happen if a person is shot in more or less this way. SPECTER: Do you think it is as likely that the damage would have been inflicted on the Governor's wrist as it was, with the bullet passing only through the Governor's chest as opposed to passing through the President's neck and the Governor's chest? LIGHT: I think the difference in likelihood is negligible on that basis alone. SPECTER: So the damage on the Governor's wrist would be equally consistent . . . with (A) passing only through the Governor's chest, or (B) passing through the President's neck and the Governor's chest? LIGHT: Yes. (WCHE, v.5, p.96)

Light has stumbled upon a serious contradiction in Specter's argument, namely that he needs the velocity of the bullet to be mostly *maintained* after passing through Kennedy's neck, in order to have enough energy to inflict all of Connally's wounds. But then he also needs the bullet's velocity to be significantly *reduced* in passing through Kennedy's neck, because he wants to argue that Connally's wrist wound would have been much more severe if the bullet had not been slowed down by passing through Kennedy first. He can't have it both ways – either the bullet's velocity is maintained passing through Kennedy, or it is significantly reduced, but it cannot be both. Dr. Light's testimony brings this contradiction out, although the obvious implications were not drawn when the Warren Commission set about writing their report.

Conclusion:
The testimony from the doctors and the ballistics experts provides little support for Specter's theory of a single bullet passing through Kennedy's neck and going on to cause all of Connally's wounds. Several of the experts emphasize the uncertainty of trying to predict what would necessarily happen in a situation where there can be great variety in the results, even from the same initial conditions. While

most of the witnesses concede that it is *possible* that both men could have been hit with the same bullet, they also point out that other results are equally consistent with the initial assumptions. It is important to emphasize that this uncertainty in the expert witness testimony is achieved without the usual cross-examination of witnesses and presentation of defense experts that would be expected in a real criminal trial. Specter is questioning the witnesses under the most favorable conditions: government-selected witnesses, a free hand in questioning them without regard for normal criminal procedure and rules of evidence, no cross-examination by the defense, and no defense experts to provide opposing opinions. Even with all these advantages, Specter is unable to elicit firm support for the single bullet theory. But if this theory collapses, then there must have been two assassins firing from behind, because in a two-shot scenario in which Kennedy and Connally were both hit from behind approximately one-and-a-half seconds apart, it would not have been possible for a single gunman to operate the Italian rifle fast enough to fire these two shots within such a short time interval.

PICTURES, PRINTS, AND PARAFFIN

Expert witnesses were invited to testify on other topics, such as the authenticity of the backyard photos of Oswald holding a rifle and wearing a pistol, fingerprints at the scene of the crime and on the alleged assassination weapon, and the results of paraffin tests to determine whether Oswald had recently fired a weapon. We will not go into great detail on these topics, because they do not contribute to answering the central question of whether Oswald shot President Kennedy. The main point to take away here is that the Warren Commission made a great show of presenting expert testimony on these topics, especially on the photos and the fingerprints. But despite the parade of distinguished witnesses, this evidence still suffers from the problem we have already encountered, namely the inability of the commission to logically connect this evidence with the actual commission of the assassination. The evidence may be "consistent with" Oswald's guilt, but it does not prove it.

The backyard photos

The main expert witness for the backyard photos of Oswald holding a rifle was FBI documents expert Lyndal Shaneyfelt. These photos are reproduced in the WCHE as Commission Exhibits 133, 134 (WCHE, v.16, p.510), 746, 747, 748, and 749. (WCHE, v.17, pp.517-523) Shaneyfelt examined the photos to determine their authenticity, or whether they were composites where Oswald's head was superimposed on another person's body, as Oswald himself alleged in his interview with Capt. Fritz. (Testimony of Det. Guy Rose, WCHE, v.7, p.231)

Shaneyfelt testified that in his opinion the photos are not composites, with the reservation that "an extremely expert composite" cannot be completely ruled out. (WCHE, v.4, p.288) Based on microscopic characteristics of the negative,

Shaneyfelt also found that the negative for CE749 was definitely taken by an Imperial Reflex Duo Lens camera which Robert Oswald identified as belonging to his brother Lee. (WCHE, v.4, p.284)

The authenticity of the backyard photos is further supported by George de Mohrenschildt's story about finding such a photo in between some old phonograph records that his wife had given to Marina Oswald to help her learn English. On the back of this picture was the inscription, "To my friend George from Lee Oswald" and the date April 5, 1963. (George de Mohrenschildt, *Lee Harvey Oswald as I Knew Him,* p.97. Unpublished manuscript edited and annotated by Michael A. Rinella and published by University Press of Kansas. Original title: *I am a Patsy!*) For de Mohrenschildt, this discovery constitutes "proof that the picture was genuine." (de Mohrenschildt, p.95) Lee Oswald's mother, Marguerite, told the commission that on Friday, November 22, after Lee had been arrested, Marina showed her a similar picture of Lee with a rifle, which had been stored between the pages of a book among Lee's belongings. (WCHE, v.1, p.146)

The existence of these two copies of the pictures makes it even more unlikely that the photos in the commission's exhibits were faked. But even though the photos are probably genuine, the existence of the backyard photos of Oswald brandishing the rifle seven months before the assassination have no value in proving that he killed the President. As Marguerite Oswald told the commission, "Anybody can own a rifle, to go hunting. You yourself [addressing Earl Warren] probably have a rifle. So I am not connecting this with the assassination. . . . No one is going to be foolish enough if they mean to assassinate the President, or even murder someone, to take a picture of themselves with that rifle, and leave that there for evidence." (WCHE, v.1, p.146)

A lawyer defending Oswald might easily concede the authenticity of the backyard photos without jeopardizing his client's case in any way. The photos are only important as a rhetorical tool to portray Oswald as a crazed ideological maniac, who might be capable of doing anything, including shooting the President. But this is not evidence. It is only a rhetorical distraction. Marguerite Oswald was right: Anybody can own a rifle.

The fingerprints

Fingerprints on the rifle

Sebastian Latona was the FBI fingerprint expert who testified to the existence of Oswald's prints on the rifle, the homemade paper bag, and a book carton from the sixth floor of the TSBD.

Latona did not find any identifiable prints on the rifle. He told the commission, "I was not successful in developing any prints at all on the weapon. I also had one of the firearms examiners dismantle the weapon and I processed the complete weapon, all parts, everything else. And no latent prints of value were developed." (WCHE, v.4, p.23) Then on November 29, 1963 Latona received a card with a print covered by cellophane, labeled as "off underside of gun barrel near end of foregrip

C 2766" which is the serial number of the rifle. Latona recognized this print as a latent palmprint. (WCHE, v.4, p.23); He received this new print from the Dallas FBI office, who told him that the print "had been developed by the Dallas Police Department." He identified this new print (CE637) "as the right palmprint of Lee Harvey Oswald."(WCHE, v.4, p.24) Lt. J. C. Day of the Dallas police crime lab told the commission that he had lifted this print on November 22 from the underside of the barrel in an area which would have been covered up by the wooden stock when the rifle was fully assembled. Day testified that "on the bottom side of the barrel which was covered by the wood, I found traces of a palmprint. I dusted these and tried lifting them, the prints, with scotch tape in the usual manner. A faint palmprint came off." At this point Day "received instructions from the chief's office to go no further with the processing, it was to be released to the FBI for them to complete. I did not process the underside of the barrel under the telescopic sight, did not get to this area of the gun." (WCHE, v.4, p.260) Day testified that he sent the lift from the underside of the barrel (CE637) to the FBI four days later, on November 26. (WCHE, v.4, p.261)

The absence of any identifiable prints from the exposed surfaces of the rifle is explained by Latona as resulting from the poor quality of the rifle. Latona describes the CE139 rifle as "a cheap old weapon. The wood is to the point where it won't take a good print to begin with hardly. The metal isn't of the best, and not readily susceptible to a latent print." (WCHE, v.4, p.29) Thus, Oswald's prints were not found on the surfaces of the rifle that would normally be in contact with a shooter's hands and fingers. This is awkward for the commission's theory of the crime, and would ordinarily mean either that Oswald had not recently held the weapon, or that he took the time to wipe his prints off the rifle after he had fired the shots, which would have added to the time required to descend the stairs and meet Roy Truly and Officer Baker on the second floor. No experimental results were presented to the commission to verify Latona's excuse that the wood and metal were in too poor a condition to retain a print.

Oswald's palmprint on the barrel does nothing to establish his guilt in the assassination. At best, all it proves is that his palm was in contact with the barrel at some point while the gun was disassembled. Since we already have evidence that he ordered the rifle, this print does nothing to advance the connection between Oswald and the rifle. It doesn't even prove that he was alive when the print was deposited on the barrel, or that the print that Day claimed to have lifted from the barrel actually came from the barrel. Since the rifle was sent back to the Dallas police on November 24 (the day of Oswald's death) and remained in the DPD's possession until November 26 (WCHE, v.4, p.262), there would have been the opportunity to plant Oswald's print on the barrel after Oswald was dead and before the rifle and the print were sent back to the FBI on November 26. To say that this was *possible* does not, of course, mean that it is proven. But it does mean that such a falsification cannot be ruled out. It remains a viable hypothesis which is consistent with the known evidence and gives rise to reasonable doubt about Oswald's guilt.

This is how a case is weakened by a faulty chain of possession in handling the evidence. The fact is that no identifiable prints belonging to Oswald were found on the alleged murder weapon in a location that would be consistent with his actually firing the fully assembled rifle.

Fingerprints and fibers from the paper bag

Lt. J. C. Day told the FBI that "he found the brown paper bag (CE142) shaped like a gun case near the scene of the shooting on the sixth floor of the [TSBD]". (CD5, p.129) It is not clear exactly which features of the bag make it "shaped like a gun case". From its appearance, it could just as easily be used for carrying curtain rods – or long-stemmed flowers. Latona identified Oswald's palmprint and a fingerprint on this makeshift paper bag. These were the only identifiable prints on the bag. (WCHE, v.4, p.5) The presence of a single fingerprint and a single palmprint would seem to be consistent with Oswald's having *carried* the bag in his hand. But *making* the bag would seem to require more contact with the surfaces of the paper. Thus one could plausibly argue that the presence of only two prints is evidence against Oswald's having made the bag himself.

FBI documents expert James Cadigan compared the paper bag to a roll of wrapping paper from the TSBD's shipping department, and found that they were identical on every point measured – visually, microscopically and UV characteristics. (WCHE, v.4, p.97) The Warren Commission goes to some length in describing Cadigan's tests on the wrapping paper and the tape found at the TSBD, and his opinion that they were indistinguishable from samples taken from the TSBD shipping room. Noticeably absent from the report's narrative is any evidence that the rifle was ever in the bag. The commission relied only on the presence of the bag in the southeast corner of the sixth floor to conclude that it had contained the rifle. "The presence of the bag in this corner is cogent evidence that it was used as the container for the rifle. At the time the bag was found, Lieutenant Day of the Dallas police wrote on it, 'Found next to the sixth floor window gun fired from. *May have been used* to carry gun." (WCR, p.135)

The FBI found the rifle to have been recently oiled, yet there is no mention of any traces of oil on the paper "gun case". In a letter from J. Edgar Hoover to the commission, dated August 20, 1964, Hoover stated that "the firing pin and spring of this weapon are well oiled and the rust present [on the firing pin and spring] necessarily must have formed prior to the oiling of these parts." (CE2974 at WCHE, v.26, p.455a)

The Warren Report's only attempt to connect the bag with the gun by means of visible evidence is based on several fibers found in the bag, which fiber expert Paul M. Stombaugh said "matched some of the brown viscose fibers from the blanket [taken from the Paine garage] in all observable characteristics." But Stombaugh could not even say that the fibers found in the bag *probably* came from this blanket. He can only say that "it is *possible* that these fibers could have come from this blanket." (WCR, p. 137) The strongest connection that Melvin Eisenberg can drag out of Stombaugh is the following:

> EISENBERG: Now, let me ask you a hypothetical question, Mr. Stombaugh. First, I hand you Commission Exhibit 139, which consists of a rifle found on the sixth floor of the Texas School Book Depository Building, and I ask you, *if* the rifle had lain in the blanket, which is [CE]140, and were then put inside the bag, [CE]142, *could it have* picked up fibers from the blanket and transferred them to the bag? STOMBAUGH: Yes. (WCHE, v.4, p.81)

Despite this feeble connection, the commission concluded that Oswald carried the rifle into the TSBD in the CE142 paper bag on the morning of November 22, 1963. (WCR, 137) But when Buell Wesley Frazier was shown this bag by the Dallas police, Frazier said he did not think it resembled the bag he saw Oswald carrying in Frazier's car that morning. Frazier "stated that the crinkly brown paper sack that Oswald had when he rode to work with him that morning was about two feet long. ... Detective Lewis stated that if this was not identical with the sack that was turned over to the [FBI] it is possible that Oswald may have thrown it away." (CD7, p.291) So here we have a new detail about the package that Oswald placed into Frazier's car: the wrapping paper was "crinkly", not like the heavy wrapping paper found in the TSBD. We have confirmation of this fact in an FBI interview of Frazier on the day of the assassination. Frazier told FBI agent Richard Harrison that the bag that Oswald carried with him on the morning of November 22, 1963 was like "the kind of sacks that one obtains in a 5 and 10 cent store." (CD5, p.317) Such bags are not made of the heavy wrapping paper used to ship packages. Thus, we have evidence that the bag known as CE142 is not the same bag that Oswald carried to work on the morning of November 22, and therefore that CE142 was not used to carry the rifle into the building.

It is clear that the commission has no evidence whatsoever that the rifle was ever actually in this bag, no evidence that Oswald constructed the bag, and no evidence that CE142 is the bag that Oswald carried to work in Frazier's car. The paper bag is worthless in establishing the case against Oswald.

Fingerprints on the 6th floor book cartons.
Latona found 13 identifiable prints on one of the book cartons (CE641) in the corner of the sixth floor. He was able to identify one fingerprint and one palmprint as belonging to Lee Oswald. (WCHE, v.4, p.32, 34) In his commission testimony, Latona did not associate any of the other prints with specific individuals. Since Oswald worked with the book cartons on the sixth floor, the discovery of his prints on one of the cartons would not be at all unusual. The commission only noted that this particular type of book carton – containing the "Rolling Readers" – was not typically found in this particular corner of the floor. The Warren Report noted the

presence of an unidentified palmprint on one of the book cartons, but dismisses the significance of this, saying "the presence on these cartons of unidentified prints . . . does not appear to be unusual since these cartons contained commercial products which had been handled by many people throughout the normal course of manufacturing, warehousing, and shipping. . . . These cartons could contain the prints of many people having nothing to do with the assassination." (WCR, p.249) The report ignores the obvious inference that Oswald himself may have been one of these many individuals who handled the boxes without having anything to do with the assassination.

An undated typewritten note in the FBI's Warren Commission file gives more specific information about the prints on the book cartons. The FBI note states that the Dallas police department developed one palm print from the four book cartons found at the sixth floor window. This palm print was identified as belonging to Oswald. The FBI was able to develop "an additional 20 latent fingerprints and 7 latent palm prints. One fingerprint and palm print was identified as Oswald's, one palm print and 5 fingerprints were identified as those of Dallas clerk, Forest L. Lucy, who wrapped the cartons. The 14 remaining fingerprints and 4 palm prints were identified as those of [Dallas police] officer Robert Lee Studebaker. One latent palm print remains unidentified. The Commission has stated that as many latents as possible should be identified to preclude speculation that Oswald had a coconspirator. . . . [The Commission} desired all TSBD employees be printed." (FBI 62-109090 Warren Commission HQ File, Section 19, p.59) However, not all TSBD employees were fingerprinted. At the request of superintendent Roy Truly, only those employees who would routinely handle book cartons near the sixth floor window were fingerprinted by the FBI. Truly requested that other TSBD employees not be fingerprinted. According to an FBI memo dated June 16, 1964, prints were taken only for the following TSBD employees: Danny Arce, Jack Dougherty, Buell Wesley Frazier, Charles Givens, James Jarman, Frankie Kaiser, Roy Edward Lewis, Billy Lovelady, Eddie Piper, William Shelley, Troy Eugene West, and Bonnie Ray Williams. (CD1136, "FBI Letterhead Memorandum of 16 Jun 1964 re: TSBD Employees' Fingerprints & Palmprints") Thus, the only TSBD employees who were fingerprinted were those who would have had a plausible reason to handle the boxes. There is no way to know whether the unidentified palm print found on one of the cartons belonged to some other TSBD employee who did not normally handle these cartons, or whether it was left by some outside person. The possibility that it could have been left by an assassin other than Oswald, or by an accomplice, remains undetermined, because Roy Truly blocked the FBI from taking fingerprint samples from his other employees.

The paraffin tests

Paraffin casts were made of Oswald's hands and his right cheek to determine if gunpowder residue was present. Dr. M. F. Mason of the Dallas City-County Criminal Investigation Laboratory at Parkland Hospital told the FBI that "that he had conducted an examination of three paraffin casts brought to him on November 23, 1963 by Captain George M. Doughty and Officer Bobby G. Brown of the [DPD] as being paraffin casts made of the right hand, left hand, and right cheek of Lee Harvey Oswald. . . . After his examination was completed, he found no evidence of nitrate in the paraffin cast of the right cheek. In the paraffin casts of the right and left hands, he found punctate traces of nitrate, which would be *consistent with* a person who had handled and/or fired a firearm." (CD5, p.147) Once again here, we have the consistency argument. This means nothing more than that a given hypothesis cannot be ruled out based on the evidence, but it does not mean that the hypothesis is proven. This is the case with the paraffin tests. The absence of nitrate on Oswald's cheek does not rule out the hypothesis that he fired a rifle on November 22, and the presence of nitrate on his hands does not rule out the possibility that he fired no shots on that day. Testimony from various experts demonstrates that the paraffin test is not probative in determining whether an individual has fired a gun.

Cortlandt Cunningham, the FBI firearms expert, testified that the paraffin test to determine whether a suspect has fired a gun is unreliable and results in many false positives. (WCHE, v.3, p.486-487) Cunningham was questioned by staff counsel Melvin Eisenberg:

> EISENBERG: A paraffin test was also run of Oswald's cheek and it produced a negative result. . . . Do your tests, or do the tests which you ran, or your experience with revolvers and rifles, cast any light on the significance of a negative result being obtained on the right cheek?
> CUNNINGHAM: No, sir, I personally wouldn't expect to find any residues on a person's right cheek after firing a rifle due to the fact that . . . the cartridge itself is sealed into the chamber by the bolt being closed behind it, and upon firing the case, the cartridge case expands into the chamber filling it up and sealing it off from the gases, so none will come back in your face. And so by its very nature, I would not expect to find residue on the right cheek of a shooter." (WCHE, v.3, p.492)

Cunningham explains that false positives can result because gunpowder is not the only substance which contains nitrates. He states that besides gunpowder, urine, tobacco, cosmetics, pharmaceuticals, soil, fertilizer and other substances will react positively with the chemical reagents used in the paraffin cast test. (WCHE, v.3, p.486)

Sgt. W. E. Barnes of the Dallas police made the paraffin casts for Oswald's hands and cheek. Barnes agrees with Cunningham's assessment, that "common sense will tell you that a man firing a rifle has got very little chance of getting powder residue on his cheek." (WCHE, v.7, p.283) In his deposition of April 7, 1964, Barnes was examined by staff attorney David Belin:

BELIN: Suppose you were to examine my hands and you were to find no nitrate deposits at all. Would you say that this conclusively shows that I did not fire a pistol?

BARNES: No.

BELIN: Well, does it conclusively show I had not fired a pistol within the last 6 or 8 or 10 hours?

BARNES: No. . . . A lot would depend what kind of pistol. . . . Then it would depend on whether you had cleaned your hands or whether you had had gloves on. . . . Washing your hands would make a difference." (WCHE, v.7, p.280)

Detective J. B. Hicks, who assisted in making the paraffin casts for Oswald, concurs that they are of limited value in determining whether a person has fired a firearm. Hicks testified that "my own personal opinion is that it is not an exact conclusive evidence, that . . . anything containing nitrate might show up on a test of that sort." (WCHE, v.7, p.288)

J. Edgar Hoover wrote to the commission to tell them that the paraffin casts of Oswald's cheek and hands were subjected to neutron activation analysis at the Oak Ridge National Laboratories to determine whether the traces of nitrate on the paraffin casts contained "any primer deposits from the rifle cartridge cases found in the [TSBD] following the President's assassination. As a result of these examinations, the deposits found on the paraffin casts from the hands and cheek of Oswald could not be specifically associated with the rifle cartridges." (WCHE, v.25, p.604a) Hoover goes on to say that the residues could not be associated with the revolver cartridges either. No characteristics were found which would be able to distinguish residue from the rifle cartridges from the revolver cartridges. (WCHE, v.25, p.604b)

Clearly the paraffin tests provide no evidence for determining whether Oswald fired any type of weapon at all on November 22, 1963. The lack of nitrate on his cheek does not rule out the possibility that he may have fired a rifle. And the presence of nitrate traces on his hands does not prove that he fired either a rifle or a revolver, since other common substances can produce a positive result on this test.

THE SHOTS

HOW MANY SHOTS WERE THERE?

The Warren Commission inferred that three shots were fired based on the fact that three shells were discovered near the sixth floor window. "The most convincing evidence relating to the number of shots was provided by the presence on the sixth floor of three spent cartridges which were demonstrated to have been fired by the same rifle that fired the bullets which caused the wounds." (WCR, p.110-111) The "earwitnesses" varied considerably on how many shots they heard, but there was a clear majority who said they had heard three. However, there were some who heard more, and some who heard fewer shots. Here is an inventory of who heard how many shots:

Witnesses who testified to hearing three shots: Victoria Adams (CD5, p.39); Danny Arce (CD205, p.7); Virgie Baker (CD5, p.66); Police officer Marrion Baker (WCHE, v.24, p.199b); Secret Service agent Glen Bennett (WCHE, v.18, p.760); Jane Berry (CD5, p.42); Deputy Sheriff Eugene Boone (WCHE, v.19, p.508); Lee Bowers (CD5, p.43); Charles Brehm (WCHE, v.22, p.837b-838a); Police officer E. V. Brown (WCHE, v.6, p.233); Dallas mayor Earle Cabell (WCHE, v.7, p.478); Elizabeth Cabell (WCHE, v.7, p.486); Vice-presidential aide Cliff Carter (WCHE, v.7, p.475); Governor Connally heard the first and third shots, and felt the second shot hit him. (WCHE, v.4, p.132-133); Nellie Connally (WCHE, v.4, p.147); news photographer Malcolm Couch (CD5, p.18); Deputy Sheriff Roger Craig (WCHE, v.19, p.524); Police chief Jesse Curry (WCHE, v.12, p.28); Mrs. Joseph Eddie Dean (CD5, p.44); Deputy Sheriff Harold Elkins (WCHE, v.19, p.540); Deputy Sheriff Jack Faulkner (WCHE, v.19, p.511); Police officer J. W. Foster (WCHE, v.6, p.251); Secret Service agent Will Greer, who was driving the Presidential limousine (WCHE, v.2, p.118); Postal inspector Harry Holmes (WCHE, v.7, p.291); Emmet Hudson (WCHE, v.19, p.481); Police officer Douglas Jackson who rode alongside the Presidential limousine (*FBI 62-109060 JFK HQ File, Section 181, pp.94*); News photographer Robert Jackson (CD5, p.15); James Jarman (CD5, p.335); Secret Service agent Lem Johns (WCHE, v.18, p.773-774); Ladybird Johnson (WCHE, v.5, p.565); Deputy Sheriff C. M. Jones (WCHE, v.19, p.512); Secret Service agent Roy Kellerman (at least 3 – WCHE, v.2, p.76); Secret Service agent Sam Kinney (WCHE, v.18, p.732); Secret Service agent Jerry Kivett (WCHE, v.18, p.778); Dolores Kounas (CD5, p.68); Patricia Ann Lawrence (CD5, p.51); Secret Service agent Winston Lawson (WCHE, v.4, p.353); Deputy Sheriff C. L. "Lummie" Lewis (WCHE, v.19, p.526); Billy Lovelady (WCHE, v.24, p.214b); Police officer B. J. Martin (WCHE, v.6, p.291); Secret Service agent William McIntyre (WCHE, v.18, p.747-748); Austin Miller (WCHE, v.19, p.485); Mary Ann Mitchell (WCHE, v.6, p.176); Deputy Sheriff Luke Mooney (WCHE, v.19, p.528); Mary Muchmore

(CD735, p.8); Harold Norman (CD5, p.26); Presidential assistant Lawrence O'Brien (WCHE, v.7, p.464); Presidential assistant Kenneth O'Donnell (WCHE, v.7, p.448); Eddie Piper (WCHE, v.6, p.385); Presidential assistant David Powers (WCHE, v.7, p.473); Frank Reilley (CD205, p.29); Texas Highway Patrol officer Joe Henry Rich, who drove the Vice-presidential follow-up car (WCHE, v.18, p.800); James Romack (WCHE, v.6, p.280); Arnold Rowland (WCHE, v.26, p.166a-b); William Shelley (WCHE, v.24, p.226a); James Simmons (WCHE, v.22, p.833a); Deputy Sheriff L. C. Smith (WCHE, v.19, p.516); Secret Service agent Forrest Sorrels (WCHE, v.21, p.548); Pearl Springer (WCHE, v.24, p.523a); Deputy Sheriff Allan Sweatt (WCHE, v.19, p.531); James Tague (CD205, p.31); Secret Service agent Warren Taylor (WCHE, v.18, p.782-783); Roy Truly (WCHE, v.24, p.227b); Police officer Buddy Walthers (WCHE, v.7, p.545); Sheriff's Department radio operator Watson (WCHE, v.19, p.522); Deputy Sheriff Harry Weatherford (WCHE, v.19, p.502); Deputy constable Seymour Weitzman (WCHE, v.24, p.228a); Otis Williams (CD5, p.64); Linda Kay Willis (WCHE, v.7, p.498-499); Phillip Willis (WCHE, v.7, p.495); Deputy Sheriff John Wiseman (WCHE, v.19, p.535); Mary Woodward (WCHE, v.24, p.520a); Secret Service agent Rufus Youngblood (WCHE, v.18, p.768)

Witnesses who reported hearing four or more shots: Robert Edwards (4) (WCHE, v.19, p.473; v.6, p.205); Amos Euins (4) (CD205, p.12), Ronald Fischer [3 in his statement to the Sheriff's office (WCHE, v.19, p.475); 4 in his deposition (WCHE, v.6, p.195)]; Ruby Henderson (4) (WCHE, v.24, p.524a-b); Jean Hill (4 to 6) (WCHE, v.6, p.207); S. M. Holland (4) (WCHE, v.19, p.480; v.6, p.244); A. J. Millican (8, in three separate volleys) (WCHE, v.19, p.486); Mary Moorman (3 or 4) (WCHE, v.19, p.487); Jesse Price (5 or 6) (WCHE, v.19, p.492); Royce Skelton (4, including 1 that hit the pavement) (WCHE, v.19, p.496; v.6, p.238); Carolyn Walther (at least 4) (WCHE, v.24, p.522b); James Worrell (4) (WCHE, v.16, p.959; v.2, p.193)

Witnesses who reported hearing fewer than three shots: Howard Brennan (2) (WCHE, v.3, p.144); John Chism (at least 2) (CD205, p.38); Marvin Faye Chism (2) (WCHE, v.19, p.472); Jack Dougherty (1) (WCHE, v.6, p.379), Police officer Bobby Hargis, whose motorcycle was traveling at the left rear of the President's car (2) (WCHE, v.6, p.294); Charles Hester (2) (WCHE, v.19, p.478); Secret Service agent Clint Hill (2) (WCHE, v.2, p.139), Jacqueline Kennedy (2) (WCHE, v.5, p.180); Secret Service agent Paul Landis (2) (WCHE, v.18, p.754-7555); F. Lee Mudd (2) (WCHE, v.24, p.538a); Thomas J. Murphy (2) (WCHE, v.22, p.835b); Jean Newman (2) (WCHE, v.19, p.489); Emory Roberts (2 or 3 per his report of 11/22/63 (WCHE, v.18, p.739); 3 in his report of 11/29/63 (WCHE, v.18, p.734)); Bonnie Ray Williams (2 in his affidavit to police (WCHE, v.24, p.229a); 3 in his testimony to the commission (WCHE, v.3, p.179)); Abraham Zapruder (2) (WCHE, v.7, p.571)

Evaluating the testimony on the number of shots

Given the variety in the number of shots heard by witnesses, it would be easy to throw up our hands and dismiss "earwitness" testimony as totally unreliable. But this would be going too far. Given the principles we considered earlier for evaluating witness testimony, we should first determine whether apparently conflicting statements can be reconciled. The Warren Report acknowledged that "the difficulty of accurate perception of the sound of gunshots required careful scrutiny of all of this testimony regarding the number of shots. The report noted that a gunshot makes several separate sounds: the muzzle blast, the shock wave, the impact on the target. "Each noise can be quite sharp and may be perceived as a separate shot. The tall buildings in the area might have further distorted the sound." The commission decided that three shots were fired, but this was not determined on the basis of what the witnesses heard, nor on the basis of bullets recovered, but on the fact that three cartridge shells were found at the sixth floor window. (WCR, p.110)

There is no way to tell from the witness testimony alone the precise number of shots fired. Two simultaneous shots might be heard as a single shot, especially if the witness was situated an equal distance between them. Thus, a witness who heard three shots is not necessarily in conflict with one who heard four or more, if they heard the shots from different locations. Several witnesses gave testimony indicating the possibility of near-simultaneous shots. Secret Service agent Roy Kellerman said one of the noises sounded "like a double bang". (WCHE, v.2, p.76) Secret Service agent Clint Hill, riding in the car immediately behind Kellerman, also said that the second explosion "had almost a double sound". (WCHE, v.2, p.144) Witness Jean Hill referred to the final sound as a "flurry of shots". (WCHE, v.6, p.207). Although it is possible that these witnesses heard multiple shots grouped closely together, their perception could also be explained by hearing as separate noises the muzzle blast and ensuing shock wave produced by a high powered rifle. All we can say is that the fact that a majority of the witnesses testified to hearing three shots does not require us to rule out the possibility that four or more shots were actually fired. Indeed, simultaneous shots are exactly what we would expect in an ambush where separate snipers were all instructed to fire at the moment when the car arrived at a predetermined spot on the street. In that case, three noises, or "explosions", could be produced by four or more separate shots.

We are probably safe in concluding that at least three shots were fired, but not because three shells were found. Having rejected the single bullet theory as being in conflict with the physical and eyewitness evidence, we can say that at least three shots were fired based on the wounds received by the two men in the car. Kennedy was hit in the back with the first shot. Connally was shot through the back and chest with the second shot. And Kennedy was hit in the head with the final shot. We cannot rule out the possibility that multiple simultaneous shots were fired, leading to a total of as many as 5 or 6 shots. For example, a shot fired into Kennedy's neck from the front at the same time as the shot to the back. Or two simultaneous head shots – one from the front right, and one from the back. The earwitness testimony can help us rule out the likelihood of missed shots, since no one reported hearing shots before about frame 210 of the Zapruder film – when Kennedy was hit in the back and possibly the throat – or after the head shot at frame 313.

WERE THE SHOTS EVENLY SPACED?

The spacing of the shots carries grave consequences for the Warren Commission's theory of the crime. Many witnesses noticed a greater pause between shots 1 and 2 than between 2 and 3 – so many, in fact, that commission member Allen Dulles commented on it during a commission session. During the testimony of Robert Frazier, Dulles noted: "There has been a certain amount of testimony indicating there was a longer pause between the report of the first shot or what is believed to be the report, explosion of the first shot and the second and third shots, that is not absolutely unanimous but I would say it is something like 5 to 1 or something of that kind, what would you say, 2 to 1, 3 to 1? . . . I think if you will read the testimony you will find it at least 2 to 1 except for the people in the car." (WCHE, v.5, p.174) The Warren Report itself notes that "a substantial majority of the witnesses stated that the shots were not evenly spaced. Most witnesses recalled that the second and third shots were bunched together." (WCR, p.115) Of course if they were bunched together, closer than 2.3 seconds apart, they could not both have been fired from the Italian bolt-action rifle.

Witnesses who discerned a longer time between the first and second shots than between the second and third included:

- Danny Arce: "I heard something like a gun shot and then a second and third shot close together." (CD205, p.7)
- Deputy Sheriff Eugene Boone: "There seemed to be a pause between the first shot and the second shot and third shots – a little longer pause." (WCHE, v.3, p.292)
- Lee Bowers: "I heard three shots. One, then a slight pause, then two very close together." (WCHE, v.6, p.287)
- Deputy Sheriff Roger Craig: There was "quite a pause" between the first and second shots. "Not more than 2 seconds" between the second and third shots. "They were real rapid." (WCHE, v.6, p.263)
- James Crawford: "I heard the first report. . . . The second shot followed some seconds, a little time elapsed after the first one, and followed very quickly by the third one." (WCHE, v.6, p.172)
- Harold Elkins: "I heard a shot ring out, a couple of seconds elapsed and then two more shots ring out." (WCHE, v.19, p.540)

- Secret Service Agent Will Greer: "The last two [shots] were closer together than the first one. It seemed like the first one, and then there was, you know, bang, bang, just right behind it almost. . . . The last two seemed closer to me than the other." (WCHE, v.2, p.130)
- Secret Service Agent George Hickey: He reported that the second and third shots were so close together that "there seemed to be practically no time element between them." (WCHE, v.18, p.762)
- News photographer Robert Jackson: He told an FBI agent "that there was a pause after the first shot, which was followed by the second and third shots in rapid succession." (CD5, p.15)
- James Jarman: He heard a shot. Then, "after an elapse of three or four seconds, he heard a second shot. . . He said a third shot was heard by him closely following the second shot, possibly within a second or two afterward." (Jarman was standing on the 5th floor, just below where the shots were said to have been fired.) (CD5, p.335)
- Ladybird Johnson: "Suddenly there was a sharp loud report – a shot. . . . Then a moment and then two more shots in rapid succession." (WCHE, v.5, p.565)
- Secret Service Agent Roy Kellerman: He answered "Yes" when Senator Cooper asked him whether there was "a longer interval between the first shot and the second shot as compared to the interval between the second shot and the third shot." (WCHE, v.2, p.77)
- Secret Service Agent Winston Lawson: After the first sound he "heard two more sharp reports. The second two were closer together than the first. There was one report, and a pause, then two more reports closer together. (WCHE, v.4, p.353)
- Billy Lovelady: "There was a slight pause after the first shot then the next two was right close together." (WCHE, v.24, p.214b)
- Mary Ann Mitchell: "I heard some reports. . . . There were three, the second and third being closer together than the first and second." (WCHE, v.6, p.176)
- Deputy Sheriff Luke Mooney: "The second and third shot was pretty close together, but there was a short lapse there between the first and second shot." (WCHE, v.3, p.282)
- Arnold Rowland: "I heard a noise which I thought to be a backfire. . . . Then in about 8 seconds I heard another report and in about 3 seconds a third report." (WCHE, v.19, p.494)
- Barbara Rowland: "The second and third [shots] were closer than the first and second." (WCHE, v.6, p.184)
- William Shelley: "I heard something sounded like it was a firecracker and a slight pause and then two more a little bit closer together." (WCHE, v.6, p.329)
- Pearl Springer: "She recalled that after the first shot there was a pause, then two more shots were fired close together." (WCHE, v.24, p.523a)

- Chief Criminal Deputy Allan Sweatt: "I heard a shot and about 7 seconds later another shot and approximately 2 or 3 seconds later a third shot." (WCHE, v.19, p.531)
- James Tague: According to the FBI report, "He heard a loud noise. . . . He then heard two more loud noises in quick succession." (CD205, p.31)
- Deputy Constable Seymour Weitzman: He described the spacing as "First one, then the second two seemed to be simultaneously." (WCHE, v.7, p.106)
- Bonnie Ray Williams: "The second and the third shot was closer together than the first shot and the second shot, as I remember." (WCHE, v.3, p.175)
- Linda Kay Willis: "I heard one [shot]. Then there was a little bit of time, and then there were two real fast bullets together." (WCHE, v.7, p.498)
- Secret Service Agent Forrest Sorrels: "There was to me about twice as much time between the first and second shots as there was between the second and third shots." (WCHE, v.7, p.345)
- Mayor Earle Cabell: "Approximately 10 seconds elapsed between the first and second shots, with not more than 5 seconds having elapsed until the third one." Asked if this was a 2-to-1 ratio, Cabell replies, "Approximately that. And again I say that, as you mentioned, as a matter of being relative. I couldn't tell you the exact seconds because they were not counted." (WCHE, v.7, p.478)

The importance of this unevenness in the shot pattern has not received enough attention in the assassination literature. We noted earlier that this uneven spacing places an additional constraint on the time limit for the shots. If these witnesses were correct in perceiving a longer interval between the first two shots, and if this interval was about 2 to 1, as testified by Secret Service Agent Sorrels and Mayor Cabell, then the absolute minimum time required to fire the three shots is not 4.6 seconds, or even 5.6 seconds, but 6.9 seconds. And this assumes the fastest possible firing time between shots of 2.3 seconds. The more realistic time of 3.1 seconds for operating the rifle and re-aiming between shots, as calculated in the Liebeler memo, would give us a minimum of 9.3 seconds to fire three shots, if we assume that the time interval between the first two shots was double that of the second and third shots. The same reasoning would apply to those few witnesses who perceived a shorter interval between the first and second shots than between the second and third.

That the shooting spree lasted only 5.6 seconds is confirmed by Zapruder's movie, and so the uneven spacing between shots wreaks havoc with the Warren Commission's claim that three shots could be fired from the Italian rifle CE139 within the timeframe established by the film. We must conclude that it was not possible for three shots to have been fired from this rifle in 5.6 seconds, if the interval spacing heard by the overwhelming majority of earwitnesses is accepted. The only way around this dilemma is for one of the shots to have wounded both Kennedy and Connally, *and* for another one of the shots to have been fired outside the 5.6 second interval. The commission achieves this by inventing the single bullet theory (one bullet penetrating Kennedy's neck and Connally's chest, wrist, and thigh) and by assuming that one of the shots missed and is not observable on the film. But the missed shot is speculation, and the single bullet theory is contradicted by the other evidence.

WAS THERE A MISSED SHOT?

The official position of both the Warren Commission and the FBI was that three shots were fired in Dealey Plaza. The FBI Summary Report on the assassination, released before the Warren Commission was even appointed, found that all three shots hit their mark. "Two bullets struck President Kennedy, and one wounded Governor Connally." (CD1, p.1) The Warren Report, on the other hand, acknowledged the possibility that one of the three shots missed and did not hit the car. "From the initial findings that (a) one shot passed through the President's neck and then most probably passed through the Governor's body, (b) a subsequent shot penetrated the President's head, (c) no other shot struck any part of the automobile, and (d) three shots were fired, it follows that one shot probably missed the car and its occupants. The evidence is inconclusive as to whether it was the first, second, or third shot which missed." (WCR, p.111) In other words, after months of investigation and hearings, and after multiple viewings of the films and photos, the commission was unable to determine the sequence of shots during the assassination. At the end of their proceedings, in the commission's view, any one of the following shot sequences was still considered as a possibility: (1) miss, magic bullet, head shot; (2) magic bullet, miss, head shot; (3) magic bullet, head shot, miss. The commission did not even entertain the possibility that there was a fourth bullet which missed, which would have been a plausible scenario, given that multiple witnesses testified that they had heard more than three shots. But this would have required introducing a second shooter, and this hypothesis was off limits. Thus, the missed shot discussion took place in the context of the three shot limit, which became a strait jacket that hampered the commission's ability to consider alternative hypotheses. The commission's justification for this constraint, given the variety in witnesses' testimony on the number of shots, was based primarily on the fact that three shells were discovered near the sixth floor window of the TSBD. (WCR, p.110-111) As we have seen, the chain of possession for these shells is non-existent, and there is no evidence that these three shells represent actual shots fired from the sixth floor window during the assassination. But even assuming the discovery of three shells, if an empty shell had been ejected from the rifle before the gunman began to fire, then three empty shells could have been found even if only two shots were fired.

The possibility of a missed shot forced itself upon the commission because a bystander, James Tague, reported having been hit in the cheek by a projectile of some kind, when either a bullet or a bullet fragment hit the curb near where he was standing at the entrance to the triple underpass between Commerce and Main

Streets. "Whatever it was that hit him broke the skin and caused about two drops of blood to flow. He thought possibly that one of the bullets had hit the curb near his feet and possibly a piece of the curbing had hit him in the cheek. He did look around the curb, and near where he was standing there was a chip missing, which he stated looked fresh." (CD205, p.31)

But even without the Tague injury, the commission would have needed a missed shot because of the time constraints imposed by the Zapruder film. Without the film, the commission could have adopted the position taken by the FBI report, that Kennedy was hit in the back with the first shot, then Connally was hit in the back with the second shot, and finally Kennedy was hit in the head – three bullets, three hits. But the Zapruder film showed that the two shots from the back occurred too close together to have been fired by the Italian bolt-action rifle. Therefore, the single bullet theory was adopted to account for all the injuries to Kennedy and Connally except for the head wound. This left one shot unaccounted for. Since there were no signs that it hit the car, it must have hit elsewhere – i.e., it missed.

Tague himself was uncertain which shot produced the fragment which hit him in the cheek. During his deposition, Tague was questioned by commission counsel Wesley Liebeler:

LIEBELER: Do you have any idea which bullet might have made that mark?
TAGUE: I would guess it was either the second or third. I wouldn't say definitely on which one.
LIEBELER: Did you hear any more shots after you felt yourself get hit in the face?
TAGUE: I believe I did.
LIEBELER: You think you did?
TAGUE: I believe I did.
LIEBELER: How many?
TAGUE: I believe that it was the second shot, so I heard the third shot afterwards.
LIEBELER: Did you hear three shots?
TAGUE: I heard three shots, yes sir. (WCHE, v.7, p.555)

The first shot did not miss.

No witnesses reported hearing a shot that occurred before the first shot which hit the President as he disappeared behind the freeway sign in the Zapruder film. The Secret Service summary of the assassination stated that the first "sharp report" was heard when the car was about 200 feet down Elm Street. (CD3, p.31) This shot was followed by "two more sounds like gunfire" in rapid succession. (CD3, p.32) This location for the first shot being fired after the car had passed the TSBD on Elm Street is consistent with all the eye- and ear-witness testimony, that no shot occurred before about frame 210 of the Zapruder film. The Warren Report itself

113

acknowledged that the President was "probably hit by frame 225", but certainly not before frame 210. (WCR, p.105) If this is the case, it means that a prior (missed) shot must have been fired no later than the interval from about frame 168 to 183 (taking 42 frames as the absolute minimum interval between shots – 2.3 seconds per shot times 18.3 frames per second). But during a Secret Service re-enactment it was found that the view from the sixth floor window would have been blocked by the oak tree between frames 166 and 210. (WCR, p.98) Thus a prior missed shot would have had to occur before frame 166, unless the sniper had been firing blindly through the tree leaves. There is no testimony for any such shot. Indeed, the Warren Report calls attention to numerous witnesses whose testimony "supports the conclusion that the first of the shots fired hit the President." One of these witnesses was Phillip Willis, who snapped a picture at the moment when he heard the first shot. "Analysis of his photograph revealed that it was taken at approximately frame 210 of the Zapruder film. . . . If Willis accurately recalled that there were no previous shots, this would be strong evidence that the first shot did not miss." (WCR, p.112)

The commission pointed out that even before frame 166, "the President was in clear view of the assassin as he rode up Houston Street and for 100 feet as he proceeded down Elm Street until he came to a point denoted as frame 166 on the Zapruder film." (WCR, p.98) It is astonishing that a lone gunman perched in the sixth floor window of the TSBD did not take advantage of the clear shot down Houston Street, but instead allowed the car to pass under a tree, and waited until the car was nearly 200 feet away, traveling downhill and away from the gunman before firing the first shot. This is an implausible scenario, given a lone assassin, and the commission perhaps tried to render it more plausible by suggesting (but not proving, or even believing) that a prior shot was attempted as the car approached the building, but missed. (The clear shot which the gunman passed up as the car drove down Houston Street is shown in CE875 at WCHE, v.17, p.875.)

The evidence indicates that the first shot from behind was fired between frames 210 and 225 and hit President Kennedy in the back. There was no prior missed shot. This much is acknowledged even by the Warren Report.

The second shot did not miss.

In our previous chapter where we discussed the shots from the rear, it was shown that Governor Connally was hit within 1.8 seconds of the shot that hit Kennedy in the back. Thus the second shot did not miss, and the interval of 1.8 seconds does not allow for a missed shot between the hits to Kennedy's back and Connally's back.

The commission itself pointed out the flaws in postulating a second shot that missed. The Warren Report noted that this would require the second shot to occur precisely in the middle of the 5.6 second timeframe, given the time needed to operate the bolt between shots. While acknowledging that "this possibility was buttressed by the testimony of witnesses who claimed that the shots were evenly spaced", the report admitted that "most witnesses recalled that the second and third shots were bunched together." (WCR, p.115) These witnesses would have to be ignored if the commission held to the notion that the second shot missed. A scenario where the second shot missed could explain the hit on the curb near James Tague, but would not buy the commission any additional time for the gunman to get his shots off. The Warren Report does not press very hard for this option.

The third shot did not miss.

The Warren Report finds a missed third shot as plausible, given that the distance between the gunman and the car was greatest at that point, but it finds that the weight of witness testimony is on the side of the third and last shot being the one that hit Kennedy in the head. It cites Associated Press photographer James Altgens, who testified that the shot which hit the President's head was the last shot. (WCR, p.115) Altgens stated confidently, "There was not another shot fired after the President was struck in the head. That was the last shot – that much I will say with a great degree of certainty." (WCHE, v.7, p.518) The Warren Report acknowledges "the preponderance of the eyewitness testimony that the head shot was the final shot." (WCR, p.117) Certainly when the sniper saw Kennedy's head explode after the third shot, he would have had no reason to fire a fourth shot, since his mission had been accomplished.

What hit James Tague?

Rejecting the separate hypotheses that either the first, the second, or the third shot missed, we are left with James Tague, whose cheek injury from a flying projectile must be explained. A letter from FBI Director Hoover to the commission presented the results of an analysis of the section of curb which was struck on the south side of Main Street near where Tague was standing. Hoover reported that the curb section, which had been removed and sent to the FBI Laboratory, displayed small smears of metal foreign to the curb. "These metal smears were spectrographically determined to be essentially lead with a trace of antimony. No copper was found. The lead could have originated from the lead core of a mutilated metal-jacketed bullet. . . . The absence of copper precludes the possibility that the mark on the curbing section was made by an unmutilated military-type full metal-jacketed bullet such as the bullet from Governor Connally's stretcher [CE399] or the bullet or bullets represented by the jacket fragments [CE567 & 569] found in the Presidential limousine. Further, the damage to the curbing would have been much more extensive if a rifle bullet had struck the curbing without first having struck some other object. Therefore, this mark could not have been made by the first impact of a high velocity rifle bullet." (WCHE, v.21, p.476)

So the projectile which hit Tague was either a bullet fragment that ricocheted off the curb, or was a piece of concrete dislodged from the curb by a bullet fragment. But Tague's injury cannot have been caused by a missed shot.

Conclusion:

In the end, the commission comes to no conclusion as to "which shot missed". (WCR, p.117) The Warren Report itself has ruled out in sequence a missed first shot, a missed second shot, and a missed third shot. yet it holds absurdly to the finding that "one shot probably missed the car and its occupants." (WCR, p.111) It is not a simple matter of determining "which shot missed" as the Warren Report puts it. Once these three alternatives have all been ruled out, the commission has proven that there was no missed shot. If there was no missed shot, then all three shots must have been fired within the 5.6 second Zapruder timeframe. But with an uneven spacing of shots, and a minimum of 2.3 seconds between each shot, the minimum time to fire the three shots is pushed beyond the allowable 5.6 seconds. Therefore, there had to be at least one other gunman firing during these 5.6 seconds.

THE MEN IN THE WINDOW

The evidence of the wounds proves that multiple shooters were firing at President Kennedy in Dealey Plaza. The next question to consider is whether Lee Oswald was one of those shooters. Having dismissed the lone gunman theory, we are now left with two possibilities: Either Oswald shot at the President from the TSBD window while two other snipers targeted him in a crossfire, or someone else was the TSBD rifleman and Oswald was downstairs, calmly eating his lunch and drinking a Coke, unaware that he had been set up to take the blame for the assassination.

The Commission relied heavily on the testimony of eyewitnesses in Dealey Plaza and in the Texas School Book Depository to establish that Oswald was in the southeast corner window of the sixth floor with a rifle at the time of the assassination. In evaluating this testimony, the commission selectively interpreted the evidence, giving great weight to testimony that supported the commission's theory of the crime, while ignoring or discounting those witnesses who provided conflicting evidence – for example, that they saw two men in the window, or that they saw Oswald downstairs close to the time of the shooting.

THE MAN IN THE WINDOW WITH THE RIFLE

Howard Brennan – Star Witness

There was only one witness who said he saw a man in the window with a rifle and identified that man as Lee Oswald. This was Howard Brennan, who was a steamfitter working with a construction company in the neighborhood of the TSBD. He watched the Presidential motorcade from the southwest corner of Elm and Houston, across from the TSBD. The Warren Report states confidently that "Howard L. Brennan was an eyewitness to the shooting", and that he "testified that Lee Harvey Oswald, whom he viewed in a police lineup on the night of the assassination, was the man he saw fire the shots from the sixth floor window of the Depository building." (WCR, p.143) Before testifying in a commission session on March 24, 1964, Brennan had given a written statement to the Dallas County Sheriff's Department, and was interviewed at least twice by the FBI. His shifting and indecisive testimony undermines the confidence that the commission placed in his statements. It will therefore be instructive for us to examine his testimony in some detail.

On the afternoon of the assassination, Brennan gave a statement to the Sheriff's Department, in which he said that before the President's car arrived, he had seen a man in the southeast window of the TSBD, in the second row of windows from the top. According to Brennan, this man "was just sitting up there looking down apparently waiting . . . to see the President." Brennan does not say that he saw a rifle in the man's hands until the sound of the first shot. At that time, Brennan says he "looked up at the building. I then saw this man I have described in the window and he was taking aim with a high powered rifle. I could see all of the barrel of the gun. I do not know if it had a scope on it or not. I was looking at the man in this window at the time of the last explosion. Then this man let the gun down to his side and stepped down out of sight. He did not seem to be in any hurry." (WCHE, v.19, p.470)

Although he says he witnessed at least one shot, Brennan does not say anything about seeing the man operate the bolt action between shots, or after the final shot. From other witnesses we know that Capt. Fritz ejected a live round from the rifle shortly after it was discovered. (WCHE, v.7, p.109; WCHE, v.4, p.205) This means that after firing the last shot, the presumed shooter would have had to operate the bolt action to eject the last empty shell and move the live round into the firing chamber. But Brennan does not report seeing any such operation of the bolt after the final shot. He says that the man simply "let the gun down to his side and stepped out of sight." Now, if the rifle was found with a live cartridge in the chamber, and the gunman was not seen to eject an empty shell after firing the last shot, how did the live round get into the chamber? The gunman could have ejected the shell after moving away from the window, but what purpose would this have served if he had already hit his target and was in a hurry to make his escape?

Brennan was interviewed by the FBI the day after the assassination. He told the agents that he heard a loud noise when the President's car was about 30 yards past where Brennan was seated. The FBI report states that Brennan "said he does not distinctly remember a second shot but he remembers more than one noise . . . and consequently he believes there must have been a second shot before he looked in the direction of the [TSBD] building." (CD5, p.12) Brennan thus stands out as being one of the few witnesses who had no clear recollection of how many shots they heard, even though he was standing right under the window from which all three shots were supposed to have been fired. After hearing the loud noise, Brennan tells the FBI agents that he "saw a man in a window on the sixth floor near the southeast corner of the building" holding what appeared to be a "heavy rifle" in his hands. (CD5, p.12) Then Brennan "saw this person take 'deliberate aim' and fire a shot. He then observed this person take the rifle from his shoulder and hold it by the barrel of the rifle, as if he were resting the butt of the rifle on the floor. He said this individual observed the scene on the street below, momentarily, and then stepped back from the window." Brennan estimated the distance from his position to the window as "approximately 90 yards [sic]." Brennan was brought to the police station later to view a lineup, in which "he picked Lee Harvey Oswald as the person most closely resembling the man he had observed with the rifle in the window of the [TSBD]. He stated, however, he could not positively identify Oswald as the person he saw fire the rifle." (CD5, p.13)

Brennan was interviewed again by the FBI several weeks after the assassination, on December 17, 1963. At this interview, Brennan "stated that he now can say that he is sure that Lee Harvey Oswald was the person he saw in the window at the time of the President's assassination. He claimed to have felt that a positive identification was not necessary when he observed Oswald in the police line-up at the Dallas Police Department at about 7 p.m., November 22, 1963, since it was his understanding Oswald had already been charged with the slaying of Dallas Police Officer J. D. Tippit. . . . [Also] he felt that since he had seen Oswald on television before picking Oswald out of the lineup at the police station that it tended to 'cloud' any identification he made of Oswald at that time." (CD205, p.15) Brennan added that "he was able to observe Oswald's head and shoulders in the window and possibly down as far as Oswald's belt." (CD205, p.16)

When Brennan finally testified before the commission on March 24, 1964, he came up with a new explanation for not identifying Oswald in the police lineup. He says he could have positively identified him in the lineup, but was afraid to because of "security reasons". Brennan thought that the assassination was a communist plot, and that if word got out that Brennan had identified the shooter, he and his family might be in danger. (WCHE, v.3, 148) This explanation did not come up in his FBI interview of December 17, 1963. During his commission testimony, Brennan said the gunman appeared to be "standing up and resting against the left window sill, with gun shouldered to his right shoulder, holding the gun with his left hand and taking positive aim and fired his last shot. . . . He drew the gun back from the window as though he was drawing it back to his side and maybe paused for another second as though to assure himself that he hit his mark, and then he disappeared." (WCHE, v.3, p.144) Brennan cannot be right about the man standing up, because the window only opens halfway, and there is no very great distance between the bottom of the window frame and the floor. (See building photos, CE481, 484, 485, 510.) So it would be impossible for a person to fire a rifle while standing at the window, unless the top frame of the window was pulled down, which it was not, according to photos taken immediately after the assassination. But if the gunman was sitting down, Brennan would not have been able to view him "down as far as [his] belt" as Brennan told the FBI. Furthermore, a gunman standing up would not be able to use the makeshift gun rest constructed from the book boxes. The Warren Report describes the so-called "sniper's nest", telling us that "a carton had apparently been placed on the floor at the side of the window so that a person *sitting* on the carton could look down Elm Street toward the overpass and *scarcely be noticed from the outside*. Between this carton and the half-open window were three additional cartons arranged at such an angle that a rifle resting on the top carton would be aimed directly at the motorcade as it moved away from the building." (WCR, p.8) The commission's vision of a sniper barely visible from the outside, sitting at a half-open window, with the rifle resting on a book carton conflicts dramatically with Brennan's testimony of a sniper standing in plain view of the crowd below, resting against the window sill of what could only be a window opened from the top. And yet the commission has relied completely on Brennan's testimony to positively place Oswald in the window firing a rifle.

There are several anomalies to be noted in Brennan's statements to the FBI and to the commission. First, he omits any reference to the shooter operating the bolt action of the rifle, despite his having a good enough view to see the man firing and to estimate the man's age (early 30's), height (about 5'10"), and weight (around 165 pounds). So we are still left with the question of how the live round ejected by Fritz got into the chamber. Second, he testified that the man was standing up at the window, although that would have made it impossible for Brennan to see his upper body, and impossible for the man to have aimed at the motorcade. Third, Brennan's ability to positively identify Oswald as the man in the window changed over the course of time, as did his explanations of why he was at first unable to positively identify him. Fourth, although Brennan estimated his distance from the window as about 90 yards, the commission put it at about 40 yards (120 feet). (WCR, p.144) Thus, Brennan's estimate of the distance was off by a factor of more than 2. Finally, even though Brennan was standing right across the street from the TSBD, he is not sure how many shots he heard. He can say positively that there were two. He cannot say for sure whether there were more. (WCHE, v.3, p.144) If indeed three evenly spaced shots were fired from the sixth floor window right in front of Brennan, it is incredible that he would not have clearly heard and remembered them. These types of inconsistencies would have given the commission ample reason to dismiss the testimony of any witness whose testimony proved inimical to the lone gunman theory. But Brennan's testimony is key to the commission's case, so they go lightly in judging his inconsistencies, because Brennan is the only witness who even comes close to identifying Oswald in the window with a rifle.

Other witnesses who saw a man or a rifle in the window

Howard Brennan is not the only witness who said he saw a man and/or a rifle in the sixth floor window of the TSBD, although he is the only one who positively (maybe) identified Oswald as the man he saw.

- *Amos Euins*, a high school student, was standing across from the TSBD near the corner of Houston and Elm Streets. Immediately after the assassination he told the Sheriff's Department that he heard a shot as the Presidential car went down Elm St. Euins looked up at the TSBD and "saw a man in a window with a gun and I saw him shoot twice. He then stepped back behind some boxes. I could tell the gun was a rifle and it sounded like an automatic rifle the way he was shooting." (WCHE, v.16, p.963) Later, Euins told the FBI that he could see a bald spot on the man's head, but he did not see the man's face and could not identify him. "He said he was sure this man was white, because his hand extended outside the window on the rifle." Euins thought he heard four shots, and after the fourth shot he saw the man begin to look around, withdraw the rifle, and step back from the window. (CD205, p.12)
- *Robert Edwards* of the Dallas County Auditor's Office was watching the motorcade with his friend Ronald Fischer at the corner of Elm and Houston,

and happened to look up at the TSBD shortly before the motorcade arrived. Edwards told the FBI that he "saw a man on the sixth floor of the [TSBD] who was apparently *standing so he could be seen* in the corner window. He described this person as a white man, wearing a light colored sports shirt, open at the neck, and having short, light, sandy hair. . . He did not see a gun at any time, and his attention was diverted from this man when the Presidential motorcade appeared." (CD205, p.21) "Lee Harvey Oswald's photograph was exhibited to Edwards and he could not be sure this was a photograph of the same party he had seen in the window." (CD205, p.22) Edwards' companion, Ronald Fischer, gave similar information, adding "All I could see was his head." (WCHE, v.19, p.475)

- *James Worrell* saw a rifle barrel sticking out of an upper window of the TSBD, shortly after he heard the first shot. The gun fired again while he was looking at it. Afterwards, he said he saw a man wearing a dark shirt or jacket run from the back of the TSBD (WCHE, v.16, p.959), and he recognized this man as Lee Oswald from pictures on TV and in the newspapers. (WCHE, v.24, p.294a-b)
- *Robert Jackson,* a photographer for the Dallas Times Herald, while riding in the motorcade looked up after the third shot and reported that he "saw the rifle or what looked like a rifle . . . [being] drawn fairly slowly back into the building, and I saw no one in the window with it." (WCHE, v.2, p.159)
- *Malcolm Couch*, a photographer for WFAA-TV in Dallas, while riding in the motorcade, recalled looking up after the third shot and "seeing about a foot of a rifle being – the barrel brought into the window." (WCHE, v.6, p.157)

Based on the testimony of these witnesses, it seems clear that *someone* was standing or sitting in the sixth floor window at the southeast corner of the TSBD with a rifle. Whether this person was Oswald is the critical question. Some witnesses provided testimony indicating that someone other than Oswald was present on the sixth floor, or on a different floor, at the time of the shooting. Some saw two men in the window. Other than Howard Brennan (maybe), no one positively identified Oswald as being one of the men they saw, but several did describe a slender white male, around 5'8" to 5'10", wearing a light-colored shirt, as one of the men visible from the window when the motorcade approached.

- *Richard Randolph Carr* told the FBI on February 1, 1964 that he had been on the scaffolding of the new courthouse being constructed at the corner of Houston and Commerce Streets on the day of the assassination. He was at about the sixth floor level when he looked toward the TSBD and "observed a man looking out of a window of the top floor of the [TSBD]. This man, a heavy set individual, who was wearing a hat, a tan sport coat and horn rimmed glasses, was not in the end window next to Houston St., but was I believe in the second window over from Houston St." When Carr heard the noise of the shots, he looked toward the triple underpass, because "it seemed to me that the noises I had heard came from this direction." After he descended to the street level, Carr saw a man near Houston and Commerce who he believed was "identical with the man I had earlier seen looking out of the window of the [TSBD]. This man, walking very fast, proceeded on Houston St., south to Commerce St., then east on Commerce St. to Record St. which is one block from Houston St. This man got into a 1961 or 1962 grey Rambler station wagon which was parked just north of Commerce on Record St. The station wagon, which had Texas license and was driven by a young Negro man, drove off in a northerly direction." (CD385, p.24-25) Carr emphasizes that he did not see anyone with a gun and he does not intend to imply that the man in the tan sport coat was the man who shot President Kennedy, but simply that Carr had seen him in the window. (CD385, p.27) A light-colored Rambler station wagon also figures in the testimony of Roger Craig, who said he saw a man who looked like Oswald running down the slope of the grassy knoll several minutes after the assassination and get into a waiting white Rambler station wagon driven by a dark-skinned man. (WCHE, v.24, p.23a-b) Another witness, Marvin Robinson, also reported seeing a light-colored Nash station wagon in the same place reported by Craig. Robinson saw a white male come down the grassy slope and get into the station wagon, which drove off in the direction of Oak Cliff. (CD5, p.70) Despite having information from three witnesses who testified to seeing a Nash station wagon picking up suspicious men from the TSBD, the Warren Commission takes no note of Carr's information and does not pursue the clue of the Nash station wagon. Neither Carr nor Marvin Robinson were called to testify before the commission, nor were their depositions taken. The commission failed to follow up on the man in the tan sport coat to determine if his presence in the TSBD window was somehow connected with the assassination.

- *Arnold Rowland* was watching the motorcade with his wife Barbara. Around 12:15 to 12:20, Rowland looked at the TSBD, and on the second floor from the top (i.e., the sixth floor) he saw a man standing back from the window, holding "what appeared to be a hi powered rifle." The man was of slender build and had dark hair. (WCHE, v.19, p.494) But Rowland says this man was in the *southwest* corner window, i.e., the window nearest the overpass, not the southeast window where the alleged sniper's nest was located. (WCHE, v.26, p.167a) Rowland called his wife's attention to the man and assumed that he was a Secret Service agent. He described this man as a slender white male with a light-colored shirt. (WCHE, v.16, p.953) At the same time, and on the same floor, Rowland said he saw a black man hanging out the window "on the east end of the building, the one that they said the shots were fired from." (WCHE, v.2, p.175) Responding to questions from the commission, Rowland said that he told FBI agents "I did see the Negro man there, and they told me it didn't have any bearing or such on the case right then. In fact, they just the same as told me to forget it now." (WCHE, v.2, p.183) He was not able to identify the rifleman in the window as Oswald or any other specific person. (WCHE, v.2, p.185)

- *Carolyn Walther,* who watched the motorcade from a point on Houston Street, about 50 or 60 feet south of Elm Street, told the FBI that around 12:25 she saw a man in either the fourth or fifth floor in the southeast corner window. This man was standing up leaning out the window with both his hands extended outside the window ledge. In his hands, this man was holding a rifle with the barrel pointed downward, and the man was looking south on Houston Street. The man was wearing a white shirt. She did not notice a scope or a sling on the rifle. (WCHE, v.24, p.522a) In the same window, to the left of this man, she could see a portion of another man standing by the side of this man with a rifle. But the window was dirty and she could not see his head. "She is positive this window was not as high as the sixth floor. This second man was apparently wearing a brown suit coat, and the only thing she could see was the right side of the man, from about the waist to the shoulders." Almost immediately after seeing these men, the motorcade approached her position. (WCHE, v.24, p.522b)

- *Johnny L. Powell,* who was incarcerated in the county jail across Houston Street at the time of the assassination, told the Dallas Morning News in 1978 that "he and others in his cell watched two men with a rifle in the 6th-floor window of the Texas School Book Depository across the street. When he looked, the men were 'fooling with' a scope on the rifle, Powell said." (Earl Golz, "Witnesses overlooked in JFK probe", Dallas Morning News, December 19, 1978, p.7A. Reproduced in HSCA Administrative folder: Press Clippings for Kennedy, v.2, p.93-94) The commission did not interview Powell or any of the other prisoners in the county jail who watched the event from their cell window, but this was not because the commission was unaware of their existence. Stanley Kaufman, an attorney for one of these prisoners, told commission counsel Leon Hubert during a deposition on June 27, 1964, that his client, Willie Mitchell, told him that he and the other prisoners "had a good view of what took place, and he described to me exactly. . . . I thought it might be helpful to the commission to know that there were people in jail who saw the actual killing." (WCHE, v.15, p.525-526) Despite this advice, the commission chose to ignore these witnesses who had a bird's eye view of the assassination.

Evaluating the eyewitness testimony

What are we to make of these diverse statements from the eyewitnesses who saw activity at the windows of the TSBD? There is great variety in these statements. Some only saw a rifle sticking out the window, some saw a man, whose description resembled Oswald, holding the rifle. Others saw a second man, described variously as a dark-skinned male or a white man wearing a brown or tan sport coat. In its report, the Warren Commission clearly favored those witnesses whose observations were consistent with the commission's theory of the crime – i.e., those who saw only one man with a rifle in the southeast corner window, or who saw only a rifle barrel being withdrawn from that window. The Warren Report's section on the eyewitness accounts begins with the sentence, "Eyewitnesses testified that they saw a man fire a weapon from the sixth-floor window." (WCR, p.63) While true, this is a gross oversimplification of the testimony. Witnesses who saw something else were simply ignored – except for Arnold Rowland, who received a different treatment. Rowland was invited to give his testimony before the commission. After describing what he saw, Rowland was asked by Arlen Specter about his grades in high school and about his IQ. Rowland responded that he got straight A's in high school until his senior year, when he got a couple of B's. He reported his IQ as 147. (WCHE, v.2, p.188) Within two weeks after his commission testimony, the FBI submitted a background report on Rowland, including a statement from his high school principal that Rowland's IQ was only 109 when tested in 1959. (WCHE, v.25, p.903a) The FBI obtained report cards from Rowland's high school showing that he indeed received many A's but also several B's and C's. (WCHE, v.25, p.903b-904b) Both the assistant principal of the high school and the dean of the technical school which Rowland attended told the FBI that Rowland could not be trusted. The assistant principal told the FBI that Rowland "would not hesitate to fabricate a story if it was of any benefit for Rowland to do so." (WCHE, v.25, p.905b) Dean Edith McKissock of the Crozier Technical High School stated that Rowland "could not be trusted and would not tell the truth regarding any matter. She stated he was a conniver and prevaricated whenever it was to his advantage to do so." (WCHE, v.25, p.907a) Based on the FBI background report, the Warren Report discounted Rowland's testimony, noting that "numerous statements by Rowland concerning matters about which he would not normally be expected to be mistaken – such as subjects he studied in school, grades he received, whether or not he had graduated from high school, and whether or not he had been admitted to college – were false." The report does not explain why these subjects were even brought up at all during Rowland's testimony. The report also quoted Rowland's wife as saying, "At times my husband is prone to exaggerate." (WCR, p.251) With this exercise in character assassination, the commission dismissed Rowland's account of having seen a possible accomplice – a dark-skinned man on the same floor as the man with the rifle. This is a perfect example of the commission's rejecting a witness's testimony because of his perceived – or manufactured – character flaws, and not assessing the credibility of the statements themselves. It is a classic case of the ad hominem argument against a witness whose testimony challenges the commission's theory of the crime.

The statements of the witnesses cited above contain several clues which would have been worth pursuing if the commission had really been serious about ruling out a conspiracy – the Nash station wagon, the man in the tan sport coat, the dark-skinned man in the window. But the committee chose to ignore or reject testimony that did not fit the lone gunman theory of the crime. Even those witnesses who said they saw a lone gunman firing shots from the sixth floor window hardly supported the Warren Commission's theory of a sniper huddled behind a stack of boxes to avoid being seen. The commission claimed that the cartons were arranged around the window "so that a person sitting on the carton could look down Elm Street toward the overpass and scarcely be noticed from the outside." (WCR, p.8) Detective Robert L Studebaker told the commission that the arrangement of the boxes was a good configuration for a gun rest. And he said that another advantage to the sniper was that when sitting on the boxes "nobody could see him from the street." (WCHE, v.7, p.149) But the witnesses spoke of a man standing up, hanging out the window, and brandishing a rifle in plain view of the crowd below, almost as though he were trying to attract attention. How is this consistent with the elaborately constructed "sniper's nest" designed to conceal the assassin lying in wait for his target to pass by? The Warren Report does not address this inconsistency. And we have already noted that those witnesses who said they observed shots being fired did not report seeing the man pull the trigger or operate the bolt of the rifle.

There are two plausible conjectures which could explain these anomalies. (1) Either the gunman was not using the Mannlicher-Carcano, but another rifle which was semi-automatic and which had no bolt action, or (2) the gunman seen in the sixth floor southeast corner window was not firing shots at all but was only a decoy, a distraction, while the actual shots were being fired by someone else from farther inside the building, away from the window and invisible to the crowd below. After all, in order to shoot someone from a tall building it is not necessary to be positioned at the window itself. Any position from inside the building will work, provided that there is an unobstructed view to the target. The witnesses saw the man with the rifle and simultaneously heard shots, assuming naturally that the man they saw was the one shooting. But this may be a false inference.

There is some support for both of these possibilities. Governor Connally thought that whoever was firing at the car must have been using an automatic rifle because of the rapidity of the shots. (WCHE, v.4, p.134) Amos Euins told the Sheriff's Department that the gun he heard "sounded like an automatic rifle". (WCHE, v.16, p.963) Garland Slack told the Sheriff's Department that the shots sounded like they "came from away back or from within a building. I have heard this same sort of sound when a shot has come from within a cave, as I have been on many big game hunts." (WCHE, v.19, p.495) James Jarman, who watched the motorcade from the fifth floor window in the southeast corner of the TSBD, had the impression that the shots came from below him, not from the floor above. (WCHE, v.3, p.209)

WHERE WAS OSWALD DURING THE SHOOTING?

Despite their inconsistencies, the eyewitness statements do not rule out the possibility that Oswald was indeed the man seen in the window and that he fired at least some shots during the assassination. But neither do they positively identify him as the shooter. The eyewitness testimony is ambiguous and we must look elsewhere for an answer to the question of whether Oswald was the man seen in the window firing a rifle. There is some evidence regarding Oswald's whereabouts inside the TSBD during, before, and after the assassination. If this evidence shows Oswald to have been elsewhere in the building at the time of the shooting, then he could not have been firing a rifle from the window.

Oswald's alibi

During the interrogation, Capt. Fritz asked Oswald where he was during the shooting. Oswald "said that he was having his lunch about that time on the first floor." Fritz also asked him where he was when he was challenged by Officer Baker, and Oswald replied that he was "on the second floor drinking a Coca Cola when the officer came in." (WCHE, v.24, p.265a) If these statements are true, then Oswald could not have been on the sixth floor shooting at the President. And if he was drinking a Coke when Officer Baker accosted him, this would have added more time to his presumed escape from the sixth floor sniper's nest before Baker met him. According to Fritz's notes, Oswald "said he ate lunch with some of the colored boys who worked with him. One of them was called 'Junior' and the other one was a little short man whose name he did not know." (WCHE, v.24, p.267b)

But FBI agent James Bookhout, who was present during Fritz's interrogation of Oswald, recalls the conversation differently. According to Bookhout, Oswald did not claim to have eaten lunch with Junior Jarman or with anyone else. According to Bookhout's version of the interview, "Oswald stated that on November 22, 1963, he had eaten lunch in the lunch room at the Texas School Book Depository alone, but recalled possibly two Negro employees walking through the room during this period. He stated possibly one of these employees was called 'Junior' and the other was a short individual whose name he could not recall but whom he would be able to recognize." (CD5, p.100)

When James "Junior" Jarman was interrogated before the commission, he was asked about eating lunch with Oswald:

BALL: After his arrest, [Oswald] stated to a police officer that he had had lunch with you. Did you have lunch with him?
JARMAN: No, sir, I didn't. (WCHE, v.3, p.201)

The Warren Report relies on Jarman's testimony to reject Oswald's alibi, saying that Oswald claimed to have been eating lunch with Jarman at the time of the shooting, but that "Jarman testified that he ate his lunch on the first floor around 5 minutes to 12, and that he neither ate lunch with nor saw Oswald." (WCR, p.182) One of the sources cited by the Warren Report for Oswald's claim is CE1988, which is Bookhout's report in which he explicitly stated that Oswald told Fritz he was eating alone and had only seen "Junior" walk through the lunchroom at that time. Thus, Oswald's alibi does not depend on his having "eaten lunch with" Junior but on the fact that he saw Jarman walk through the lunchroom while he was eating alone, and Oswald would have had no way of knowing that Jarman had been there if Oswald himself had not been in the lunchroom to see him. But Oswald is not yet in the clear with this alibi, because at the time of the shooting Jarman was on the fifth floor watching the motorcade with Bonnie Ray Williams and Harold Norman. (WCHE, v.3, p.203-204) Jarman therefore could not have seen Oswald in the lunchroom *at the time of the shooting*, although he may have seen him earlier when he went to get his sandwich for lunch. Jarman testified that he stopped for his lunch break about 11:55 a.m. and went downstairs to the restroom and washed up for lunch. Then he got his sandwich from the lunchroom and went up to the second floor lounge to get a soda. (WCHE, v.3, p.201) This is the point where Oswald could have seen him, but it is not close enough to the time of the shooting to provide Oswald with a firm alibi.

Bonnie Ray Williams confirms Junior Jarman's estimate of 11:55 as the time they stopped working on the new flooring being laid on the sixth floor and went downstairs for lunch. (WCHE, v.3, p.167) This group of employees took both elevators downstairs, but Oswald, who was also working on the sixth floor, did not go with them. Williams testified that "Oswald hollered, 'Guys, how about an elevator'" or words to that effect. Oswald then said, "Close the gate on the elevator and send the elevator back up." (WCHE, v.3, p.168) So at 11:55 a.m., Oswald signaled his intention to go downstairs for lunch. No one testified to seeing him go downstairs, but Williams returned to the sixth floor to eat his own lunch, because he thought the other workers would be watching the motorcade from that floor. (WCHE, v.3, p.169) Williams was eating his lunch on the sixth floor at about 12:00 noon. He said it took him maybe 10 or 12 minutes to finish his lunch. He did not see anyone else on the sixth floor at this time. (WCHE, v.3, p.170) Williams, whose lunch consisted of perhaps the most famous chicken sandwich in U. S. history, left his lunch bag containing some chicken bones on the sixth floor and went down to the fifth floor where he found Jarman and Norman waiting for the motorcade, and he joined them. (WCHE, v.3, p.171) Williams said he finished his sandwich around 12:10 to 12:15, and got down to the fifth floor about 12:20, but he says these times are only estimates. Still, based on Williams' testimony, Oswald was nowhere to be seen on the sixth floor at roughly 12:15. This is consistent with his being downstairs eating, or with his hiding on the sixth floor behind a stack of boxes, invisible to Williams. So far, with this testimony, nothing is proven about Oswald's whereabouts at 12:15.

However, we have evidence from several street-level witnesses that *someone* was visible on the sixth floor around this time, and specifically at the time of the shooting. See the testimony cited above from Arnold Rowland, Robert Edwards, James Worrell, Richard Carr, and others The question is whether Oswald can be ruled out as the man, or one of the men, seen on the sixth floor from the street.

The best evidence for substantiating Oswald's alibi of having been downstairs at the time of the shooting comes from Carolyn Arnold, who worked as a secretary at the TSBD. She was not asked to testify before the commission, and her deposition was not taken. The Warren Report does not mention her. An FBI report dated 11/26/63 states that Arnold left her second floor office between 12:00 and 12:15 on November 22 "to go downstairs and stand in front of the building to view the Presidential motorcade. As she was standing in front of the building, she stated she thought she caught a fleeting glimpse of Lee Harvey Oswald standing in the hallway between the front door and the double doors leading to the warehouse, located on the first floor. She could not be sure that this was Oswald, but said she felt it was and believed the time to be a few minutes before 12:15 p.m." (CD5, p.41) In a statement dated March 18, 1964, Arnold said, "I did not see Lee Harvey Oswald *at the time President Kennedy was shot.*" But she does confirm 12:25 p.m. as the time she exited the building. (WCHE, v.22, p.635a)

When interviewed in 1978 by Dallas journalist Earl Golz, Arnold disputed the FBI's version of her statements. She specifically challenged the phrase "fleeting glimpse", which the FBI report attributed to her. Arnold told Golz, "That is completely foreign to me. . . . It would have forced me to have been turning back around to the building when, in fact, I was trying to watch the parade. Why would I be looking back inside the building? That doesn't make any sense to me." In the 1978 interview, Arnold told Golz that "she saw Oswald in the 2nd-floor lunchroom as she was on her way out of the depository to watch the presidential motorcade Nov. 22, 1963. She left the building at 12:25 p.m." (Earl Golz, "Was Oswald in Window?, *Dallas Morning News,* November 26, 1978. Available online at jfk.hood.edu.)

Carolyn Arnold's information in the Earl Golz interview is the only testimony we have of someone who saw Oswald downstairs in the TSBD at a time when other witnesses were reporting a man, or two men, in an upper floor window of the TSBD. If Arnold's statements to Golz are correct that Oswald was in the downstairs lunchroom at 12:25 then Oswald is exonerated. He could not have fired any shots from the sixth floor of the TSBD. Arnold gives the impression of being a credible witness. As we shall see, she is not the only witness who reported that their testimony had been distorted or falsified by the FBI or by the commission. It is perhaps revealing that Carolyn Arnold did not even have her deposition taken by the commission. This would lead us to think that the commission thought no good could come from interviewing her and perhaps opening up an issue that would be better left untouched – at least from the perspective of the commission's theory of the case.

Escape from the sixth floor

Outside of Carolyn Arnold's story in the Earl Golz article, we have several witnesses who saw Oswald shortly before noon downstairs in the TSBD, and a police officer, Marrion Baker, who encountered Oswald downstairs in the second floor lunchroom shortly after the shooting. During one re-enactment, Baker reached the second floor lunchroom from the street outside within a minute and fifteen seconds after the last shot. Another trial resulted in a time of one minute thirty seconds. (WCHE, v.3, p.252) On the afternoon of the assassination, Baker was apparently traveling at a good pace, because Roy Truly told the commission that while he was still outside, he saw the officer "run up to the building, . . . He ran right by me. And he was pushing people out of the way. . . . He ran up the stairway." (WCHE, v.3, p.221) All this running would suggest that the shorter re-enactment time of a minute and fifteen seconds would be more likely to coincide with Baker's actual pace on November 22. Here we have a new time constraint. Would it have been possible for Oswald to have fired the shots from the sixth floor window and appeared on the second floor in time to meet Baker and Roy Truly less than a minute and a half after the last shot? If not, then this would rule out Oswald as the shooter in the window.

In addition to re-enacting his entry into the building after the shots were fired, Officer Baker testified that he and commission counsel David Belin ran two time trials of Oswald's presumed escape route from the sixth floor window to the second floor lunchroom. They timed it as 1:18 on the first run, and 1:14 on the second. (WCHE, v.3, p.254) The FBI also conducted tests to see how long it would take to descend from the sixth floor window to the first floor exit. (CD5, p.120-121) The time required to reach the second floor lunchroom where the Coke machine was located would have been a little less than the FBI re-enactment times, but judging by the floor plans, the difference could not have been more than 10 to 15 seconds, if that, adjusting for the additional distance from the lunchroom to the first floor exit. The fastest time clocked by the FBI, to the front door, was 1 minute 45 seconds. (CD5, p.120) This was the route presumed to have been taken by Oswald, and consisted of "walking from window on sixth floor to stairway, walking down stairway to first floor, and walking from stairway to front door." This is the only route that could be consistent with Oswald meeting Baker and Truly on the second floor within 1 minute 30 seconds of the final shot, provided that we subtract 15 seconds from the FBI timing for the portion of the route between the lunchroom and the front door. This exceeds both of Baker's re-enactment times for the same route. The FBI trials were done "at a fast walk except in areas where an individual would have walked at a normal pace so as not to arouse suspicion." (CD5, p.120)

If Baker was in the lunchroom within 1:15 of the last shot, and if it would have taken Oswald 1:30 to get to the lunchroom from the sixth floor window, then Oswald could not have been shooting at the President from the window and still have met Baker and Truly on the second floor. Oswald must have been downstairs the whole time. Even allowing for some imprecision in the timings, the best that can be said for the commission's theory is that it might have been *barely possible* for Oswald to have done the shooting and then arrived on the second floor when Baker entered the lunchroom. But for this to work, any measurement errors must break in the commission's favor.

Note, however, that these re-enactment times do not include time for hiding the rifle, nor for possibly wiping fingerprints off the rifle – or for buying the Coca Cola that Oswald was seen with on the second floor. (Testimony of Mrs. Robert A. Reid at WCHE, v.24, p.223b; WCHE, v.3, p.274) It cannot be determined from the testimony whether Oswald had already bought the Coke before meeting officer Baker, or whether he bought it afterwards. He definitely had the Coke in his hand at the time Mrs. Reid saw him. Mrs. Reid said that Oswald "was very calm" (WCHE, v.3, p.274), and officer Baker described Oswald as calm and collected, and not out of breath. (WCHE, v.3, p.252). Whenever he bought the Coke, Oswald did not give the appearance of someone who had just committed a sensational murder and then hurried down four flights of stairs. Also, although Harold Norman, at the fifth floor window, reported hearing shells being ejected above him, neither Norman nor his companions Bonnie Ray Williams and James Jarman reported hearing the footsteps of someone walking across the sixth floor from the sniper's nest to the stairway at the opposite corner of the building. (For a diagram of the second floor of the TSBD, see CE497 at WCHE, v.17, p.212, showing the location of the lunchroom and Coke machine, and the location where Mrs. Reid encountered Oswald after she came back into the building.)

Also, the eyewitnesses who claim to have seen the final shot being fired said that the gunman did not seem to be in a hurry. He did not leave the window immediately after firing the last shot, but lingered to observe the results. Recall that Robert Jackson saw the rifle barrel being "drawn fairly slowly back into the building." (WCHE, v.2, p.159) Howard Brennan said the man "did not seem to be in any hurry." (WCHE, v.19, p.470) Amos Euins saw the man "looking around" before withdrawing the rifle and stepping back from the window. (CD205, p.12) So the FBI re-enactment times are quite generous on the commission's behalf. To make them realistic we would have to add a few seconds for lingering at the window and for stashing the rifle in between the cartons near the stairway and possibly for wiping off the fingerprints.

Testimony of Victoria Adams

The claim that Oswald descended the stairs from the sixth floor to the second floor lunchroom is dealt a blow by the testimony of Victoria Adams. Adams worked on the fourth floor of the TSBD for the Scott Foresman Publishing Company. She watched the motorcade from a fourth floor window along with co-worker Sandra Styles. According to an FBI report dated November 24, 1963, Adams said that after they heard the three shots, "she and her friend then ran immediately to the back of the building to where the stairs were located and ran down the stairs. No one else was observed on the stairs at this time, and she is sure that this would be the only means of escape from the building from the sixth floor." (CD5, p.39) In this FBI interview, Adams is not quoted as having seen William Shelley or Billy Lovelady on the first floor, as her deposition transcript records. In the deposition, taken April 7, 1964 by David Belin, Adams again stated that after the third shot she went down the back stairs to the first floor and then out of the building via the Houston Street dock, accompanied by Sandra Styles. Adams says these are the only stairs leading down from the 4th floor. (WCHE, v.6, p.388) She told Belin that she did not see, hear, or encounter anyone on the stairs. When she got to the first floor, the deposition transcript says she saw Bill Shelley and Billy Lovelady. (WCHE, v.6, p.388, 389) Adams estimated that between 15 and 30 seconds elapsed between hearing the last shot and her starting to move toward the stairway. She estimates that it took her one minute from the window to the bottom of the stairs on the first floor. She again states that she did not see or hear Oswald on the stairs, although this is precisely the time during which he would have had to be in the stairway, according to the Warren Commission's version of Oswald's movements. (WCHE, v.6, p.392)

The key in evaluating the credibility of Adams' testimony is the presence or absence of Shelley and Lovelady on the first floor when Adams exited from the stairway. In his deposition taken by Joseph Ball, Bill Shelley said that he and Billy Lovelady were out in front of the TSBD when the motorcade passed and they heard three loud noises, which sounded like they came from the west. After Gloria Calvery ran up crying that the President had been shot, Shelley said that he and Lovelady "took off across the street to that little old island and we stopped there for a minute." They walked down to the railroad yards and watched the police search the cars in the parking lot. After several minutes, Shelley and Lovelady came back inside the TSBD. (WCHE, v.6, p.329-330) Since Shelley and Lovelady were gone from the building for several minutes, if Victoria Adams had seen them on the first floor when she came out of the stairway that would mean that she actually descended the stairs several minutes later than she claimed, which would have allowed Oswald (or anyone else) to walk down from the sixth floor to the lunchroom without being seen on the stairway, before Adams and Styles were on the stairs. Under this scenario, Adams' testimony would not be damaging to the commission's version of events.

But Adams was interviewed several years later by journalist Barry Ernest, and after Ernest showed her a copy of her deposition transcript, she wondered if the statement about seeing Shelley and Lovelady on the first floor was inserted later, without her knowledge. She told Ernest that Shelley and Lovelady "weren't there . . . I honestly can't remember seeing them. . . . No, I don't remember them being there." (Barry Ernest, *The Girl on the Stairs,* 2013, p.255-256)

Shelley and Lovelady said nothing to support the government's version of events when they were deposed by commission counsel Joseph Ball. In Shelley's deposition, Ball asked who was present on the first floor when the two men returned to the building.

BALL: When you came into the shipping room did you see anybody?
SHELLEY: I saw Eddie Piper. . . .
BALL: Who else did you see?
SHELLEY: That's all we saw immediately.
BALL: Did you ever see Vickie Adams?
SHELLEY: I saw her that day but I don't remember where I saw her.

BALL: You don't remember whether you saw her when you came back?
SHELLEY: It was after we entered the building.
BALL: You think you did see her after you entered the building?
SHELLEY: Yes, sir. I thought it was on the fourth floor awhile after that.
(WCHE, v.6, p.330)

Obviously, Shelley is telling Ball that he saw Adams on the fourth floor, some time after he returned to the building – not on the first floor at the time he entered.

Ball fares no better with Billy Lovelady. He tries to establish whether Lovelady saw Adams when he re-entered the building with Shelley several minutes after the shooting. It's clear from his responses that Lovelady knows Ball is asking about Victoria Adams, before Ball even mentions her name. This gives the appearance of some pre-deposition coaching from Ball.

BALL: You came in through the first floor?
LOVELADY: Right.
BALL: Who did you see in the first floor?
LOVELADY: I saw a girl but I wouldn't swear to it it's Vickie.
BALL: Who is Vickie?
LOVELADY: The girl that works for Scott Foresman.
BALL: What is her full name?
LOVELADY: I wouldn't know.
BALL: Vickie Adams?
LOVELADY: I believe so.
BALL: Would you say it was Vickie you saw?
LOVELADY: I couldn't swear. (WCHE, v.6, p.340)

The commission did not try to corroborate Adams' timeline by asking her co-worker Sandra Styles to testify. Styles did not appear before the commission, nor was her deposition taken. An FBI report with Styles appears among the commission's documents, in which she describes hearing the shots as they watched from the fourth floor window, then "Victoria Adams and I left the office *at this time*, went down the back stairs and left the building at the back door." (CD706, p.90)

Adams' supervisor, Dorothy Ann Garner, also confirmed that Adams and Styles went downstairs *before* Roy Truly and Officer Baker came up. In a letter to Warren Commission general counsel Lee Rankin, dated June 2, 1964, Assistant U.S. Attorney Martha Joe Stroud wrote that "Miss Garner, Miss Adams' supervisor, stated this morning that after Miss Adams went downstairs, she (Miss Garner) saw Mr. Truly and the policeman come up." (Letter reproduced in Barry Ernest, *The Girl on the Stairs,* p.298*).* This would mean that Adams could not have waited several minutes as the Warren Report claimed (WCR, p.154), but must have come down the stairs within seconds after hearing the shots fired. Dorothy Garner also was never called by the commission to testify in corroboration of Adams' testimony, despite the fact that Adams' timeline is absolutely critical to the commission's theory that Oswald descended the stairs immediately after the shooting. None of the other escape routes timed by the FBI would have allowed Oswald to get to the second floor in time to meet Officer Baker in the lunchroom. Adams' testimony is therefore highly damaging to the government's case, and if there were any way to refute it, one would think the commission would have jumped at the chance. The fact that they chose not to interview Styles and Garner shows that the commission's lawyers were afraid of what they might say. Adams' testimony by itself was bad enough, but standing alone it could be altered, falsified and rendered harmless in the record. It would have been much harder to do the same to three witnesses on this important point.

Conclusion

The validity of Oswald's alibi depends in large part on the credence given to Carolyn Arnold's story. If she was accurate in recalling her testimony of 15 years prior, and if Golz was accurate in his reporting in 1978, then Oswald was downstairs at 12:25, just before Kennedy was shot, and therefore he could not be the assassin. This also would mean that the FBI deliberately falsified Arnold's testimony on November 26, 1963. Corroborating Arnold's testimony is the testimony of Victoria Adams, which eliminates the stairway as Oswald's escape route from the sixth floor. Sandra Styles and Dorothy Garner both confirm Adams' account of descending the stairs immediately after the shots were fired. Without this escape route, the commission has no way to place Oswald in the second floor lunchroom in time to meet Officer Baker, unless Oswald was on the second floor the whole time and not on the sixth floor during the assassination at all. Also, the timing re-enactments are damaging to the commission's case. According to Officer Baker, he may have been in the building confronting Oswald within as short a time as 1 minute, 15 seconds from the final shot, but the FBI re-enactment indicates that Oswald's escape from the sixth floor to the second floor lunchroom probably took at least 1 minute, 30 seconds. This is too long. It would make Oswald late for his meeting with Baker. In order to salvage the commission's case, we must assume that Baker's estimate for his entry into the building was too short, and that the FBI's estimate of Oswald's escape route was too long. Both these measurement errors must break in the commission's favor, or else we must conclude that Oswald was downstairs during the entire assassination.

Thus, the preponderance of the evidence leans in the direction of Oswald not being on the stairs, and therefore not having been on the sixth floor shooting the President. By all appearances, Oswald looked like a person who had been sitting calmly in the lunchroom drinking a Coke when he was supposed to have been assassinating President Kennedy. The evidence leads us to conclude that Oswald was *not* one of the shooters in the sixth floor window.

WHO WAS THE MAN IN THE WINDOW, IF NOT OSWALD? WAS THERE AN OSWALD DOUBLE?

The existence of an Oswald double or lookalike is a topic which strikes some serious researchers as bordering on the fringe of credibility. Yet there is credible evidence that there was an Oswald double and that he was in the TSBD at the time of the assassination. This Oswald lookalike was seen escaping from the building shortly after the assassination and was seen later making his escape from Dallas by plane. There are at least four witnesses whose testimony supports this scenario, although there is convincing evidence that the real Lee Oswald went back to his rooming house in Oak Cliff by bus and taxi. The presence of an Oswald double in the sixth floor window would easily reconcile the discrepancies between the testimony of the street level witnesses and the witnesses inside the TSBD. But it would obviously prove the existence of a conspiracy in the President's murder.

Testimony of Roger Craig

After giving his testimony to the Warren Commission, and especially after his name was mentioned in some of the early books that were critical of the commission's findings, Deputy Roger Craig was subjected to harassment, surveillance, and ostracism from his fellow law enforcement officers at the Dallas Police and Sheriff departments. He told journalist Barry Ernest that Sheriff Bill Decker "gave me strict orders not to talk to anybody about it, to keep my mouth shut." (Barry Ernest, *The Girl on the Stairs,* p.124) What did Roger Craig tell the commission that provoked such a reaction?

Shortly after the assassination, Craig was checking the south curb of Elm Street, where he had reason to believe a bullet had hit the pavement. In his report to the Sheriff, dated November 22, 1963, Craig wrote: "I heard a shrill whistle and I turned around and saw a white male running down the hill from the direction of the Texas School Book Depository Building and I saw what I think was a light colored Rambler station wagon with luggage rack on top pull over to the curb and this subject who had come running down the hill get into this car. The man driving this station wagon was a dark complected white male. I tried to get across Elm Street to stop the car and talk with subjects, but the traffic was so heavy I could not make it. I reported this incident at the time to a Secret Service officer, whose name I do not know, then I left this area and went at once to the building and assisted in the search of the building. Later that afternoon, I heard that the City had a suspect in custody and I called and reported the information about the suspect running down the hill and getting into a car to Captain Fritz and was requested to come at once to City Hall. I went to the City Hall and identified the subject they had in custody as being the same person I saw running down this hill and get into the station wagon and leave the scene." (WCHE, v.19, p.524) The subject in custody was, of course, Lee Oswald.

Craig told the same story on the same day to FBI agents who interviewed him, except that the FBI reports that he described the driver of the station wagon as a "Negro male" instead of a dark complexioned white man. This FBI report states that Craig "is positive that Oswald is identical with the same individual he observed getting into the Rambler station wagon as mentioned above." (CD5, p.69)

In yet another FBI interview on November 25, Craig re-told the same story, except that upon reflection he has now decided that the driver of the station wagon was actually a dark complexioned white male, and not a black man. He described the man who ran down the hill as a white male, 5'9" in height, weighing 140 pounds, slender build, sandy hair, dressed in a brown shirt and blue trousers." After hearing that a suspect was in custody at the police station, Craig "stated he subsequently went to Dallas Police Department and there identified Lee Harvey Oswald as the person he had seen running from Texas School Book Depository. Mr. Craig further stated there is no doubt in his mind that the man he observed running from the Texas School Book Depository and the person he viewed at Dallas Police Department are identical." (CD5, p.71-72)

In describing the meeting with Oswald in Capt. Fritz's office, Craig testified in his deposition that Fritz asked Oswald, "What about this station wagon?" Craig reports Oswald's response as "That station wagon belongs to Mrs. Paine . . . Don't try to tie her into this. She had nothing to do with it." (WCHE, v.6, p.270) Fritz later denied that Craig was present during Oswald's interrogation. Fritz claimed that he vaguely recalled some deputy sheriff who started to tell him some things that "wouldn't help us" and that "his story that he was telling didn't fit with what we knew to be true." (WCHE, v.4, p.245) The Warren Report allowed that Craig "may have seen a person enter a white Rambler station wagon 15 or 20 minutes after the shooting and travel west on Elm Street, but the Commission concluded that this man was not Lee Harvey Oswald, because of the overwhelming evidence that Oswald was far away from the building by that time." (WCR, p.160-161)

Even if the man was not Oswald, we must surely think that the commission would have been interested in finding this man who was seen fleeing the scene of a sensational crime and jumping into a getaway car which sped off across the river. This interest should have been even stronger considering that both the man and the car were noticed by other witnesses besides Craig. We have already seen that Richard Randolph Carr stated that the man in the tan sport coat, whom he previously had seen in the TSBD window, got into a Rambler station wagon shortly after the shooting. (CD385, p.24-25) And the fleeing man described by Craig was also seen by another witness, Marvin Robinson. The fact that the commission showed no interest in pursuing these leads demonstrates that their purpose was not to solve the case, but simply to close it, by identifying Oswald as being solely responsible for the assassination.

Testimony of Marvin C. Robinson

On the day after the assassination, Marvin Robinson told the FBI that he was driving west on Elm Street shortly after the shooting. Robinson stated that "after he had crossed Houston Street and was in front of the Texas School Book Depository building a light colored Nash station wagon suddenly appeared before him. He stated this vehicle stopped and a white male came down the grass covered incline between the building and the street and entered the station wagon after which it drove away in the direction of the Oak Cliff section of Dallas. Robinson stated he does not recall the license number on the station wagon or whether or not it bore a Texas license plate." Robinson told the FBI agents that he does not think he would be able to identify the individual who ran down the hill. (CD5, p.70) Robinson was not asked to testify before the commission, nor was his deposition taken. The Warren Report makes no mention of him.

Testimony of James Worrell

James Worrell, who said he witnessed shots being fired from the sixth floor window, told police officer K. L. Anderton that shortly after the shooting, he had run to a point on the north side of the TSBD, where he "saw a man run out of the building in a southerly direction." This would have been toward the front of the building. "He said when he got home and saw pictures of Lee Harvey Oswald in the newspapers and on television, he recognized him as the man he saw run from the building." (WCHE, v.24, p.294a-b) The report does not say which side of the building the man was on. If he was seen on the west side of the building, i.e., the side nearest the triple underpass, this would be consistent with the information given by Roger Craig and Marvin Robinson.

Since there is credible evidence that the real Lee Oswald was on a bus or in a taxi on his way to Oak Cliff when the unknown man was running down the hill to the Rambler station wagon, the weight of the evidence points to the second man as not being Oswald. Despite some inconsistencies and vagueness in the testimony, the evidence that Oswald proceeded to his rooming house via bus and taxi is strong. Bus driver Cecil McWatters remembers a man who pounded on the door of his bus on Elm Street between two stops and boarded the bus, only to get off two blocks later when the bus was caught in heavy traffic. McWatters recalls giving a transfer to this man, and Oswald was arrested with a bus transfer in his shirt pocket, according to Detective Sims and Capt. Fritz. (WCHE, v.7, p.173; WCHE, v.24, p.267a) A copy of the bus transfer is in evidence as CE381. (WCHE, v.16, p.974) However, McWatters told the commission that he would be unable to positively identify the man he gave the transfer to. (WCHE, v.2, p.283) Mary Bledsoe, a former landlady of Oswald, just happened to be on McWatters' bus during this trip, and said she recognized Oswald when he got on the bus looking like "a maniac". (WCHE, v.6, p.409)

Oswald was positively identified in a police lineup by taxi driver William Whaley, who said that Oswald was the man he picked up near the Greyhound bus station in downtown Dallas. In an affidavit given to Dallas police on November 23, 1963, Whaley said he drove the man to the 500 block of North Beckley. Whaley described his passenger: "This boy was small, five feet eight inches, slender, had on a dark shirt with white spots of something on it. He had a bracelet on his left wrist. He looked like he was 25 or 26 years old." (WCHE, v.24, p.228b) According to his wife Marina, Lee wore a bracelet in place of his watch, after his watch stopped working. (WCHE, v.23, p.521b) Whaley later amended his story during his deposition, to say that he actually dropped his passenger off in the 700 block of North Beckley. (WCHE, v. 6, p.434)

Although the testimony of McWatters, Bledsoe, and Whaley puts Oswald on his way to Oak Cliff during the half hour following the assassination, Craig was adamant that the man he saw running down the grassy slope was Oswald, so we must conclude that this man at least bore a striking resemblance to Oswald, to the point where the two could be confused with each other during a brief glance from 50 or 60 feet away, by someone who had never seen Oswald before. We are thus led to ask whether this second man was the rifleman who was seen in the TSBD window, and whether he was in fact an Oswald "double" or "lookalike".

The notion that a man resembling Oswald took part in the assassination is not a far-fetched idea. There was already a man working in the TSBD who was acknowledged by co-workers to be an Oswald "lookalike". This was Billy Lovelady. The resemblance was so striking that the FBI felt it necessary to interview Lovelady to establish that it was Lovelady, and not Oswald, who was standing on the front steps of the TSBD in a photo taken at the time of the assassination. (CD385, p.8) [The photo is CE203 at WCHE, v.16, p.584.] Lovelady, of course, was not the man seen escaping down the grassy slope into the waiting Rambler station wagon. But this example shows how easy it may be to find two people who resemble each other very closely, to the point where an observer unacquainted with them might identify them as the same person.

Robert Vinson's story

Perhaps the most credible – and spectacular – witness testimony of a second Oswald comes from Robert Vinson. His story is told in *Flight from Dallas (2007)* by James P. Johnston and Jon Roe. Vinson was an Air Force Sergeant who worked for the North American Air Defense Command (NORAD) at the time of the assassination. He was born in Alabama, but was distantly related to the Vinson family of Georgia, whose members included U. S. Representative Carl Vinson, chairman of the House Armed Services Committee, and Fred Vinson, Chief Justice of the U. S. Supreme Court.

In November 1963, Robert Vinson was stationed at Colorado Springs, CO, where he was an administrative supervisor for the electronics division of NORAD. (*Flight from Dallas,* p.19) Concerned about an expected promotion which he felt was being overly delayed, Vinson decided to fly to Washington to lobby for his promotion in person. While in Washington, on Thursday, November 21, 1963, Vinson paid a social call to his distant cousin, Representative Carl Vinson, and then met with a Colonel Chapman, who referred him to an office in the Pentagon where he could get help with his promotion. While in Chapman's office, Vinson overheard Chapman taking a phone call, in which Chapman told the caller: "We have information, and I strongly recommend that the president not go to Dallas." This phone conversation ended quickly, and Chapman gave Vinson the information about who he should see at the Pentagon to discuss his promotion. (*Flight from Dallas*, p.20-21)

After receiving a favorable response to his promotion concerns, Vinson spent the night of November 21 in Washington, expecting to catch a military shuttle flight the next day back to Colorado Springs. The flight would be free to service personnel in uniform. But to Vinson's surprise, when he showed up at Andrews Air Force Base on Friday morning, November 22, he was told that the usual Friday shuttle to Colorado Springs would not be flying that day. Vinson decided to remain at the base on standby, and he told the airman at the check-in desk to let him know if any unscheduled flights happened to be going his way and had space available for a passenger. Soon afterwards, as Vinson was eating his breakfast in the base restaurant, he was paged over the intercom. Arriving back at the check-in counter, the airman behind the counter pointed to a C-54 out on the runway and said that it was going to Lowry Air Force base near Denver. He told Vinson he could hitch a ride on it.

Arriving at the plane, Vinson was struck by the fact that there were no other passengers on it, and no markings, "except for an emblem on its tail that appeared to be a graphic of the earth, rust brown with white grid marks on it separating latitude and longitude." Although clearly a military plane, this aircraft was not marked with "USAF" and did not have a serial number printed on its tail. (*Flight from Dallas*, p.22-23) [The graphic on the plane's tail was associated at that time with CIA planes.] Vinson climbed aboard. No one asked his name. Two men climbed into the plane and entered the cockpit, which they shut behind them. Neither of them spoke to Vinson, who was the only passenger on the plane. The plane took off and headed west. The flight was uneventful until around 12:30. As the plane was over Nebraska, one of the men in the cockpit "announced in a flat, unemotional voice over the loudspeaker that the president had been shot at 12:29. That's all he said." (*Flight from Dallas*, p.24)

Immediately after this announcement, the plane turned south. Between 3:30 and 4:00 p.m. Central time, Vinson noticed that they were approaching Dallas. Vinson related that the plane made a rough landing on a bare strip of land alongside the Trinity River. There was a Jeep nearby, from which two men jumped out and boarded the airplane. "One of the crew came out of the cockpit to unhinge and shove open the passenger door so the two men could board the plane." One of the two men looked like a Cuban, the other was a white male, about 5'7" to 5'9" and weighing about 150 to 160 pounds. The two men did not speak to each other or to Vinson. (*Flight from Dallas,* p.26)

Vinson eventually made his way back to Colorado Springs, via Roswell, New Mexico. The other two passengers also disembarked at Roswell, without saying a word to each other or to Vinson. Late on Saturday, November 23, while watching assassination coverage on TV with his wife, Vinson saw Lee Oswald on the screen. He told his wife, "That guy looks just like the little guy who was on the airplane." He wife replied, "Are you nuts? It couldn't be him. He's in jail." And Vinson insisted, "I swear, that's the little guy who got on the plane." "Well," his wife warned, "keep quiet about it." (*Flight from Dallas,* p.29) And he did keep quiet about it for quite some time, but was eventually tracked down and offered a lucrative job with the CIA, which would keep him at a restricted site 40 miles northwest of Las Vegas. It was made clear to Vinson, that he had no choice about this re-assignment. When the new job offer came, his supervisors called him in and said "We're sorry to lose you, Bob, but these orders came down from headquarters, and we can't do anything about them." (*Flight from Dallas,* p.37)

Clearly the agency was taken by surprise at the unexpected passenger on the C-54, and went to some pains to track Vinson down and investigate his background before deciding how to handle this awkward situation. The fact that Vinson was given a job with the CIA – and did not simply disappear – is evidence that the CIA trusted him not to tell what he saw on November 22, 1963. But now that the story has come out, it is clear that this is additional proof of an Oswald lookalike at the assassination scene.

Explaining the two "Oswalds"

To explain the escape from the TSBD, we can now construct a plausible scenario, which is based not on pure speculation, but is a model which fits the available evidence. The man with the rifle in the sixth floor window was not Lee Oswald, but bore a strong resemblance to him. He may have fired shots from the window, or his role in the conspiracy may have been to help frame Oswald by simply making himself conspicuous to the crowd below. After the shots were fired, this man left the TSBD by the back exit, ran around to the west side and entered a waiting Rambler station wagon as observed by Roger Craig and Marvin Robinson. Perhaps changing vehicles along the way, this man and a confederate made their way to the primitive landing strip near the Trinity River, where the C-54 carrying Robert Vinson picked them up. This Oswald lookalike would not have faced the same time constraints as the real Oswald when exiting the TSBD, because there is no encounter with a police officer requiring him to be downstairs within a minute and a half after the shooting. This second man could have taken his time in leaving the building unobserved. In the meantime, the real Lee Oswald was on his way to his rooming house on Beckley Street, via bus and taxi. There is conflicting testimony as to when or whether the TSBD building was fully sealed off, but we know that at least 7 minutes after the assassination, at 12:37, there had not yet been any instructions issued to prevent people from entering or leaving the building, according to Inspector Herbert Sawyer. (WCHE, v.6, p.320)

OSWALD SIGHTINGS BEFORE NOVEMBER 22, 1963

There were a number of witnesses who testified that in the days and weeks before the assassination, they had seen Oswald at various locations in the Dallas area. These witnesses were clear in saying that they saw "Oswald", not just someone who looked like Oswald. These sightings have been the subject of additional conjectures about a second Oswald, but the evidence is strong that the witnesses in these incidents saw the real Lee Oswald. To assume that they saw an Oswald lookalike is an unnecessary complication. As a general rule, we choose the least complicated explanation for an event. While we must concede the *possibility* that these were sightings of a different man who resembled Oswald, the evidence best fits the hypothesis that the real Oswald was the man they saw, and this is the simplest way to account for their testimony.

We will examine four such sightings: at the gun range, the furniture store, the car dealership, and Oswald the hitchhiker. Each of these incidents is attested by multiple witnesses. The Warren Report discounted all of them, probably because they threatened the commission's portrait of Oswald in several ways, either by suggesting that Oswald was not a loner and may have had unknown accomplices in planning the assassination, or that Oswald really was able to drive a car, or that he was making plans which were inconsistent with murdering the President – namely, plans to buy a new car and furniture for a new apartment. Also, if these witnesses are right about seeing Oswald at the places and times given, then this would mean that certain witnesses on whom the commission relies (in particular, Ruth Paine and Marina Oswald) would have been wrong in some of their critical testimony, and this would seriously weaken the government's case against Oswald. In the commission's view, the credibility of Ruth Paine and Marina Oswald must be upheld at all costs.

OSWALD AT THE GUN RANGE

Testimony of Malcolm Howard Price

Malcolm Howard Price was a part-time, occasional employee of the Sports Drome rifle range, which was owned and operated by Floyd and Virginia Davis. In an interview with the FBI on December 1, 1963, Price told the agents that he "believed that he sighted in a scope for Lee Harvey Oswald on Saturday, October 26, 1963." On viewing a photo of Oswald at the Dallas Police Department, Price said "he was sure that this was the same person for whom he sighted in the scope. He said this man had a 7.6 rifle that had been sporterized." Price recalled that the alleged assassination rifle shown in the newspapers was definitely not the same gun that he sighted in on October 26, 1963." (WCHE, v.26, p.366a) Price also told the agents that this man "visited the range four or five days in succession, arriving about 4 p.m. and staying until dark." (WCHE, v.26, p.366b)

At his deposition, while being questioned by Wesley Liebeler, Price told essentially the same story, but mistakenly said the date was in September, not October. Liebeler helpfully suggested September 28 as the date, and Price agreed. (WCHE, v.10, p.370) The Warren Report used this mistaken date to discredit Price's testimony, saying that on September 28, Oswald was known to be in Mexico City, so could not have been at the rifle range. (WCR, p.319) However, it is clear that Price meant the date to be October 26, because not only did he give the October date to the FBI agents who interviewed him, but the owners of the range, Floyd and Virginia Davis, testified that the range did not open for business until October 26. (WCHE, v.26, p.391b, 392b)

During his deposition testimony, Price provided additional details about Oswald's visit to the gun range. The first time he came, says Price, "it was just about dusky dark and he came in in an old model car, I would judge it was possibly a 1940 or 1941 model Ford. . . . He was by himself, and I have heard that he couldn't drive, but he was driving that day because he was the only one in the car, and he came down and inquired if there was anyone there that could set a scope." Price sighted the scope for him and zeroed it in on 100 yards, firing the rifle 12 to 18 times. Then he gave the rifle to Oswald who fired 3 shots in a bull's eye and told Price he was satisfied with the scope. Price continued, "He didn't talk too much, and I was kind of surprised that he didn't fire the rifle more. He just fired the three shots and said, 'Well, that's good enough.'" Price said the man picked up all the shell casings from the rifle and took them with him. (WCHE, v.10, p.370) Price testified that he saw this same man two more times at the gun range. On the third occasion, Price asked the man if the scope was still set and Oswald told him it was working fine. On this occasion, Oswald asked Price to look through the scope, which was of Japanese manufacture, and Price said it was brighter and clearer than three American scopes he compared it to. (WCHE, v.10, p.372) On this day, Price handled the rifle and had an opportunity to view it close up. "It was a Mauser-type rifle." (WCHE, v.10, p.373) During his deposition, Liebeler handed Price a picture of Oswald handing out leaflets in New Orleans, and Price identified Oswald from the picture as the same man he saw at the rifle range. (WCHE, v.10, p.375)

In a deposition taken April 1, 1964, Virginia Louise Davis, co-owner of the Sports Drome rifle range, vouched for Price's character and truthfulness. "Howard Price, he is the kind of person that you can believe what he says. He is intelligent. When he says he knows a rifle, he knows that rifle. . . . and he remembered that gun." (WCHE, v.10, p.368) Davis also mentions that several other customers also told her they had seen Oswald at the range. (WCHE, v.10, p.367)

Testimony of Sterling Wood and Dr. Homer Wood

Malcolm Price was not the only witness to observe Lee Oswald at the Sports Drome rifle range. Sterling Wood, the 13-year-old son of Dr. Homer Wood, went to the range with his father on the Saturday before the assassination, November 16, 1963. Sterling told the FBI in an interview on December 3, 1963, that while he was shooting, he noticed "a man shooting from an adjoining booth whom he believed is identical with Lee Harvey Oswald. He explained this identification by the fact that upon seeing Oswald's picture on television and in the newspapers on November 22 and 23, 1963, he immediately believed that Oswald was the man using the booth next to him." During a break in the shooting, Sterling went down to examine his own target and also looked at the target used by Oswald. Sterling "noted that all but two of the shots fired by Oswald were in three- or four-inch bullseyes on the target. He noted that these shots were fired from a distance of 100 yards, and he was impressed by the marksmanship of Oswald." (WCHE, v.26, p.368a); "He described this man whom he believes is Oswald as a white male, 25 to 30, 5'7"-5'8", slender build, sharp facial features, black hair, and wearing dark pants with a blue shirt having white stripes. . . . Sterling Wood observed the gun used by the person next to him and noted that it was a rifle that he believed was of Italian make. He described the gun as a bolt action carbine with a shoulder strap and barrel extending beyond the stock only three or four inches. He asked this person whether the gun was a 6.5 Italian carbine and was advised that it was. He then asked whether the telescopic sight was a four-power scope and was advised that that was correct. This was the only conversation he had with this man. During the firing, he observed flame coming from the muzzle of the gun when it was fired. He was unable to explain the reason for this flame." (WCHE, v.26, p.368b); Sterling said that "after seeing Oswald's photograph in the news, he is satisfied in his own mind that the person in the booth next to him . . . was actually Lee Harvey Oswald." (WCHE, v.26, p.369a)

In a second interview with the FBI the following day, Sterling was shown a photo of the Italian rifle from the TSBD and was asked whether he had seen it before. He told the FBI agents that the rifle in the photo "was not the one he had observed being fired at the firearms range on November 16, 1963, inasmuch as the sling strap and swivel on the gun he had observed were attached to the bottom of both the butt and fore end of the rifle, rather than on the side of the butt and fore end, as on the rifle in the photograph. He stated further that there was a difference in the telescope as between the rifle he had observed and the one in the photograph, in that the telescope he saw had an enlarged eyepiece, or ocular lens, of greater diameter than the body of the telescope and that the telescope tapered to a smaller diameter immediately ahead of the eyepiece. He stated emphatically that there was no enlargement of the housing of the objective lens at the forward end of the telescope on the gun he saw." (WCHE, v.26, p.369b) At his deposition on April 1, 1964, Sterling told Wesley Liebeler that the man left the range with another man in a newer model car, which looked like a Ford. He said Oswald was not driving. Sterling described the man's appearance: "The man out at the rifle range had a mean, stern face. you could tell he was a cold man, and that is what made me look at him more than I did anybody else. So when I saw the picture on television that night, I was sure it was him." (WCHE, v.10, p.393) When Liebeler showed Sterling the photos of Oswald in Pizzo Exhibits 453-B&C, Sterling identified the man in those pictures as identical to the man he saw at the gun range. (WCHE, v.10, p.395)

Sterling's father, Dr. Homer Wood, testified to Sterling's knowledge of guns. He told Liebeler that his son knows more about guns than Dr. Wood himself does. (WCHE, v.10, p.387) Dr. Wood also saw the same man at the gun range and told Liebeler "in my mind there is no doubt" that the man at the range was Lee Oswald. (WCHE, v.10, p.389)

Testimony of Garland Slack

Garland Slack was present in Dealey Plaza when the assassination occurred. He was also at the Sports Drome gun range on Sunday, November 10, 1963. He told the FBI that on that date "he saw a man believed to be identical with Oswald at which time the man was accompanied by another man described as tall, as having a lot of dark hair, dark complexion, and a full beard. . . . Slack observed the person he believed to be Oswald and the second man get into an old jalopy which Slack could not further describe. . . . The two men had three rifles which he observed them putting into the back seat. . . He said all the rifles appeared to be of the same make. On November 10, 1963, Slack estimated Oswald fired between 50 to 70 rounds of ammunition while practicing. . . . He recalled the man as firing in bursts of three shots at a time in rapid succession. . . . He observed the man believed to be Oswald was an expert shot." (WCHE, v.26, p.365a); The FBI interview goes on to say that when shown a photograph of Oswald taken November 23, 1963 by the Dallas police, "Slack stated upon observing this photograph he feels positive the individual he observed at the Sports Drome Rifle Range is identical with Oswald except the photograph shows dark hair and . . . the individual at the range had blond hair." (WCHE, v.26, p.365b) The bearded man seen with Oswald was later identified as Michael Bentley Murph. Slack said at his deposition that he had read in the newspaper that this man had no connection with Oswald except that he had just driven Oswald to the range, and Slack believes that Oswald just hitched a ride with Murph. (WCHE, v.10, p.381) When the gun range was conducting a "turkey shoot" contest, Slack noticed that Oswald was shooting rapid fire in bursts of three or four shots. Slack told him, "You're not going to win no turkey shooting rapid fire." (WCHE, v.10, p.380) Slack testified that the picture of the Mannlicher-Carcano rifle in the newspapers was not the rifle he saw when Oswald was shooting at the range. (WCHE, v.10, p.381) When Slack is shown the photo of Oswald in Pizzo Exhibit 453-C (WCHE, v.21, p.140) he tells Liebeler, "That is the man I saw at the rifle range." (WCHE, v.10, p.383)

After he recognized Oswald on TV, Slack went back to the gun range where "these four or five other people knew he had been there, but they were afraid to say anything about it. But when I asked the manager, I said, 'Oswald was over here,' and he said, 'Yes, I know he was.' And they were afraid it would hurt their business." (WCHE, v.10, p.380)

Conclusion

The man seen at the Sports Drome gun range by Price, Slack, and the Woods was in all likelihood Lee Oswald. The idea that he was an Oswald double whose job was to attract attention to Oswald as an expert marksman introduces unnecessary complications. There is no need to go to such extravagant lengths to explain these sightings.

From these witnesses we have consistent stories by multiple reliable witnesses who saw Oswald multiple times and testified in detail to the events they observed. The evidence that Oswald was at the gun range is stronger than the evidence that he fired shots from the sixth floor window. If these same witnesses had given similar testimony about seeing Oswald firing a rifle from the TSBD instead of at the gun range, their statements would have been enthusiastically and uncritically accepted by the commission. Instead, the commission uses the false opening date of September 28 to reject the testimony of both Price and Slack, when there was ample evidence that the opening date of the gun range was actually October 26. The Woods' testimony is rejected because it conflicts with the testimony of Ruth Paine, who denied that Oswald had been out of her sight on the relevant dates for a long enough period of time to have gone to the range. (WCR, p.319) Also, the commission discounts the testimony of these witnesses because their descriptions of the rifle do not correspond to the Mannlicher-Carcano rifle found at the TSBD. (WCR, p.320) Thus, the commission takes its preferred scenario as given, and evaluates all other testimony on the basis of whether it corresponds with or contradicts this scenario. It is critical for the commission's theory that Ruth Paine's veracity must not be challenged. Although there are many points in the gun range stories which support the commission's preferred scenario – e.g., that Oswald was an expert marksman and had practiced extensively before the assassination – the acceptance of the gun range testimony would deal a blow to the Oswald timelines established by Ruth Paine's testimony, and this would discredit the prosecution's most important witness. Also, the testimony of the gun range witnesses is inconsistent with the Italian rifle CE139 being the assassination weapon. For these reasons, the gun range stories must be discredited.

OSWALD AT THE FURNITURE STORE

Testimony of Edith Whitworth

Edith Whitworth worked at a used furniture store known as the Furniture Mart. It had previously housed a gun shop, and in early November 1963 there was still a sign out front advertising gun repair. In an interview with FBI agents, Whitworth said that around November 6 to 8, a man came into her shop inquiring about gun repair. She later recognized this man from TV pictures as Lee Oswald. She advised him that there was no longer a gun repair shop in her building, and directed him to a nearby gun shop. The FBI report goes on to say that Whitworth stated that "Oswald inquired as to both a living room and dining room set, stating that he would need both in the near future. While Oswald was in the store, his wife, carrying a small baby and leading a small girl, came in and observed Oswald's activities but never made any statement or said anything. . . . On leaving the Furniture Mart . . . the Oswalds made a U-turn and left driving against the traffic on East Irving Boulevard in the direction of the gun repair shop in either a 1956 or 1957 two-tone blue and white Ford or Plymouth." (CD205, p.65) During a special deposition session, Wesley Liebeler arranged for Whitworth to meet Marina Oswald, along with her daughter June. Whitworth noticed a resemblance to the woman who was in her store in November 1963, but says, "She doesn't look like she does today, because her face was fuller then and it might have been because she just had this baby then and still hadn't gone back like she was . . . But this little girl – it definitely was her." Marina denied ever having been in the store (WCHE, v.11, p.277) and denied ever seeing Lee drive a car. (WCHE, v.11, p.280)

Testimony of Gertrude Hunter

Gertrude Hunter was in the Furniture Mart with Edith Whitworth at the time the Oswalds came into the store. She testified that a man drove up in front of the store, came in, and asked for a gunsmith. She said the car was a two-tone blue Ford, probably a 1957 or 1958. She is specific about the car because a friend of hers has a similar Ford. At some point during this visit, the man went out of the store and came back in with the woman and the two children. (WCHE, v.11, p.255) Hunter stated that the wife did not say anything while in the store, nor did she show the baby to the two women. (WCHE, v.11, p.256) After the couple left the store, Hunter saw them get into the car, and start to drive the wrong way on the one-way street. She corrected them and told them to go the other way. (WCHE, v.11, p.258) When several photos were shown to Hunter, she could not identify any of them as definitely being the man who came into the store, but she said that Garner Exhibit 1 (a photo of Oswald passing out leaflets) could be him. Pizzo Exhibit 453-C (also Oswald, after his arrest) "could look like him some, but he was not dressed that way." (WCHE, v.11, p.262)

Conclusion

The consistent and detailed testimony of Whitworth and Hunter must lead us to conclude that Oswald was probably in the furniture store with Marina and the children, and that he probably drove a car to get there. The children were of the same ages as Oswald's children. The wife's behavior in the store – i.e., not speaking to the two women and not even showing off the baby – is completely consistent with Marina's inability to speak English fluently. Oswald's search for a gunsmith is entirely consistent with his activities at the gun range observed by Price, Slack, and the Woods. That Oswald was interested in furniture is consistent with Marina's statement that on the evening of Thursday, November 21, Lee "suggested that we rent an apartment in Dallas. . . . [He] wanted me to live with him in Dallas." (WCHE, v.11, p.393)

Here again the commission rejects credible, consistent testimony from reliable witnesses because it conflicts with the storyline given by Ruth Paine. The Warren Report dismissed the testimony of Whitworth and Hunter, on the grounds that Oswald would have been working at the TSBD during the time he was said to be at the Furniture Mart, and "there is no evidence that he left his job during business hours." (WCR, p.317) But the sighting of Oswald at the Furniture Mart is evidence that he did just that. Also, TSBD employee Bonnie Ray Williams testified that at lunchtime Oswald would often go out for a walk, "and I assume he would come back." (WCHE, v.3, p.164) So in Williams' testimony we have evidence that Oswald did leave the building during working hours on multiple occasions.

The testimony of Whitworth and Hunter must also be rejected, the commission tells us, because "Ruth Paine has stated that she always accompanied Marina Oswald whenever Marina left the house with her children and that they never went to the Furniture Mart, either with or without Lee Harvey Oswald, at any time during October or November 1963." (WCR, p.317) Furthermore, both Ruth Paine and Marina Oswald insisted that Oswald did not know how to drive a car. Instead of weighing the testimony of Whitworth and Hunter against that of Ruth Paine, Paine's testimony is taken as an unquestioned standard by which to judge the testimony of the other witnesses. In the Furniture Mart story, there is nothing that would rule out Oswald as lone assassin. The visit to the store is consistent with either a lone gunman theory or a conspiracy scenario. The real danger in this story is that, if true, it would cast doubt on the reliability of Ruth Paine, and the commission's case relies too heavily on her to allow her veracity to be questioned.

OSWALD AT THE CAR DEALERSHIP

Testimony of Albert Guy Bogard

Bogard was a car salesman employed by Downtown Lincoln Mercury in Dallas. In an interview on December 9, 1963, Bogard told FBI agents that "on Saturday, November 9, 1963, at about 3:00 to 4:00 p.m., a young man came in the showroom at Downtown Lincoln-Mercury, and stated he was interested in a car. . . . This man said his name was Lee Oswald." (WCHE, v.26, p.450b) Bogard stated that he took the man outside to the lot and the man "seemed interested in a red Comet hardtop." Bogard offered to let him take a test drive. When Bogard asked how the man planned to pay for the car, the man replied that "he had some money coming in within two or three weeks and would pay cash for the car." Bogard stated that during the test drive the man "drove at speeds up to 75 to 85 miles per hour." After the test drive, Bogard was unsuccessful in getting the man to make a down payment, fill out a sales order, or give his address and phone number for followup contact. (WCHE, v.26, p.451a) Bogard stated that he wrote the man's name "Lee Oswald" on the back of a business card and put the card into his pocket. On the afternoon of the assassination, Bogard heard the name "Lee Oswald" on the radio as being the suspect, whereupon he showed the card to some other employees of the showroom and "threw the card in the waste basket," remarking, "He isn't a prospect any more." Bogard concluded, "I am positive that this Lee Harvey Oswald, who was arrested in connection with the death of President Kennedy, is the same person who came to my place of business on November 9, 1963, and gave me his name as Lee Oswald." (WCHE, v.26, p.451b)

Bogard was again interviewed by the FBI on January 24, 1964 and told the agents he was sure that November 9, 1963 was the date of the demonstration ride with the man he identified as Oswald. He was sure of this because the car shown to the man was only available for demonstration on that date. (CD385, p.80)

Yet another FBI report dated February 25, 1964 summarizes the results of a polygraph exam given to Bogard. Bogard was asked a series of questions regarding the incident involving Oswald and the demonstration ride. The report concludes: ""No significant emotional responses were recorded by the polygraph, when Bogard was asked relevant questions concerning his report. The responses recorded were those normally expected of a person telling the truth." (WCHE, v.26, p.577b)

Once again, the Warren Report dismissed this Oswald sighting, as it did the appearances at the gun range and the furniture store, on the grounds that on the date of the test drive, "Oswald's whereabouts on November 9, as testified to by Marina Oswald and Ruth Paine, would have made it impossible for him to have visited the automobile showroom as Mr. Bogard claims." (WCR, p.321) As usual, the timelines given by Ruth Paine and Marina Oswald are taken as established facts, and any witness whose testimony conflicts with them is deemed untrustworthy. A more logical approach would be to take a skeptical view of the Ruth Paine and Marina Oswald stories, given that a significant number of credible witnesses have testified that Oswald was not where these two women said he was on the dates in question. Even though Bogard stated that Oswald identified himself by name, and even though Bogard passed a polygraph test, the commission still dismissed his testimony. His identification of Oswald is much stronger and more definite than that of Howard Brennan, yet the commission chose to base its case against Oswald on Brennan's shaky testimony while rejecting the testimony of credible witnesses such as Bogard, whose stories were much more consistent and credible.

Testimony of Eugene Wilson

Like Bogard, Eugene Wilson was an auto salesman for Downtown Lincoln-Mercury in Dallas. Wilson was not asked to testify before the commission, nor was his deposition taken. However, in an interview with the FBI on September 8, 1964, Wilson corroborated portions of Bogard's story. Wilson recalled that early in November, Bogard had come to him with a customer who had "no cash, no credit, and had been employed on his job for only a short period of time, and Bogard had not been able to sell him a car. Wilson said he talked to this customer for only a minute or so, and told him that if he did not have a credit rating, or a substantial amount of cash, and had not been employed on his job for some time, they would be unable to sell him a car. This customer then said, rather sarcastically, 'Maybe I'm going to have to go back to Russia to buy a car." Wilson also stated that Bogard told him that on the demonstration ride, "the customer drove like a madman, driving much too fast. . . . Wilson described this customer as a white male, between 26 and 30 years old, weighed about 135 pounds, and was only about five feet tall." (WCHE, v.26, p.685a)

Since Wilson was not asked to testify before the commission, there was no opportunity to question him to verify whether the FBI report is correct in saying that Wilson told them the man was only five feet tall. However, if we put the estimated weight of 135 pounds and the alleged height of five feet into a Body Mass Index calculator, we come up with a body mass index of 26.4 which is in the "overweight" category. Bogard had described the customer as "medium build" (WCHE, v.10, p.353), and no one at the dealership described him as "overweight". So we are left to wonder whether the height of five feet was correctly recorded in Wilson's FBI interview.

Wilson told the FBI that "the next day after President Kennedy was assassinated, Bogard walked up to Wilson and mentioned that the man who had shot President Kennedy was the customer to whom Bogard had introduced Wilson." Wilson was not able to identify pictures of Lee Oswald as being the same man he saw with Bogard at the car dealership, claiming that he has poor vision due to cataracts, and has seen so many customers since November 9 that he cannot remember exactly what this customer looked like. (WCHE, v.26, p.685b)

Incidentally, the date of Wilson's interview with the FBI, September 8, 1964, just as the Warren Report was on the verge of being printed, indicates the commission's eagerness to dispose of Bogard's story, which challenged the reliability of the commission's key witnesses – i.e., Ruth Paine and Marina Oswald, and also refuted the commission's claim that Oswald did not know how to drive a car. In Wilson's description of the car customer as being only five feet tall, the commission found the evidence it needed to completely dismiss Bogard's story. Oswald could not have been the customer seen by Bogard, the commission reasoned, in part because Oswald was much taller than five feet. (WCR, p.321)

Testimony of Frank Pizzo

Frank Pizzo was the assistant manager of Downtown Lincoln-Mercury in the fall of 1963. At his deposition on March 31, 1964, Pizzo told commission counsel Albert Jenner that on the day of the assassination, a number of the car salesmen were listening to the radio, and Pizzo overheard one of them say, "Al Bogard lost his prospect." (WCHE, v.10, p.345). Pizzo testified further that "this salesman made the remark that Al Bogard . . . said, 'Well, there goes my prospect,' when he heard the name Lee Harvey Oswald, so he dumped it [the business card on which he had written Oswald's name] in the wastebasket. . . . One of the boys said the next day that he had lost his customer and the guy that they have got is the man that Bogard has as a prospect." (WCHE, v.10, p.346) Jenner showed Pizzo several photos, including one of Oswald after his arrest (Pizzo Exhibit 453-C) but Pizzo doesn't think that the hairline is the same as he saw on the man at the dealership, but he said that the man in Pizzo Exhibit 453-C has the correct facial features. (WCHE, v.10, p.349) The commission seized on the hairline differences to conclude that the customer that Pizzo saw with Bogard could not have been Lee Oswald. (WCR, p.321)

Conclusion

Bogard, Wilson, and Pizzo all agreed that in early November, around November 9, a customer came in to the dealership and Bogard discussed selling a car to him. Wilson remembers Bogard telling him about the wild test drive that he took in which this customer drove at high speed. Wilson and Pizzo both confirmed that Bogard had mentioned losing his prospect after Oswald's name was heard on the radio following the assassination. The customer's comment about having to go "back to Russia" in order to buy a car, strongly suggests that the customer was in fact Lee Oswald. The customer's remark about coming into some money in 2 or 3 weeks is consistent with his remark to Edith Whitworth at the furniture store that he would be needing new furniture soon. Bogard's identification of Oswald as this customer is confident and firm. Although Wilson and Pizzo are not so certain about the identification, Bogard was the one who spent the most time with the customer and his memory is obviously much more definite that that of the other two men, who only saw the customer briefly.

The commission once again used the testimony of Ruth Paine and Marina Oswald as a yardstick to assess Bogard's credibility. But considered on its own merits, Bogard's confident identification of the man as Oswald, plus the confirmation from Wilson and Pizzo that such an event actually occurred around the time stated by Bogard, must lead us to the conclusion that it is highly probable that Oswald was in fact the customer in the car dealership on November 9th and that he took the test drive with Bogard in a red Comet Caliente, in anticipation of receiving a large sum of money in the near future, notwithstanding the alternative "facts" given by Ruth Paine and Marina Oswald.

OSWALD THE HITCHHIKER

Testimony of Ralph Yates

Ralph Yates was a refrigerator serviceman with the Texas Butcher Supply Company. On November 26, 1963, just 4 days after the assassination, he told the FBI that a couple of days before the assassination, probably Wednesday, November

20, he picked up a hitchhiker near the Beckley Street entrance to the expressway. "Yates said after seeing photographs and television pictures of Lee Harvey Oswald, he is of the opinion that this man was identical with Oswald. He told the agents that when the hitchhiker walked up to get into the pickup truck, he was carrying a package wrapped in brown wrapping paper about 4 feet to 4-1/2 feet long. Yates said he told this man he could put the package in the back of the truck, but the man said that the package contained curtain rods and he would carry it with him in the cab of the truck. Yates brought up the fact that the President would be in town soon. (CD5, p.417) "Yates stated the man then asked Yates if he thought a person could assassinate the President. Yates replied that he guessed such a thing could be possible. The man then asked Yates if it could be done from the top of a building or out of a window, high up, and Yates said he guessed this was possible if one had a good rifle with a scope and was a good shot. Yates advised about this time the man pulled out a picture which showed a man with a rifle and asked Yates if he thought the President could be killed with a gun like that one. Yates said he was driving and did not look at the picture but indicated to the man that he guessed so. [In a later FBI interview, Yates said the man in the picture with the rifle was Oswald himself. (CD205, p.45)] Yates said that the man then asked if he knew the President's route for the parade in Dallas and Yates replied that he did not know the route but that it had been in the paper. He said the man then said that he had misunderstood him and that actually he had asked Yates if he thought that the President would change his route. Yates said he replied that he doubted it unless they might for safety reasons." Yates said he dropped the man off downtown at the corner of Elm and Houston Streets. (CD5, p.418)

At a second interview with the FBI on December 10, 1963, Yates stated: "I have been shown a photograph of Lee Harvey Oswald . . . This is a photograph of the man that I picked up and gave a ride to, and had the conversation with as set forth above in this statement." (CD205, p.46)

Yates was not called to testify before the commission, nor was his deposition taken. The Warren Report does not mention Yates or his story.

Testimony of Dempsey Jones

Yates' co-worker, Dempsey Jones, confirmed to the FBI that Yates had told him about the hitchhiker after Yates returned to work that day. Jones said that "Yates told him he had picked up a boy in Oak Cliff and taken this boy to Houston and Elm in Dallas. Yates said this boy had a package not described at that time, but after the death of the President, Yates described the package as a 'long package' and then on telling the facts over again, Yates said this man told him it was some window shades." Jones said that Yates told him that the man mentioned "that one could be in a building and shoot the President as he, the President, passed by." After the President was shot, Yates told Jones that he believed the man he had picked up was "the man who shot and killed the President, and he was going to call it in and tell them what he knew about it. Jones described Yates as "a big talker who always talks about a lot of foolishness". (CD5, p.420)

Conclusion

The details in Yates' story are persuasive that it is highly probable that the man he picked up was Lee Oswald:

- The man was picked up near Beckley Street in Oak Cliff, the same street and neighborhood where Oswald's rooming house was located.
- The curtain rod story was the same one that Oswald told to his co-worker Wesley Frazier on the morning he brought a package to work in Frazier's car. But Yates' estimate of the package size was larger than the one seen by Frazier, and the package in Yates' truck was long enough to have contained the Italian rifle allegedly recovered from the sixth floor of the TSBD.
- The hitchhiker brought up the subject of assassinating the President with a rifle from the window of a tall building – exactly the same scenario that unfolded, according to official accounts, on November 22.
- Yates dropped the man off at the corner of Houston and Elm Streets, where Oswald worked at the Texas School Book Depository.
- On the same day that he picked up the hitchhiker, Yates told his co-worker Dempsey Jones about the incident, mentioning the same details which Yates later gave to the FBI.

There can be no reasonable doubt that one or two days before the assassination Ralph Yates picked up Lee Oswald and gave him a ride from Oak Cliff to the TSBD in downtown Dallas. Oswald's questions to Yates about the possibility of assassinating the President are curious, and can be taken in more than one way. But it is difficult to imagine, if Oswald was himself planning to assassinate the President, that he would discuss these plans openly with a stranger just a day or two before the event. The Yates encounter fits more comfortably into a scenario where Oswald is either involved in, or has infiltrated, a plot to kill the President, and he is seeking confirmation from Yates that the plot will fail, either because the rifle is not adequate to the job, or because the President's route will be changed. Alternatively, he may have been spilling these details to Yates in the hope that Yates would go to the police to report a possible assassination plot.

THE MEMOIR OF JUDYTH VARY BAKER

Support for the view that Oswald was a reluctant participant in a conspiracy to kill the President comes from the autobiographical memoir *Me and Lee,* by Judyth Vary Baker, who tells the story of her relationship with Oswald in the summer and fall of 1963. A thorough assessment of her credibility would take us too far from our purpose in this volume, but suffice it to say that she strikes me as being a credible witness in what she describes, although we cannot be sure that Oswald was always truthful with her. So while we might believe her account of what she saw and heard, we might still be skeptical of anything that Oswald told her. There is, however, a document in the Warren Commission's collection which corroborates one detail of Baker's story.

Baker writes that on November 20, 1963, while at her job in Florida, she tried to reach Oswald at the TSBD, using a pre-arranged signal. She placed a person-to-person call to the TSBD and asked to speak to "the new janitor", Lee Oswald. After checking, the person who answered at the TSBD told her that Oswald refused the call, which indicated to Baker that he was there, but unable to talk at that moment. (Baker, *Me and Lee,* p.519)

This call which Baker reportedly made to the TSBD finds corroboration in Commission Document 75 (FBI DeBrueys Report of 02 Dec 1963). We find on page 180 a report of an FBI communication with Ed Turnley, Security Manager for Southern Bell Telephone Company in New Orleans. The FBI reports that Turnley provided the following information: "On November 24, 1963, Yvonne Cooper . . . Operator Number 19, Covington, Louisiana, notified her supervisor that two or three days previously she had handled a prepaid long distance, person-to-person call to Lee Harvey Oswald at the 'Texas State Book Depository', Dallas, Texas. Mrs. Cooper recalled that it was necessary for her to contact the Dallas information operator for this information. She specifically remembered the words 'Book Depository' in her request to Dallas Information. She stated she obtained this number and was connected without any difficulty. Mrs. Cooper stated that this call was placed by an adult female who was very polite, had no speech impediment, no accent, and who appeared to be familiar with the proceedings in placing long distance telephone calls. Mrs. Cooper stated that the answering party in Dallas . . . was asked by her for Lee Harvey Oswald. The answering party advised she did not know who Oswald was. At this point, according to Mrs. Cooper, the calling party advised Oswald is a new employee. Mrs. Cooper thinks the calling party said Oswald was the janitor. Mrs. Cooper stated that at this point the answering party said 'oh' as if she knew who it was, and the call was completed." (CD75, p.180) Turnley told the FBI that the Covington office normally handled calls from within Louisiana (CD75, p.181), but without further technical information we cannot be sure that long distance calls from Florida to Texas would not be routed through the Covington office. In most of its details, this story from the phone company manager conforms to the story about the pre-arranged signal that Baker said she used in phoning Oswald at the TSBD on November 20.

With these preliminaries, we can now turn to Baker's account of Oswald's activities during the days before the assassination. This may give us insight as to what Oswald's motive was in almost revealing the existence of an assassination plot to Ralph Yates.

Baker writes that on October 26, Oswald told her by phone that he had been "invited to be an actual participant in the assassination plans against JFK." She says that Oswald expected to be set up by the plotters and feared that he might not live to see another birthday. (Baker, *Me and Lee,* p.505) Baker wrote that Oswald called her back on the evening of November 20 and said he had "sent out information that might be able to save [Kennedy]". (Baker, p.519) Oswald told her that his CIA handler was David Phillips (Baker, p.521), and he told her that she should remember the names Bobby Baker and Billy Sol Estes, and said that the assassination was happening because of them. (Baker, p.522)

If Baker's account is true, then it suggests that Oswald had infiltrated a plot to kill the President, that he was looking for a way to foil the plot, and that his questions to Yates were intended either to reassure himself that the plot would fail, or perhaps to raise enough suspicion in Yates' mind that Yates would go to the police to report a possible assassination plot. But we can be sure that Oswald's questions to Yates are not the behavior that we would expect from a lone assassin who was planning to kill Kennedy.

EVALUATING THE OSWALD SIGHTINGS

There are some common themes that occur across the four Oswald sightings that we have examined. In all these incidents, Oswald is seen to be operating alone. Notwithstanding the large bearded man with whom Oswald may have hitched a ride to the gun range, there is no direct information to be derived from these incidents that Oswald was working with anyone on a conspiracy to assassinate the President. The sightings are consistent with both the lone gunman scenario and the conspiracy scenario. The sightings undermine the notion that Oswald could not drive a car, and that he was a poor shot. Based on the witnesses at the gun range, Oswald's capabilities as a marksman were more than adequate to do the job the commission suspected him of. Of course, this does not mean that Oswald was the shooter in the TSBD window, but only that he was not, in November 1963, the poor marksman that some of his Marine comrades testified to before the commission.

In two of the sightings – the furniture store and the car dealership – Oswald is quoted as saying that he is expecting some money in a few weeks, or that he will soon need new furniture. But this, too, is ambiguous. He could have expected money from the conspirators for doing his part in the assassination, or he could be expecting fame and fortune as the man who foiled the plot and saved Kennedy's life. Having an expectation of a financial windfall would be consistent with either of these scenarios. It would not be consistent with Oswald as lone assassin. In that scenario, where would the money come from? Thus, the expectation of imminent financial gain is inconsistent with the commission's lone gunman theory.

In the final analysis, the Oswald pre-assassination sightings do not give us any insight as to whether Lee Oswald was the man seen holding a rifle in the sixth floor TSBD window. We have seen that evidence from within the TSBD, especially from Carolyn Arnold and from Victoria Adams (supported by Sandra Styles and Dorothy Ann Garner), raises severe difficulty with the hypothesis that Oswald was the sixth floor shooter. We have also seen that there is credible evidence that an Oswald lookalike was present in the TSBD during the assassination and may have been the man seen standing at the sixth floor window and afterwards escaping in a Rambler station wagon. But the hypothesis that an Oswald double was involved in the sightings at the furniture store, the gun range, the auto dealership and the hitchhiking incident is unnecessarily complex. There is no need to postulate such an elaborate scheme in order to explain the sightings. But the correspondences between Oswald and the man observed in these sightings are too numerous to be mere coincidence. Either the man was Lee Oswald himself, which means that the Ruth/Marina timelines are unreliable, or he was a double planted by conspirators in an extravagant attempt to draw attention to Oswald in an effort to make his subsequent guilt seem more plausible. But the commission's claim that these sightings were just random encounters with men who happened to look like Lee Oswald is incredible. The commission struggled until the very end with how to handle these sightings, finally resorting to the feeble attempt to discredit the witnesses by pointing out discrepancies between their testimony and that of Ruth Paine and Marina Oswald, whose veracity was never questioned.

If the sightings at the gun range, the furniture store, and the car dealership, along with the hitchhiking incident, involved the real Lee Oswald, then many of the "facts" attested to by Ruth Paine and Marina Oswald had to be false, including his lack of practice with a rifle, his inability to drive, and the elaborately concocted story about the driving lessons given by Ruth Paine. The circumstances under which Oswald obtained the job at the Texas School Book Depository also would come under scrutiny, as Ruth Paine was instrumental in that as well.

It is not clear what might have motivated Paine to give false testimony, or what she might have been hiding. It is known that Ruth Paine's father, William Avery Hyde, had been under consideration by the CIA for a possible covert assignment in Vietnam in 1957, but according to a CIA memo, Hyde was not used in this role. (Memo Re Ruth Paine, dated December 5, 1963, NARA Record Number 104-10121-10087, released in 1999) In a CIA memo dated May 7, 1967, a Sylvia Hyde Hoke is named as Ruth Paine's sister. (Memo re Thurston, Wesley Standish, #91888, NARA Record Number: 1993.08.05.07:21:52:150037, p.6) This sister, Sylvia Hyde Hoke, was acknowledged in a CIA memo dated July 30, 1971 as having been a CIA employee. (Security File on Sylvia Hyde Hoke, NARA Record Number 1993.07.24.08:39:37:560310, p.7) The mother of Michael Paine, Ruth's husband, was a close friend of Mary Bancroft, who was the mistress of former CIA Director Allen Dulles. (David Talbot, *The Devil's Chessboard: Allen Dulles, the CIA, and the Rise of America's Secret Government,* 2015, p.537.)

Given these family connections with the CIA, Ruth Paine's role in providing cover for Lee Oswald's activities in Dallas during the fall of 1963 deserves further investigation, especially given that many other witnesses give accounts of Oswald's activities that are at variance with Ruth Paine's.

CONNECTIONS

Despite the Warren Commission's characterization of Oswald as a loner and a misfit, there is substantial evidence that he had a number of connections to other people and organizations which raise doubts about the image presented by the commission. The commission put a great deal of effort into dismissing the evidence of these associations, because they obviously conflicted with the impression the commission sought to create about Oswald's character. Nothing is more likely to create suspicion about a person than calling him a "loner", and the commission went to great lengths to stamp that label on Oswald. But whether Oswald was a loner has little bearing on the assassination. Whether loner or not, he could still have been sitting in the window shooting at Kennedy – or not. But painting Oswald as a loner served the goal of eliminating the likelihood that Oswald could have conspired with others to commit the assassination. It also served to distance him from any association with agencies of the U. S. government. The more contacts Oswald had with others, the more plausible it is that he did not act alone, but in concert with other conspirators. Therefore, this chapter will consider Oswald's connections to people and groups who may have had reason to want Kennedy removed. We will see that he had connections with organized crime, anti-Castro Cuban exiles, and U. S. intelligence. All of these groups have come under suspicion for having a motive and the means for killing President Kennedy, and Oswald's relation to them points to his involvement in a conspiracy to kill the President – either as a participant in the plot, or as an infiltrator and informant, who tried to stop it.

DID OSWALD AND RUBY KNOW EACH OTHER?

Jack Ruby's role in the assassination is a key to establishing that Kennedy was killed by a conspiracy involving at least organized crime, and very likely other actors as well, including the Dallas police and anti-Castro Cubans. Ruby, of course, murdered Oswald on live TV on the morning of Sunday, November 24, 1963, as Oswald was about to be transferred from the Dallas police department to the county jail. Ruby tried to portray the murder as a spontaneous act on his part, motivated by sympathy for Mrs. Kennedy and her children. In other words, the lone nut assassin was cut down by a lone nut avenger. For many observers, this was a hard pill to swallow. Many people who were willing to accept Oswald as an opportunistic impulsive killer had trouble accepting that two lone nuts were involved in the events of that weekend. The Warren Commission wanted us to believe that lightning had indeed struck twice in the same place, but to all appearances it looked as though Ruby had killed Oswald in order to silence him. Secret Service agent Forrest Sorrels told police chief Curry that Ruby told him, "somebody had to kill the son-of-a-bitch and the police department couldn't do it." (WCHE, v.4, p.197)

Ruby's address in Oak Cliff:

Since it will figure somewhat into the comings and goings of Ruby and Oswald, we should at this point confirm that Ruby's address in November 1963 was 223 S. Ewing Avenue, Apt. 207 in the Oak Cliff section of Dallas. An HSCA press release of 9/26/1978 gives this as Ruby's address in a list of phone calls made to and from Ruby in summer and fall 1963. (HSCA Press Release of 26 Sep 1978: Agenda, Blakey Narration, Exhibits, p.57)

Thanks to Google maps, if you enter Ruby's Ewing Avenue address along with Oswald's rooming house address at 1026 N. Beckley, and ask for directions, you get a handy map showing several routes between the two points, all of which are either 1.3 miles or 1.4 miles in length – easily within a half hour's walking distance, or even faster with a police escort. The Tippit murder site near 10th Street and Patton Ave. is between the addresses of Oswald and Ruby. If we ask, "Where was Oswald going when he encountered Officer Tippit?" it would not be unreasonable to list Ruby's apartment as one possible destination. Tenth and Patton is not a location that Oswald would have passed on a direct route from his rooming house to the Texas Theatre, where he was eventually captured. If we enter Oswald's address and the site of the Tippit killing at 10th and Patton, Google maps gives routes of 0.8 or 0.9 mile – about a 15-minute walk at a brisk pace.

Reporter Seth Kantor quotes a private communication dated May 26, 1964 from Texas Attorney General Waggoner Carr to Warren Commission counsel Lee Rankin, in which Carr suggests "that every effort be made to determine why Oswald was headed in the general direction of Ruby's house at the time he was intercepted by officer Tippit." (Seth Kantor, *The Ruby Cover-up,* Zebra Books, 1978, p.385)

Sightings of Oswald and Ruby together before the assassination

If Ruby killed Oswald in order to silence him, that does not necessarily mean that Ruby and Oswald were associated with each other before the assassination. But if they were seen together before the assassination this would lend credence to the hypothesis that they both were involved in the plot. As it turns out, there are a number of witnesses who did claim to have seen them together. These individual sightings are not always confirmed by other witnesses, although there are enough of these incidents to establish a strong suspicion that Ruby and Oswald may have been acquainted before the assassination. But the evidence is not sufficient to prove such an acquaintance beyond a reasonable doubt.

Testimony of Carroll Jarnagin:

Carroll Jarnagin was a Dallas attorney who wrote a letter which the FBI received on December 5, 1963, and which included an 8-page statement describing a meeting that he witnessed between Ruby and Oswald at the Carousel Club on October 4, 1963. Jarnagin stated he also phoned this information in to the Texas Department of Public Safety on October 5, 1963. No one at the Texas Department of Public Safety ever admitted to receiving such a letter or phone call. Jarnagin wrote in his statement to the FBI that while at the Carousel Club, "I heard Jack Ruby talking to a man using the name of H. L. Lee. These men were talking about plans to kill the Governor of Texas." Jarnagin writes that after seeing the picture of Lee Oswald in the newspaper on November 23, 1963, he realized that Oswald was the man he saw using the name of H. L. Lee. (WCHE, v.26, p.254a) Jarnagin was sitting at a nearby table with his date, a dancer who was acquainted with Ruby. Jarnagin described the conversation that he overheard between Ruby and the man calling himself H. L. Lee: Lee says he just arrived from New Orleans and needs some money. Ruby tells him he'll get the money "after the job is done". Ruby questions whether Lee can "do the job". Lee responds, "It's simple. I'm a Marine sharpshooter." The conversation suggests that "the job" is killing "the Governor". (WCHE, v.26, p.255a) After some discussion of the details of how the job is to be done, Lee spots Jarnagin and asks Ruby if Jarnagin is an FBI agent. Ruby calls the dancer over to his table and she confirms that Jarnagin is not an FBI man. After this, Ruby and Lee speak more softly and Jarnagin cannot easily overhear them. (WCHE, v.26, p.256b)

The FBI report of Jarnagin's statement added that "Jarnagin advised that he has never had a mental or nervous breakdown, but that he does have an alcoholic problem and has considered the possibility of joining Alcoholics Anonymous. He also stated that his ex-wife, in divorce proceedings, indicated that his drinking was part of the reason for her getting a divorce. Jarnagin admitted that on the night of October 4, 1963, he was drunk, but stated that he still believes he could recall the events that occurred." (WCHE, v.26, p.258a-b)

After receiving Jarnagin's statement, the FBI conducted an investigation into his background which revealed that Jarnagin "was arrested for drunk and disorderly on March 8, 1958; disposition $10 bond forfeited on March 19, 1958. Details regarding this arrest reflect that Jarnagin was arrested by a police officer after he was noticed on the street in an obviously intoxicated condition. At the time of the arrest, he became very indignant and, in securing the officer's badge number, advised the officer he was an Attorney at Law and that he intended to sue." (WCHE, v.26, p.260b); An investigation into Jarnagin's credit record found that "his credit record was satisfactory, with exception of one repossession of a washing machine in 1956." (WCHE, v.26, p.261a);

Jarnagin was not asked to testify before the commission about his report to the FBI, nor was his deposition taken. His name is not mentioned in the index to the Warren Report. His story does come up in the testimony of District Attorney Henry Wade, in response to a question by Sen. Cooper regarding rumors that Ruby and Oswald had been seen together before the assassination. Wade mentions that he talked to a Dallas attorney who related this story to him, although he says that he cannot remember the attorney's name. It is later determined that he's talking about Jarnagin. (WCHE, v.5, p.239) Wade read Jarnagin's statement when Jarnagin visited him late one night. Wade told the commission that "it didn't ring true to me.

It all deals with a conversation between Oswald and Ruby about killing John Connally, the Governor of Texas, over, he says, they can't get syndicated crime in Texas without they kill the Governor. (WCHE, v.5, p.233).

Wade told Jarnagin that he couldn't use his statement at Ruby's trial without putting Jarnagin through a polygraph test. Jarnagin agreed to take the examination, and Wade tells the commission "he took a lie detector. There was no truth in it." No questions are raised by commission members or counsel about the detailed results of the polygraph test that Jarnagin reportedly took. (WCHE, v.5, p.234) In other testimony, the commission was told of the polygraph's unreliability in detecting lies. FBI polygraph expert Bell Herndon testified that "the polygraph instrument, of course, is commonly known to the public as the lie detector. In fact it is not such a device." Arlen Specter asked Herndon, "What is its level of reliability in indicating patterns of deception? Herndon replied, "There has been no conclusive scientific objective study in that regard, and as of today there are no valid statistics with regard to its actual objective reliability." (WCHE, v.14, p.581) Thus, there is no scientific basis for rejecting a witness's testimony based on the results of a polygraph examination. J. Edgar Hoover himself told the commission, "I have seen individuals who have failed the lie detector test and who were just as innocent as they could be." (WCHE, v.5, p.103)

Jarnagin later told Texas newspaper editor Penn Jones, Jr. that he bore no ill will toward Henry Wade, telling Jones that Wade "did the only thing he could under the circumstances." Jones wrote that there were several points in Jarnagin's story that would have been worth pursuing by the commission. "For example, at the time of the assassination, Ruby was sitting in the Dallas News building in a room from which he could have watched Oswald get off his shots and thus earn his pay. . . . Oswald, after the shooting, was walking in the direction of Ruby's apartment where, one might presume, Oswald expected to pick up his pay. Apparently Oswald changed directions to the Texas Theatre after the killing of Tippit." (Penn Jones, Jr., *Pardon my Grief, v.1,* 1966, p.55) This scenario would not be consistent with the hypothesis that an Oswald double was standing in the sixth floor window, but given the conflicting witness testimony about what was going on in the window, a commission whose task was really to get to the bottom of things might have at least called Jarnagin to testify in person to answer questions about the conversation he said he witnessed.

In 1968, researcher Barry Ernest visited Jarnagin in his Dallas office. This was the second time Ernest had interviewed Jarnagin. Ernest marveled at Jarnagin's recall from the previous meeting which had taken place four months earlier. Ernest wrote that Jarnagin "proceeded to tell me my name, where I was from, and the exact date and time of our previous meeting. He brought forth details of my past I had not remembered telling him during the idle chatter I apparently had lapsed into while we had talked last March. Then he gave me a verbatim recitation of the questions I had asked him back then and the answers he had provided, all without benefit of notes. The man had total recall." (Barry Ernest, *The Girl on the Stairs,* 2013, p.114)

Whatever one's view of Jarnagin's credibility, it cannot be said that his detailed recall of the conversation between Ruby and Oswald was beyond his capability. Jarnagin told Ernest he was hesitant to reveal too much because of the number of witnesses who had already turned up dead in Dallas. He did, however, re-affirm to Ernest that the man he saw talking to Ruby was Lee Oswald. "It was Oswald I saw that night at the club. . . . I know it was him." (Ernest, p.115, 117)

Testimony of Wilbyrn Waldon (Robert) Litchfield:
Litchfield was an ex-felon, having served time for forgery when he was 19 years old. At the time of his deposition by the Warren Commission he was 30 years old and was a professional bowler and bowling instructor and a salesman for bowling trophies and supplies. He was unemployed during the latter half of 1963.

Prior to his deposition testimony, Litchfield had submitted a sworn affidavit to the Dallas police stating that he had seen Ruby and Oswald together at the Carousel Club in early November 1963. His affidavit is in the WCHE as Commission Exhibit No. 3149, along with the text of a statement he gave to the Dallas police. (WCHE, v.26, pp.840a-845b) Litchfield stated that he saw Oswald sitting at a table wearing a white V-necked sweater. "The reason I noticed this man was that everyone else in the Carousel was either in a suit, sport coat, or in uniform." There were two other people waiting to see Ruby. When Ruby came into the club, he met first with these two other people, then with Oswald. Litchfield says that Ruby and Oswald walked back toward Ruby's office and were gone about 15 to 20 minutes. Litchfield stated that "the gentleman in the V-neck white sweater and grey slacks walked by me underneath a bright light by the door. He was approximately two feet from where I was sitting. (WCHE, v.26, p.840a-b). According to Litchfield, "after President Kennedy was assassinated, and this fellow Oswald's picture was on television and in the paper, I remembered that he was the man that I saw in the white V-neck sweater the night that I was at the Carousel Club to see Jack Ruby. I didn't say anything for about a week until Sunday, December 2, 1963, and then I called Don Green, a friend of mine, and told him about it, and asked his advice. He suggested that I come in and talk to the police." (WCHE, v.26, p.841a) Litchfield explained that his friend Green is an officer on the vice squad with the Dallas police. (WCHE, v.14, p.102)

Attached to the affidavit as part of CE3149 is an unsworn statement from Detective R. D. Lewis of the Dallas police, relating the results of a polygraph examination which he said was given to Litchfield. Lewis wrote that "it is the opinion of this examiner that this person has been untruthful to the above questions." No raw data is presented to substantiate this opinion, but Lewis does state that "Mr. Litchfield tried for the first half of the examination to control his breathing pattern." (WCHE, v.26, p.841b) We have already seen in connection with the report of Carroll Jarnagin that there is no scientific basis for using a polygraph examination to determine whether a witness is testifying truthfully. But the Dallas police used the polygraph on several occasions to challenge the credibility of witnesses whose testimony was inconvenient, such as Jarnagin and Litchfield.

At his deposition on April 16, 1964, Litchfield described the polygraph examination, and his treatment by police and federal agents, to commission attorney Leon Hubert.

> LITCHFIELD: And the tests showed that I hadn't seen him because when the man giving it asked me, "Have you definitely seen him," and I said, "Yes," and it showed that I hadn't.
> HUBERT: You mean he told you the results of the test?
> LITCHFIELD: No, he didn't tell me the results of the test, but Donald [Green] did. (WCHE, v.14, p.103)
> . . . .
> HUBERT: Did you ever tell them that the man I now know is Oswald from the films and that I am now picking him out is also the man that I saw at the Carousel?
> LITCHFIELD: I did.
> HUBERT: You told them that?
> LITCHFIELD: Yes, sir.
> HUBERT: And you believe that to be true?
> LITCHFIELD: I thought it was until they convinced me I was wrong.
> HUBERT: What do you think about it now?
> LITCHFIELD: I said, "It sure as heck looked like him," that's all I can say now. Of course, I don't want to say I'm definitely positive it is – I said, "It's a heck of a close resemblance." . . . And when the police were questioning me, they said, "Are you positive, are you positive, are you positive?" I said, "It looks like him, it looks like him, it looks like him." And they come back, "Are you positive, are you positive?" And then the fact that when the Federal agents talked to me, they said, "You know, if you say you are positive and it wasn't him," it's a Federal charge, and I said, "Well, I'm not that positive." . . .
> HUBERT: Well, are you conveying to me that you really were positive, but that –
> LITCHFIELD: In my mind. . . .
> HUBERT: But, what has caused you to weaken in your opinion it was Oswald, as you tell it to me, is the fact that you got the impression that if you gave a positive identification and it proved to be false, that it would be a Federal offense, is that correct?
> LITCHFIELD: Yes. (WCHE, v.14, p.107-108)

We see here a common technique for getting a witness to waver from a positive statement. A witness who is 99.9 percent certain in their testimony can be made to admit, "Well, I'm not 100 percent sure," and having gotten this admission, the investigators can dismiss the statement on the grounds that the witness is "uncertain" in his or her testimony. In Litchfield's deposition, we must give credit to Leon Hubert for bringing out the circumstances of Litchfield's retraction, and eliciting testimony about the pressure tactics used by the police and federal agents.

The Warren Report concedes that Litchfield may have seen a man enter Ruby's office at the Carousel Club, but "there is strong reason to believe that Litchfield did not see Lee Harvey Oswald." The report goes on to describe this "strong reason": "Litchfield described the man he saw as having pockmarks on the right side of his chin; Oswald did not have such identifying marks. Moreover, the Commission has substantial doubts concerning Litchfield's credibility." The report then notes Litchfield's two convictions for forgery, without mentioning that these convictions occurred more than a decade before his testimony. (WCR, p.361) The report also mentions that two of Litchfield's poker buddies "added that Litchfield's statements were often untrustworthy." (WCR, p.362) Here we have the ad hominem argument again – if a man's character is questionable, then everything he says must be a lie. This is clearly an invalid argument. If it were valid, then prosecutors would never be able to use testimony from a jailhouse snitch to convict another prisoner, but we know this happens all the time.

Testimony of William Crowe (aka Bill Demar):

Crowe was an entertainer who worked at Ruby's Carousel Club under the name of Bill Demar as an emcee and also performed as a ventriloquist, standup comedian, and impressionist. One of his acts was a memory trick, in which several members of the audience would each call out a different object, and Crowe then would go around and name the object that each of them had called out. According to an FBI report dated November 24,1963, "a photograph of Lee Harvey Oswald . . . taken August 9, 1963 [by the New Orleans Police Department] was exhibited to Demar, and Demar said he believes this is the man he saw seated among the patrons of the Carousel Club 'one night last week'. . . . He observed Oswald seated in the group around the runway in the club and due to the seating arrangement at this club, he, Demar, would be unable to say whether or not Oswald had a party or group with him at the time he was seen. . . . He believes Oswald was among a number of persons at the club that was used by him in performing this memory demonstration." (WCHE, v.19, p.385)

On November 25, 1963, Crowe submitted a sworn statement to the Secret Service, in which he stated: "Sometime between November 11, 1963 and November 16, 1963 I think that I saw Lee Harvey Oswald in the Carousel Club. I think that he was one of the people in the club that assisted in my [memory] act. . . . Due to the dim lighting in the Carousel Club I cannot say that this was the man for sure, but after seeing his picture in the paper it looked like him." He does not recall ever seeing Oswald and Ruby talking together. (WCHE, v.19, p.386)

Crowe had been more definite in an interview reported by the Associated Press, which reads as follows: "Entertainer Bill Demar of Evansville, Ind., told the

Associated Press by telephone today he was positive Lee Harvey Oswald was a patron about nine days ago in the Dallas night club of Jack Ruby. . . . Demar, Bill Crowe in private life, had completed two weeks of a five-week engagement at Ruby's Carousel Club when it was closed indefinitely Friday. "I have a memory act," the magician-ventriloquist said, in which I have 20 customers call out various objects in rapid order. Then I tell them at random what they called out. I am positive Oswald was one of the men that called out an object about nine days ago." (AP Wire Service report dated November 24, 1963, reproduced in CD87, p.104)

Nearly six months after his statements to the FBI, the Secret Service and the Associated Press, Crowe was called in for a deposition, and was questioned by commission counsel Leon Hubert.

> HUBERT: You tell us now that you have a distinct recollection of having thought to yourself when you saw . . . Oswald's picture in the paper that 'I have seen this man and I saw him, I think, in the Carousel Club last week.' Although you didn't convey that to anybody?
> CROWE: No.
> HUBERT: That actually occurred, and that thought went through your mind?
> CROWE: I would say so, yes." (WCHE, v.15, p.107)

Crowe tells Hubert that a newsman friend of his in Evansville, Indiana – David Hoy – called him in Dallas sometime on Sunday, November 24, 1963, and told him that he [Hoy] had been contacted by a certain news service which "had suggested that he tell me to make myself scarce or to hide out or to move and let my whereabouts not be known."

> HUBERT: Did he say why you should take such action?
> CROWE: He said that it had been expressed to him that my life would be in danger.
> HUBERT: Did he tell you why he thought or he had heard that your life might be in danger?
> CROWE: Because I had mentioned about seeing Oswald in the club." (WCHE, v.15, p.110)
> . . . .
> HUBERT: Would you give us your present recollection concerning whether Lee Harvey Oswald was in the Carousel Club on the week preceding the death of the President?
> CROWE: From what I recall, the face appeared familiar, and I possibly saw Lee Harvey Oswald in the club the week before. . . . I might say this: Bill Willis, the drummer in the band at the club, said he seemed to remember Lee Harvey Oswald sitting in the front row on Thursday night right in the corner of the stage and the runway. (WCHE, v.15, p.111)

The commission chose not to interview drummer Bill Willis, relying instead on an FBI interview in which "Willis advised that he thought also that the photographs of Oswald resembled a patron who had participated in the show a few nights ago. . . . Willis stated he is not sure he has the same man in mind that Demar has referred to. He believes it is only remotely possible this man is identical to Oswald, and is personally convinced there was only a superficial resemblance." (WCHE, v.25, p.506)

The Warren Report devotes a full page and more to an effort to discredit Crowe's Oswald sighting on the basis of Crowe's "uncertainty". The report noted that "no other *employees* recalled seeing Oswald or a person resembling him at the Carousel Club." (WCR, p.361)

The treatment of Jarnagin, Litchfield, and Crowe illustrates Penn Jones' observation that "when a witness's testimony indicated a conspiracy, the Warren Commission showed flexibility of methods in destroying the credibility of such witness." (Penn Jones, Jr., *Forgive my Grief, v.1,* p.171)

Other evidence of a connection between Ruby and Oswald before the assassination:
Larry Crafard, part-time handyman and general assistant at Ruby's Carousel Club, stated in his deposition that "I believe that before I left Dallas I had heard someone state that Oswald had been in the Carousel Club on at least one previous occasion, that I wasn't positive who had made the statement, that I believed that it was made before I left Dallas. . . . I thought it had been Andrew" [Armstrong, Ruby's assistant manager]. (WCHE, v.14, p.46)

Dallas District Attorney Henry Wade testified before the commission that "we have . . . some 8 or 10 witnesses who have said they had seen Ruby and Oswald together at various times." The only one he mentions by name is Carroll Jarnagin. (WCHE, v.5, p.232)

An article in the Dallas Morning News by Earl Golz, dated March 28, 1976, quotes a Dallas deputy sheriff by the name of Billy Preston, who told the reporter that in late 1963 or early 1964 he (Preston) and constable Robie Love turned over to District Attorney Henry Wade a box of papers they received from a Dallas woman several weeks after the assassination. The woman's roommate had been hiding the papers for her boy friend, who was described as a "Latin American". In addition to Preston, deputies Ben Cash and Mike Callahan had examined the contents of the box. "Preston and Cash also said they saw a receipt for a motel near New Orleans dated several weeks before the assassination with Oswald's and Ruby's names on it. The receipt showed several telephone calls to numbers in Mexico City which were later found to be those of the Cuban and Russian embassies." Cash is quoted in the article as saying that he and Preston kept quiet about the documents, because of the implications of tying Cuba and Russia to the assassination. "Because at that time it was a pretty hot issue, you remember. So we kept quiet and went along with the game." (Earl Golz, "Papers Link Ruby, Oswald", *Dallas Morning News*, March 28, 1976, p.30A, reproduced in FBI 62-109060 JFK HQ File, Section 185, p.106-107) The date of the motel receipt is not given in the article, so it is impossible to tell whether this incident occurred before or after Oswald's trip to Mexico. Of course the Cuba and Russia connections can be played both ways: either as evidence that Cuba and/or Russia were involved with Oswald in plotting the Kennedy assassination, or that Oswald, as a U. S. intelligence operative, was scheming to get into Cuba in order to assassinate Castro, as part of the CIA's collaboration with organized crime to overthrow Castro – a plan which was not known at the time of the Warren Commission, but was revealed in congressional investigations during the 1970s.

Conclusion

The evidence for an association between Ruby and Oswald before the assassination is inconclusive. Jarnagin's credibility is not firmly established, although it is not necessary for him to have perfect recall of the conversation between Ruby and Oswald in order to establish the fact that he saw the two men together at the Carousel Club. Litchfield's sighting is perhaps stronger, given his detailed description of the man's attire and the close-up look he had of the man's face. Crowe's identification of Oswald in the audience is vague and uncertain, under dim lighting. Crafard's assertion is hearsay and he is not even sure who he got it from. The papers turned over to Henry Wade by Deputies Preston and Cash have not turned up since then and cannot be examined to see what they actually contain. While it remains possible that Ruby and Oswald knew each other before the assassination, and that Ruby was Oswald's "handler" inside the conspiracy, we cannot say that the evidence is strong enough to draw a firm conclusion – but neither can we rule it out. There are enough witnesses who say they saw Ruby and Oswald together before the assassination that the total weight of this evidence cannot easily be put aside. On balance, we might say that the evidence tilts slightly toward a pre-assassination acquaintance between Ruby and Oswald, but not enough to meet the standard of beyond reasonable doubt.

Seth Kantor adopts a cautious approach when he says, "Ruby and Oswald probably didn't know each other; yet both could have been used as separate parts of a conspiracy to commit murder in Dallas on the weekend of November 22-24, 1963. Oswald on Friday. Ruby on Sunday. Two men separately manipulated by the same power." (Kantor, *The Ruby Cover-up,* p.397)

We might mention here that Judyth Vary Baker, in her book *Me and Lee,* describes in some detail numerous pre-assassination encounters between Oswald and Ruby, whom she knew as "Sparky" Rubenstein. She also describes an association between Oswald and organized crime boss Carlos Marcello of New Orleans. As we noted earlier, we will not undertake a detailed assessment of Baker's credibility here, but her book is an important contribution to the assassination literature and must be reckoned with by anyone seeking to fill in the gaps of Oswald's activities in the summer and fall of 1963.

WAS OSWALD A COMMUNIST?

Being a Communist could mean many things in 1963. It could mean that you were a card-carrying member of the American Communist Party, or it might mean you were in favor of school integration and equal rights for black people. You might also have been called a communist if you were in favor of peaceful coexistence with the Soviet Union instead of advocating a fight to the death to destroy the Soviet tyranny before it engulfed the entire free world.

While acknowledging that it could find no single motive that prompted Oswald to assassinate the President, the Warren Commission did find that "his commitment to Marxism and communism appears to have been [one] important factor in his motivation." (WCR, p.423) This was an easy sell in 1963. Most Americans would have agreed with the premise that communism was the mortal enemy of the United States. It was only natural that our mortal enemies would try to do us harm, and so assassinating our President was only to be expected from a communist. The fact that the vast majority of American communists had no such violent tendencies was a detail that did not come into the discussion. And the commission made no effort to determine whether assassinating President Kennedy would actually further the interests of either the Soviet or Cuban regimes.

Oswald's career as a "Communist agitator"

FBI agent John Fain submitted a report dated August 30, 1962, on his observation of Oswald. Fain reported that his confidential informants informed him that neither Oswald nor his wife Marina were members of the U. S. Communist Party in Fort Worth, nor had they been engaged in any party activities in that area. (CE824 at WCHE, v.17, p.739) Another confidential FBI informant in the New Orleans area, who was familiar with some of the Communist Party activity in that area told the FBI on October 1, 1963 that "Oswald was unknown to the informant." (CE3037 at WCHE, v.26, p.581b) Other New Orleans informants were contacted by the FBI on December 2, 1963, and these informants advised that they did not know anyone by the name of Lee Harvey Oswald or any other Oswald or Hidell, "nor were they aware of the existence of the Fair Play for Cuba Committee (FPCC)". (CE2973 at WCHE, v.26, p.454b)

Silvia Duran, a Cuban embassy employee in Mexico City at the time of Oswald's visit in September-October 1963, told the House Select Committee on Assassinations that the identification documents shown to her by Oswald included a membership card for the American Communist Party. This immediately made Duran suspicious because membership in the Communist Party was illegal in

Mexico and actual Communist party members typically travelled only with their passports and not with any documents that could tie them to the Communist Party. (HSCA segregated CIA collection (staff notes), NARA Record Number: 180-10141-10494, released April 26, 2018, p.10) Although there is no reliable evidence that Oswald was formally a member of the American Communist Party, the FBI Summary Report on the assassination noted that during his activity "supporting the Fair Play for Cuba Committee, Oswald continued to maintain contact with the Communist Party" in the form of letters to party officials and subscriptions to party literature. (CD1, p.66)

The debate around Oswald's alleged communist activities centers on whether he was a genuine communist (whatever that might mean) or whether he was operating on behalf of U. S. intelligence as an agent provocateur for the purpose of embarrassing and discrediting left-leaning organizations like the Fair Play for Cuba Committee. Most of his actions can be interpreted either way. Were his FPCC activities motivated by a genuine admiration for the Castro regime, or by a desire to expose the FPCC as a communist front organization? Did his visits to the Cuban and Soviet embassies in Mexico City indicate a desire to reach Cuba for instructions on assassinating President Kennedy, or was he part of an CIA assassination team whose goal was to kill Castro? Or was his attempt to reach Cuba motivated by his fear that the conspiracy he had infiltrated was getting ready to sacrifice him as the patsy in the murder of President Kennedy, and getting to Cuba or Russia was the only way to save his own life? Was his "defection" to the USSR motivated by sympathy with communist ideology, or by a U. S. intelligence operation to plant U. S. service members as spies in Russia? The options are not mutually exclusive. If Oswald was acting as a double agent, he could have been playing both sides at once.

There is considerable reason to doubt Oswald's sincerity in advocating for communist causes. Even the Warren Report acknowledges that Oswald's FPCC branch in New Orleans "was a product of his imagination. . . . The chapter had never been chartered by the national FPCC organization. It appears to have been a solitary operation on Oswald's part in spite of his misstatements to the New Orleans police that it had 35 members." (WCR, p.407) Oswald explicitly rejected the plea of FPCC national director V. T. Lee that he should not establish an office for the New Orleans FPCC chapter, as it might attract the attention of the "lunatic fringe" in the community. (WCHE, v.20, p.515, 518) Oswald's FPCC activities in New Orleans attracted unfavorable media attention for the organization, while at the same time there is no evidence that he did anything substantial to promote the establishment and growth of an FPCC chapter in that city.

After his return to the United States from the Soviet Union, Oswald's alleged communist activities were sporadic and superficial. Other than a couple of street demonstrations and media appearances in New Orleans during the summer of 1963, Oswald's resumé as a communist agitator appears very skimpy. In a radio debate on August 21, 1963, Oswald argued in favor of the FPCC's position on Cuba, and his opponent argued the anti-Castro position. During the debate, Oswald was exposed as a former defector to the Soviet Union. The debate host, William Stuckey, told the Warren Commission that Oswald "handled himself very well", but Stuckey's assessment was that "we finished him on that program. I think that after that program the Fair Play for Cuba Committee, if there ever was one in New Orleans, had no future there, because we had publicly linked the Fair Play for Cuba Committee with a fellow who had lived in Russia for 3 years and who was an admitted Marxist." (WCHE, v.11, p.171) If Oswald was a genuine FPCC advocate, he certainly was not acting in such a way as to promote the organization's interests. The commission takes this as another indication that Oswald was a failure in everything he did, but given that a number of witnesses commented on Oswald's articulateness and intelligence in discussing political matters, his actions look more like deliberate sabotage of the FPCC's reputation than the actions of a committed Castro supporter.

In a handwritten manuscript, written during his residence in the USSR, Oswald wrote that "no man, having known, having lived, under the Russian Communist and American capitalist system, could possibly make a choice between them. There is no choice. One offers oppression, the other poverty. Both offer imperialistic injustice, tinted with two brands of slavery." (CE97, WCHE, v.16, p.429) In the same manuscript, Oswald wrote of the American Communist Party: "The Communist Party of the United States has betrayed itself! It has turned itself into the traditional lever of a foreign power to overthrow the government of the United States, not in the name of freedom or high ideals, but in servile conformity to the wishes of the Soviet Union and in anticipation of Soviet Russia's complete domination of the American continent." (CE97, WCHE, v.16, p.422)

In these writings, and in his actions, Oswald does not come across as the tool of a foreign power. By his actions and his associations, he looks more like an agent provocateur than a committed communist. If he has any sincere regard for communism at all, it is only an abstract, utopian, idealistic kind of communism. There is no evidence that communist ideology or allegiance to any communist state provided any sort of motive for Oswald to assassinate President Kennedy.

544 Camp Street, New Orleans

One of the strongest pieces of evidence suggesting that Oswald was acting on behalf of U. S. intelligence, or at least on behalf of right wing activists, was the address which appeared on some of the FPCC leaflets that he distributed. The address was 544 Camp Street, New Orleans. (WCHE, v.22, p.828b) The Warren Report noted that "extensive investigation was not able to connect Oswald with that address, although it did develop the fact that an anti-Castro organization had maintained offices there for a period ending early in 1962." (WCR, p.408) But Gaeton Fonzi, an investigator for the House Select Committee on Assassinations, wrote that this address was also associated with "Guy Banister, a former FBI agent who ran anti-Castro activities out of an address at 544 Camp Street, the address on the pro-Castro leaflets Oswald had been distributing." (Gaeton Fonzi, *The Last Investigation (2008)*, p.140-141) Banister's secretary, Delphine Roberts, told author Anthony Summers that in 1963, Oswald walked into Banister's office at 544 Camp Street, and asked to fill out an application for accreditation as one of Banister's agents. Roberts told Summers, "I gained the impression that he [Oswald] and Guy Banister already knew each other." (Anthony Summers, *Not in Your Lifetime* (2013), p.277)

Oswald as FBI informant

If Oswald could be shown to have been working for U. S. intelligence or law enforcement agencies this would severely undercut the claim that he was a communist and that he was motivated to kill the President by his devotion to communist ideology or by his allegiance to the communist regimes in either Cuba or the USSR. The Warren Commission sought to dispel the notion that Oswald was working on behalf of American intelligence or law enforcement by inviting CIA Director John McCone and FBI Director J. Edgar Hoover to testify before the commission. They were both asked whether Oswald had been employed or engaged in any capacity with their agencies. "No," replied McCone. (WCHE, v.5, p.120) "No," replied Hoover. (WCHE, v.5, p.98) And that was the end of that discussion.

The appearances of McCone and Hoover had been occasioned by an alarming report that Oswald may have been an FBI informant. In the commission's executive session held January 27, 1964, the minutes of which were originally marked "Top Secret", Rankin told the commission about a call he had received from Texas Attorney General Waggoner Carr, in which Carr was "quite excited". (*Warren Commission Executive Session of 27 Jan 1964*, p.128); Carr had information which had come out during proceedings in Jack Ruby's trial, to the effect that "Oswald was an undercover agent for the FBI." Rankin reported further that Carr "also knew the number that was assigned by the FBI to Oswald which was No. 179, and he knew that he was on the payroll or employed, I think that is the way he put it, employed by the FBI at $200 per month from September of 1962 up to the time of the assassination. That was all he [Carr] knew about it." Carr told Rankin that his source for this information was "a person in whom he had complete faith and could rely upon." (WC Exec Session of 27 Jan 1964, p.129) Rankin also told the commission that another source, Dallas Deputy Sheriff Allen Sweatt, had provided information to the Secret Service that "Oswald was an undercover agent and was being paid so much a month for some time back to September, and that it had a number which he gave and that report as No. 172. This report by the Secret Service agent was of a conference or inquiry that he made in the area to Sweatt back on December 17th. The report was dated January 3, and we didn't get it until January 23. . . . We wondered whether the Secret Service was withholding something from us." (WC Exec Session of 27 Jan 1964, p.131) Rankin refers to this story as a "dirty rumor that is very bad for the Commission . . . and it is very damaging to the agencies that are involved in it and *it must be wiped out* insofar as it is possible to do so by this Commission." (WC Exec Session of 27 Jan 1964, p.139)

A Secret Service report dated January 3, 1964 also named Deputy Sweatt as providing similar information to reporter Alonzo Hudkins of the Houston Post. Sweatt told Hudkins that Oswald was being paid $200 per month by the FBI as an informant in connection with their subversive investigations. (CD320, p.116) Another Secret Service report mentioned that within several days after Oswald's death, Marina Oswald was found to be in possession of a wallet belonging to Oswald, and in the wallet was $180 in cash (eight $20's and two $10's, in relatively new bills). Marina told the Secret Service agent that she did not know where the money came from, but that it was money that Oswald had been "saving". (WCHE, v.23, p.418a-b)

Supporting the allegation that Oswald was an FBI informant is the fact that when he was arrested in New Orleans, he specifically requested to speak with a representative of the FBI. The New Orleans police contacted the local FBI office, and FBI agent John L. Quigley came to visit Oswald in his cell. (WCHE, v.4, p.432) In view of the fact that some of the information that Oswald provided to Quigley about the non-existent FPCC chapter was false, one wonders whether Oswald's purpose was simply to feed the FBI enough information to keep them satisfied so that they would continue paying him the $200 per month stipend as an informant.

Oswald's connections to U. S. intelligence

The standard work on Oswald's connections with the CIA is John Newman's *Oswald and the CIA*. Newman's 600+ page book cannot be comprehensively surveyed here, but several of his conclusions can be highlighted as important for determining whether Oswald was working for the CIA, and how he might have been set up to take the rap for President Kennedy's assassination. Newman notes that when Oswald went to the Soviet Union, threatening to reveal U. S. military secrets to the Russians, the CIA did not open a personality file (known as a "201 file") on him, but the agency did add Oswald to its mail monitoring program, which allowed his mail to be opened and read. This, as Newman notes, is unusual. It "makes Oswald special . . . as if someone wanted Oswald watched quietly". Newman concludes that "the anomalies surrounding Oswald's early CIA files encourage speculation about whether or not U. S. intelligence had a hand in Oswald's defection." (Newman, *Oswald and the CIA* (2008), p.421-422, originally published 1995) Newman notes further that a review of the available CIA records on Oswald enable us to "say with some authority that the CIA was spawning a web of deception about Oswald weeks before the president's murder, a fact that may have directly contributed to the outcome in Dallas." Newman does not find documentary evidence of an "institutional plot" by the CIA, but finds that the facts may well fit into the "renegade faction" hypothesis. (Newman, p.430)

In the 2008 epilogue to his book, Newman, a history professor and former military intelligence officer, stated, on the basis of records made public up to that time, "I do not know who directly handled Oswald in 1963, but someone involved in the murder of the President did." He noted that many researchers think this was David Atlee Phillips, "who at the time of Oswald's visit to Mexico City, was head of Cuban operations at the CIA station there. . . . Whether or not Oswald's handler or handlers understood that their activities would lead to the death of the president, they were nevertheless taking cues from someone in CIA counterintelligence who was harnessed to the plot." (Newman, p.614) Newman finds reason to believe that Oswald's trip to Mexico City was designed to associate him with the Soviet and Cuban embassies there, and with Valeriy Kostikov, KGB assassination operative, who just happened to work at the Soviet embassy issuing visas. (Newman, p.615)

Newman found that CIA information on Oswald's visit to Mexico City was suppressed, resulting in a lowering of his threat profile before the assassination. This resulted in Oswald's removal from the FBI's watch list, and "ensured that Oswald would not be placed on the security index, and therefore would be on the parade route when the president's motorcade passed the Texas School Book Depository." (Newman, p.630) Whether as assassin or as patsy, Oswald was being set up to take the blame for the President's assassination.

While Newman does not find evidence that the CIA "as an organization" instigated the assassination, he does find the evidence compelling that some elements in the CIA, and one person in particular, were responsible for plotting to kill Kennedy. Newman concludes: "The person who designed this plot had to have access to all of the information on Oswald at CIA HQS [headquarters]. The person who designed this plot had to have the authority to alter how information on Oswald was kept at CIA HQS. The person who designed this plot had to have access to . . . the sensitive joint agency operation against the KGB assassin, Valeriy Kostikov. The person who designed this plot had the authority to instigate a counterintelligence operation in the Cuban affairs staff at CIA HQS. In my view, there is only one person whose hands fit into these gloves: James Jesus Angleton, Chief of CIA's Counterintelligence Staff. . . . Whoever Oswald's direct handler or handlers were, we must now seriously consider the possibility that Angleton was probably their general manager. No one else in the Agency had the access, the authority, and the diabolically ingenious mind to manage this sophisticated plot." (Newman, p.636-637) Newman notes that the cover-up was ensured by the Soviet and Cuban connections that were built in to the plot. Neither the CIA nor the FBI wanted to be seen as missing the obvious clues about Oswald's connection to the Soviet assassination expert, Valeriy Kostikov, or Oswald's urgent desire to travel to Cuba, possibly to receive instructions from Castro himself. President Johnson had no desire to let these details of a possible Cuban connection leak out, because it might lead to irresistible demands for military retaliation against Castro, which would surely lead to nuclear confrontation with the Soviet Union. Once President Kennedy had been assassinated, the entire federal government had ample reason to close the case quickly and cleanly, by blaming the tragedy on a single assassin, acting on his own.

One more confirmation of Oswald's CIA connections comes from Antonio Veciana, leader of the anti-Castro Cuban exile group Alpha 66, and participant in the CIA-assisted plots to assassinate Fidel Castro. Gaeton Fonzi, an investigator for the House Select Committee on Assassinations, conducted numerous interviews with Veciana, and in one of those interviews Veciana told Fonzi about a meeting he, Veciana, had with his CIA handler, a man known to Veciana as Maurice Bishop. In September 1963, arriving early for a meeting with Bishop in the lobby of a large office building in downtown Dallas, Veciana saw Bishop standing in a corner of the lobby talking with a young man. Bishop soon ended his conversation with the young man, and the three men walked out of the building together. After a few additional words, the young man went on his way, and Bishop and Veciana proceeded to a nearby coffee shop to discuss matters related to the activities of Alpha 66. Veciana later recognized Lee Harvey Oswald as the man he saw talking with Bishop. As Fonzi describes it, "on the day that John F. Kennedy was assassinated, Veciana immediately recognized the news photographs and television images of Lee Harvey Oswald as being of the young man he had seen with Maurice Bishop in Dallas. There was no doubt in his mind. When I asked if it could have been someone who closely resembled Oswald, Veciana said, 'Well, you know, Bishop himself taught me how to remember faces, how to remember characteristics. I am sure it was Oswald.'" (Gaeton Fonzi, *The Last Investigation,* 2008, p.141-142) Based on a composite drawing of "Bishop" drawn from Veciana's description, suspicion fell on CIA officer David Atlee Phillips as the man Veciana knew as Maurice Bishop. But there was no confirmation of this identification until Veciana, in his eighties and no longer fearing for himself or his family, positively identified David Phillips as his CIA handler during his time as leader of Alpha 66. In a book published in 2017, Veciana wrote that "my CIA case officer, the man whom I knew as Maurice Bishop, was actually David Atlee Phillips. . . . And I saw Phillips conferring with Lee Harvey Oswald in a Dallas office building not long before the killing of JFK." (Antonio Veciana and Carlos Harrison, *Trained to Kill: The Inside Story of CIA Plots against Castro, Kennedy, and Che* (2017), p.201). Veciana related that he had kept quiet about Phillips' identity for many years out of fear for his family and to show the CIA that he could be trusted, even to the point of lying under oath to the HSCA. (Veciana, p.202)

Conclusion

Was Oswald a communist? Or was his communist image just a pose to facilitate infiltration of allegedly subversive organizations like the FPCC? The evidence indicates that Oswald may have had some vague, idealistic, utopian beliefs about social justice and economic fairness. But these certainly did not rise to the level of a coherent political ideology and did not take the form of formal membership in any party or organization, other than his one-man FPCC chapter. His connections with right wing elements such as Guy Banister, and with the FBI and CIA, indicate that whatever political beliefs he may have had at a personal level, operationally he was firmly planted within the anti-communist camp of U. S. intelligence and federal law enforcement.

OSWALD AND THE ANTI-CASTRO CUBAN EXILES

The Odio incident

For the Warren Commission, one of the most disturbing reports in their investigation was the allegation that Oswald was seen in the company of two Cuban-looking men visiting the Dallas apartment of Sylvia Odio, an anti-Castro Cuban exile, whose parents were imprisoned in Castro's Cuba. The Warren Report devotes nearly three pages to this incident. (WCR, pp.321-324) Odio was the daughter of Amador and Sarah Odio, who had been early supporters of Castro but subsequently turned against him, on the grounds that Castro "betrayed the revolution". But Castro arrested both of Sylvia's parents in October 1961, and Sylvia, who had been living in Puerto Rico at the time of her parents' arrest, eventually moved to Dallas with her four children in March of 1963, having been abandoned by her husband. She maintained contact with anti-Castro Cubans in the Dallas area, had a job and an apartment, where her younger sister Annie was helping to look after the children. While in Dallas, Sylvia and her younger sisters joined the anti-Castro group known as JURE (Junta Revolucionaria). (Gaeton Fonzi, *The Last Investigation*, p.109-111)

On December 18, 1963, Sylvia Odio was interviewed by FBI agents James Hosty and Bardwell Odum. She advised the agents that "she is a Cuban refugee and a member of the organization known as Junta Revolucionaria or JURE. Miss Odio stated that in late September or early October, 1963, two Cuban men came to her house and stated they were from JURE. They were accompanied by an individual whom they introduced as Leon Oswald. Miss Odio stated that based upon photographs she has seen of Lee Harvey Oswald she is certain that Leon Oswald is identical with Lee Harvey Oswald. . . . Miss Odio stated the purpose of their visit was to ask her to write some letters to various businesses in Dallas and request funds for JURE." She told the agents that she declined the men's request because she was afraid of repercussions for her parents who were incarcerated in Cuba. (CD205, p.643)

During her deposition by Wesley Liebeler, Odio said that one of the Cubans, who went by the name "Leopoldo", called her the next day and asked her, "What do you think of the American?" And she told him, "I didn't think anything." She told Liebeler that Leopoldo said, "You know our idea is to introduce him to the underground in Cuba, because he is great, he is kind of nuts. . . . He told us we don't have any guts, you Cubans, because President Kennedy should have been assassinated after the Bay of Pigs, and some Cubans should have done that. . . . And he said, 'It is so easy to do it." (WCHE, v.11, p.372) Odio told Liebeler that as soon as she saw the pictures of Oswald on the news after the assassination, she was sure that he was the man who accompanied the two Cubans who visited her. (WCHE, v.11, p.382)

The alleged visit of Oswald to Odio's apartment was a problem for the commission because it indicated that Oswald might have had associations with anti-Castro groups who may have been accomplices in the Kennedy assassination. A second problem emerged after analyzing the timeline, because Odio testified that the visit was on a Thursday or Friday "in the last days of September" 1963. This would narrow it down to September 26 or 27. It turns out that Oswald could not have been at Odio's apartment on those days and still have been in Mexico when the commission said he was, by using public transportation. He would have had to use some form of private transportation. Since Oswald was not known to drive a car, this meant he would have been traveling with someone in order to make his bus connection to Mexico. The timing problem, plus the visit to Odio's apartment, indicated associations which implied that Oswald may have been acting with others and was not the loner the commission pictured him as. As the Warren Report put it, the commission considered Odio's testimony important "in view of the possibility it raised that Oswald may have had companions on his trip to Mexico." (WCR, p.324)

The Odio visit continued to cause discomfort for the Warren Commission well into the summer of 1964. It was still unresolved as the Warren Report was being prepared for publication. On August 28, commission counsel Lee Rankin wrote to FBI Director Hoover, telling Hoover that "it is a matter of some importance to the Commission that Mrs. Odio's allegations either be proved or disproved." (WCHE, v.26, p.595b) He continued, "Would you please conduct the investigation necessary to determine who it was that Mrs. Odio saw in or about late September or early October 1963." (WCHE, v.26, p.596a) After noting the dates of other known events, Rankin concluded that "The only time [Oswald] could have been in Odio's apartment appears to be the nights of September 24 or 25, 1963, most likely the latter. . . . Oswald could have been in Dallas on the night of September 25, 1963 and still have been on the bus on which he was seen by Dr. and Mrs. John B. McFarland, according to your letterhead memorandum on Oswald dated December 23, 1963." (WCHE, v.26, p.596b)

Hoover obliged by responding to Rankin in a letter dated September 21, 1964. Hoover advised Rankin that the FBI had "located one Loran Eugene Hall at Johnsondale, California. Hall has been identified as a participant in numerous anti-Castro activities. He advised that in September, 1963, he was at Dallas, Texas, soliciting aid in connection with an anti-Castro cause. He recalled meeting a Cuban woman, Mrs. Odio, who lived in a garden-type apartment at 1080 Magellan Circle, Dallas, Texas. He said that at the time of his visit he was accompanied by Lawrence Howard, a Mexican-American from East Los Angeles, and William Seymour from Arizona. He denied that Lee Harvey Oswald was with him during his visit to Mrs. Odio's apartment in September, 1963. Hall stated that William Seymour is similar in appearance to Lee Harvey Oswald and that Seymour speaks only a few words of

Spanish." (WCHE, v.26, p.834b) Hoover continues, "You will note that the name Loran Hall bears some phonetic resemblance to the name Leon Oswald." (WCHE, v.26, p.835a) This was the commission's escape hatch from the Odio problem. The Warren Commission submitted its final report to President Johnson on September 24. In the Warren Report, the commission explained the Odio incident as follows: "On September 16, 1964, the FBI located Loran Eugene Hall in Johnsondale, California. Hall has been identified as a participant in numerous anti-Castro activities. He told the FBI that in September of 1963 he was in Dallas, soliciting aid in connection with anti-Castro activities. He said he had visited Mrs. Odio. He was accompanied by Lawrence Howard, a Mexican-American from East Los Angeles and one William Seymour from Arizona. He stated that Seymour is similar in appearance to Lee Harvey Oswald; he speaks only a few words of Spanish, as Mrs. Odio had testified one of the men who visited her did. While the FBI had not yet completed its investigation into this matter at the time the report went to press, the Commission has concluded that Lee Harvey Oswald was not at Mrs. Odio's apartment in September of 1963." (WCR, p.324) Problem solved.

Except that on November 9, 1964, the FBI said "Never mind." Loran Hall and his friends were not at Sylvia Odio's apartment after all. But the Warren Report was already out with the now discredited story. In a letter to Lee Rankin, Hoover said the FBI's subsequent investigation found that William Seymour was working in Florida during late September and October 1963, and had never met Sylvia Odio. His presence in Florida during this time was verified by payroll records at Seymour's job. (CD1553, p.19) Lawrence Howard was also interviewed and he "denied any contact with a Cuban woman named Odio at Dallas." (CD1553, p.20). Seymour further described Loran Hall as a "loud mouthed, filthy talking liar". (CD1553, p.27) When Hall himself was re-interviewed by the FBI he recanted his story about meeting Sylvia Odio in Dallas. (CD1553, p.29)

So the Odio story remained unrefuted, and the timing problem resurfaced. But with the Warren Report safely into publication, and President Johnson safely elected to his own term as president, the Odio problem would remain buried in the 26 volumes of hearings and exhibits, which were published several weeks after the report, and after the 1964 presidential election.

The Warren Report set forth the chronology which led it to conclude that Oswald could not have been at Sylvia Odio's apartment on either September 26 or 27, 1963. The commission, it said, had "developed considerable evidence that he was not in Dallas at any time between the beginning of September and October 3, 1963. . . . Oswald is known to have been in New Orleans as late as September 23, 1963, the date on which Mrs. Paine and Marina Oswald left New Orleans for Dallas. Sometime between 4 p.m. on September 24 and 1 p.m. on September 25, Oswald cashed an unemployment compensation check at a store in New Orleans. Under normal procedures this check would not have reached Oswald's postal box in New Orleans until at least 5 a.m. on September 25. The store at which he cashed the check did not open until 8 a.m. Therefore, it appeared that Oswald's presence in

New Orleans until sometime between 8 a.m. and 1 p.m. on September 25 was quite firmly established." (WCR, p.323)

The Warren Report then notes that there is "strong evidence" that Oswald proceeded to Mexico by traveling on a Continental Trailways bus (No. 5133) which left Houston at 2:35 a.m. on September 26, bound for Laredo, Texas. Bus company records confirmed that one such ticket was sold during the night shift, and "two English passengers, Dr. and Mrs. John B. McFarland, testified that they saw Oswald riding alone on this bus shortly after they awoke at 6 a.m. [The purchase of a ticket in Houston would seem to suggest that Oswald did not arrive in Houston by bus, since if he had left Dallas, or New Orleans, by bus, he would surely have bought a through ticket that did not require him to buy another ticket in Houston for the second leg of his journey.]

The bus was scheduled to arrive in Laredo at 1:20 p.m. on September 26, and Mexican immigration records show that Oswald in fact crossed the border at Laredo to Nuevo Laredo, Mexico, between 6 a.m. and 2 p.m. on that day." (WCR, p.323) However, the Warren Report noted a gap not accounted for "between the morning of September 25 and 2:35 a.m. on September 26". But the commission rules out this time for the visit to Odio because "the only public means of transportation by which Oswald could have traveled from New Orleans to Dallas in time to catch his bus from Houston to Laredo, would have been the airlines. Investigation disclosed no indication that he flew between these points." (WCR, p.323) But the commission did not consider whether Oswald had access to private air transportation. If Oswald was indeed associating with anti-Castro Cubans, it is not inconceivable that they could have had access to private planes provided by financial backers or by their CIA partners.

In fact, this is exactly what happened, according to Judyth Vary Baker. In her memoir, *Me and Lee,* she related that Oswald got from New Orleans to Dallas on a private plane, a De Havilland Dove, owned by an oil field services company. She described Oswald leaving the New Orleans area on this plane on the morning of September 25, and traveling first to Austin, Texas and then to Dallas, as he carried out some courier errands, picking up and dropping off various bags and parcels. Baker says that Oswald arrived in Dallas around sunset, and was met by two Hispanic men who drove him around as he completed his errands, and then visited a woman "who was active in the anti-Castro community to see if she had contacts in Mexico City. After completing his tasks in Dallas, Oswald boarded the de Havilland again and was flown to Houston in time to catch the 2:35 a.m. bus to Laredo on September 26. Baker points out that numerous witnesses recalled seeing Oswald on the bus from Houston to Laredo, but no witnesses have come forward to say that they saw him on the bus from New Orleans to Houston, or Dallas to Houston. (Baker, *Me and Lee,* p.493-499) The woman he visited in Dallas could very likely have been Sylvia Odio, on the evening of September 25, 1963, which is within the timeframe when Odio recalled being visited by the three men.

There is a postscript to the Odio incident which has not been widely publicized. The Warren Commission had in its files an FBI report (CE3108) dated November 29, 1963 summarizing an interview with a Mrs. C. L. (Lucille) Connell of Dallas. Mrs. Connell was a volunteer worker with the Catholic Cuban Relief Committee. She told the FBI that she had become acquainted with Sylvia Odio in her work with the relief committee. Mrs. Connell stated that on November 28, 1963 (one day before the FBI interviewed her), she was told by Sylvia Odio in a telephone conversation that she (Odio) knew Lee Oswald, and that "he had made some talks to small groups of Cuban refugees in Dallas in the past. Odio stated she personally considered Oswald brilliant and clever, and that he had captivated the groups to whom he spoke. . . . Odio volunteered that information was . . . received from [a] New Orleans source to the effect that Oswald was considered by that source in New Orleans to be a 'double agent'. The source stated Oswald was probably trying to infiltrate the Dallas Cuban refugee group, and that he should not be trusted." (WCHE, v.26, p.738b)

For her part, Sylvia Odio (CE3147) "emphatically denied that she had ever told Mrs. C. L. Connell that Lee Harvey Oswald had made talks to small groups of Cuban refugees in Dallas. She similarly denied knowledge of ever telling Mrs. Connell that a Cuban associate of hers had called anyone in New Orleans regarding Oswald, in which this Cuban friend had been advised that Oswald was a double agent attempting to infiltrate Cuban exile groups." She attributed Mrs. Connell's statement to personal animosity, and alleged that Mrs. Connell "was trying to embarrass or get her, Miss Odio, in trouble." (WCHE, v.26, p.837b)

Odio's denial of the Connell report is in an FBI report dated September 9, 1964, nearly a year after Mrs. Connell's FBI interview, and just two weeks before the Warren Report was published. Connell's statements were obtained by the FBI just one day after the alleged phone conversation occurred. Both the Warren Commission and the HSCA were more interested in Oswald's alleged visit to Sylvia Odio's apartment, so did not devote much, if any, energy to establishing the truth of whether Odio did indeed tell Connell that Oswald had spoken to Cuban refugee groups and that he had been identified as a double agent. If we accept Connell's report at face value, then it strengthens Oswald's connection with anti-Castro Cuban exile groups, and supports the hypothesis that he was a double agent, ostensibly working for both sides of the Cuba issue. [The New Orleans source mentioned in Mrs. Connell's interview may have been Carlos Bringuier, a member of the anti-Castro Cuban Student Directorate. Bringuier told Warren Commission attorney Wesley Liebeler that he was "convinced that Oswald was not an FBI agent and that he was a pro-Castro agent." (WCHE, v.10, p.35)]

Conclusion:

The preponderance of the evidence indicates that Oswald visited Sylvia Odio in the company of two Hispanic men on the evening of September 25, 1963 in Dallas. The only way for Oswald to have been in Dallas at that time and still have been on the bus from Houston to Laredo was for him to have traveled to Dallas and then to Houston by airplane, in time to catch the 2:35 a.m. bus to Laredo. Judyth Baker's story thus fills in the gaps and provides a plausible explanation for the known evidence. This explanation is fits a scenario where Oswald is connected with clandestine groups of anti-Castro Cubans and U. S. intelligence operatives.

OSWALD'S MOTIVE?

The Warren Commission utterly failed to put forward a plausible motive for Oswald's killing of the President. The best it could do was to state weakly that "many factors were undoubtedly involved in Oswald's motivation for the assassination, and the Commission does not believe that it can ascribe to him any one motive or group of motives." (WCR, p.423) The report goes on to suggest that some of these "many factors" may have been "an overriding hostility to his environment", his inability to "establish meaningful relationships with other people", his "perpetual discontent", his "hatred for American society", his "commitment to Marxism and communism". (WCR, p.423) The best that the commission can come up with is the speculation that "out of these and the many other factors which may have molded the character of Lee Harvey Oswald there emerged a man capable of assassinating President Kennedy." (WCR, p.424) Thus, the Warren Commission attributes the assassination to Oswald's "character".

But Oswald as lone assassin makes no sense in the context of his previously stated views about President Kennedy and his policies.

Marina Oswald testified that Lee did not express any hostility toward President Kennedy. "From Lee's behavior I cannot conclude that he was against the President." (WCHE, v.1, p.22) She told the commission, "I had never heard anything bad about Kennedy from Lee. And he never had anything against him." (WCHE, v.1, p.71)

Ruth Paine testified that she "had never thought of [Oswald] as a violent man. He had never said anything against President Kennedy, nor anything about Kennedy." (WCHE, v.3, p.69)

Oswald's close acquaintance George de Mohrenschildt testified that Oswald was an admirer of Kennedy. When de Mohrenschildt expressed approval of Kennedy's civil rights policies, Oswald agreed with him, saying "Yes, yes, yes; I think [he] is an excellent President, young, full of energy, full of good ideas". (WCHE, v.9, p.255) According to de Mohrenschildt, Oswald "did not have any permanent animosity for President Kennedy." (WCHE, v.9, p.275)

De Mohrenschildt's wife, Jeanne, told the commission that Oswald had a "difficult personality", but said "he never appeared to be violent or anything" except on one occasion when the de Mohrenschildts found that he had been beating his wife. (WCHE, v.9, p.310) But she says that Oswald was very attached to his child. He was "absolutely fanatical about the child. He loved that child. you should see him looking at the child, he just changed completely." (WCHE, v.9, p.311)

Other members of the Russian emigré community in Dallas gave testimony that contradicted the commission's view of Oswald's character:

John Hall never regarded Oswald as being dangerous in any way, although "he was certainly abnormal" (WCHE, v.8, p.411)

Elena Hall had no impression that Oswald was capable of such a crime:

> E. HALL: I never thought he could do something like that.
> LIEBELER: Like shoot the President, you mean?
> E. HALL: Yes.
> LIEBELER: Did it ever occur to you prior to the time of the assassination that he was dangerous or mentally unstable in any way?
> E. HALL: No.
> LIEBELER: Were you surprised when you heard that he had been arrested in connection with the assassination?
> E. HALL: Very much so. (WCHE, v.8, p.405)

Katherine Ford testified that Marina Oswald told her that Lee "never did say anything bad about Kennedy." (WCHE, v.2, p.315) Her husband, Declan Ford was asked whether he had ever heard Oswald expressing any hostility toward President Kennedy. "No, never did," replied Ford. (WCHE, v.2, p.327) Anna Meller, another Russian emigré, never heard Oswald speak of President Kennedy. (WCHE, v.8, p.386)

One of the first questions that police ask in investigating a homicide is, "Did the victim have any known enemies?" In the absence of any stated animosity or hostility toward Kennedy, there is no evidence to prove or even suggest that Lee Oswald was an enemy of President Kennedy. The commission is left to speculate that Oswald's character and personality made him kill the President.

On February 28, 1964, commission attorney Norman Redlich wrote a memo to the commission's general counsel Lee Rankin, suggesting another possible motive for Oswald's alleged crime – that he was driven to it by a nagging and mocking wife. Redlich wrote: "There are many possible explanations for the assassination – a foreign or domestic plot, Oswald's insanity or Oswald's political motivation. Another possible explanation is that Oswald was a mentally disturbed person with delusions of grandeur who was driven on to commit this act by a wife who married him for selfish motives, degraded him in public, taunted him about his inadequacies, and drove him to prove to her that he was the 'big man' he aspired to be." Redlich goes on to say that the Commission should not prematurely ignore any of these possibilities. (HSCA, v.11, p.126)

Lee's brother Robert Oswald, in testimony before the Warren Commission, was asked if he could give the commission "any reason for why [Lee] may have done this? Robert Oswald replied, "No, sir; I could not." (WCHE, v.1, p.314) The commission made little progress on the question of motive during its proceedings that dragged through the summer months of 1964. Anthony Summers reported that "in the summer of 1964, when the Warren Report was being drafted, the alleged assassin's elder brother, Robert, received a call from a commission lawyer holed up in a cabin in Vermont, working on the chapter that would deal with the question of *why* Oswald might have killed President Kennedy. Robert Oswald was 'flabbergasted', he would recall, that the commission had yet to find a motive for the man it had pegged as the lone assassin." (Summers, *Not in Your Lifetime* (2013), p.111-112)

OSWALD'S CONNECTIONS TO CRIMINAL ELEMENTS

The House Select Committee on Assassinations reported that "the evidence that has been presented by the committee demonstrates that Oswald did, in fact, have organized crime associations." (HSCA Final Report, p.179) The committee noted that when he was 15 to 16 years old, Oswald lived with his mother at 126 Exchange Alley in New Orleans. Exchange Alley "was an area notorious for illicit activities." Aaron Kohn, managing director of the Metropolitan Crime Commission of New Orleans, told the House committee that "Exchange Alley, specifically that little block that Oswald lived on, was literally the hub of some of the most notorious underworld joints in the city." Kohn noted further that "Exchange Alley was the location of various gambling operations affiliated with the Marcello organization." (HSCA, v.9, p.93)

"Oswald's uncle, Charles Murret (commonly known as "Dutz") had for some time been involved in the New Orleans gambling circles. The committee established that he was associated with organized crime figures there, having worked for years in an underworld gambling syndicate affiliated with the Carlos Marcello crime family." During the time that Oswald lived with his mother at Exchange Alley, he regularly visited his uncle and his aunt Lillian, who was the sister of Lee's mother Marguerite. The House committee reported that "his uncle Charles Murret was a father figure of sorts. The Murrets served as the closest thing to a real family that Oswald had been exposed to up to that point in his life." (HSCA, v.9, p.95) Oswald's half-brother, John Pic, told the FBI in 1963 that "from something said to him when he was quite young, it is his impression [that] Charles Murret was a gambler and bookmaker". (FBI report dated 11/30/63 of interview 11/29/63 with John Edward Pic, HSCA Administrative folder: John Edward Pic; NARA Record Number: 124-10371-10040, p.14 of 15) The House committee noted that there was no "indication that Pic's brief information about Murret attracted any interest at the time", and added that the Warren Commission and the FBI "were not fully aware" of the uncle's organized crime connections in 1963. Lee continued to have contact with Uncle Dutz and Aunt Lillian after he returned from the Soviet Union, and when Oswald was arrested for handing out pro-Castro literature in New Orleans, he was "released from jail when a friend of Charles Murret's intervened on his behalf". (HSCA, v.9, p.95) Lillian Murret testified to the HSCA that "her husband had been 'in the gambling business' with a man named Sam Saia for a number of years."

Their son Gene testified that his father "certainly has had associations with Sam Saia." Lee Oswald's mother Marguerite told the House committee that she herself knew Sam Saia. "I knew him and Mr. Murret worked with him. They knew each other for years." (HSCA. v.9, p.96)

So who was Sam Saia? The HSCA report tells us that "Sam Saia, who died in October 1965, was identified by various Federal and State authorities as an organized crime leader in New Orleans for over 15 years. Aaron Kohn testified that Saia 'had the reputation of being very close to Carlos Marcello' and had been 'the biggest and most powerful operator of illegal handbooks and other forms of illegal gambling in the city of New Orleans.'" (HSCA, v.9, p.97)

The HSCA also found "credible evidence indicating [David] Ferrie and Oswald were seen together in August 1963 in the town of Clinton, La." (HSCA, v.10, p.203) "David Ferrie worked as an investigator for Carlos Marcello, who has been identified over the years as the organized crime boss of Louisiana and Texas." (HSCA, v.4, p.485)

While the HSCA did not find specific evidence that Lee Oswald himself had been involved in organized crime activities, it is clear from the evidence developed by the committee that Oswald was known to members of organized crime, through his uncle and other family members, and that criminal elements would have had the opportunity to use him for occasional odd jobs, and would have been well placed to identify him as a potential patsy for "the big event", as the assassination plan was known among the plotters.

RUBY'S CONNECTIONS TO ORGANIZED CRIME AND DALLAS POLICE

Jack Ruby's assassination of Oswald had all the appearance of a mob hit. If you were casting for the role of a gangster hit man in a B-movie, you wouldn't find anyone better suited for the role than Jack Ruby. He looked the part, and when Ruby burst out of the crowd of reporters and police officers to gun down Oswald on live TV, and claimed he did it to protect Mrs. Kennedy from having to return for a trial, many viewers thought this was just one lone nut too many. Speculation abounded that Ruby had killed Oswald in order to silence him and to protect others who were involved in Kennedy's assassination. But who would have put Ruby up to it? And how did he slip unnoticed into the basement garage where Oswald was to be transferred to a police car that would take him to the county jail? Only police and credentialed journalists were supposed to be allowed into the garage. If it can be shown that Ruby was tied to organized crime and had a close relationship with members of the Dallas police force, this would strengthen the hypothesis that he killed Oswald in order to prevent him from revealing information about the plot to kill the President, and that Ruby was able to gain access to the basement at City Hall through his police contacts. As the HSCA determined in 1978, "a primary reason to suspect organized crime of possible involvement in the assassination was Ruby's killing of Oswald." (HSCA Final Report, p.149)

The Warren Report claimed that the commission had investigated possible ties between Ruby and organized crime, but the section on "Ruby's Background and Associations" devotes more space to whether Ruby was involved in any pro-Communist or right wing political activities than to his possible associations with organized crime. The Warren Report concluded, "Ruby has disclaimed that he was associated with organized criminal activities, and law enforcement agencies have confirmed that denial." (WCR, p.370-371) FBI Director Hoover told the commission that Ruby was "on the fringe of what you might call the underworld" when he lived in Chicago. But Hoover said that when Ruby came to Dallas and opened up a nightclub, "it was just another nightclub." (WCHE, v.5, p.103) In its section on "Speculations and Rumors", the Warren Report stated categorically, "There is no credible evidence that Jack Ruby was active in the criminal underworld. Investigation disclosed no one in either Chicago or Dallas who had any knowledge that Ruby was associated with organized criminal activity." (WCR, p.663)

But the Warren Commission's own records contradict this innocent picture of Jack Ruby as just a regular businessman trying to make a living. Testimony from several witnesses indicates that Ruby showed no interest in running the Carousel as a profitable business and it is questionable whether it was being run as a bona fide business at all, or merely as a front. Furthermore, several witnesses told the FBI that they knew of Ruby's participation in organized crime activities, both past and present, but these witnesses were not heard by the Warren Commission.

Ruby's management of the Carousel Club

The Carousel Club was not profitable, and Ruby did not run it like a businessman who was trying to make a living from the nightclub. He received regular infusions of cash from his primary benefactor, Ralph Paul, and the club had all the appearance of being a front for other, perhaps illegal, activities.

Testimony of Andrew Armstrong: Ruby's assistant manager at the Carousel Club, Andrew Armstrong, was questioned by commission counsel Leon Hubert:

> HUBERT: What was the financial condition of the club, as far as you know?
> ARMSTRONG: Not good. . . . I would say it was making enough to pay the bills and paying overhead." (WCHE, v.13, p.319-320)

Testimony of Barry Deavenport. Deavenport, a Los Angeles architect acquainted with Ruby, told the FBI that "several years ago, he happened to be in the Egyptian Lounge operated by the Campisi brothers, and overheard one of the brothers make a statement that he was financing Ruby, or words to that effect." (WCHE, v.22, p.916a) (See below for more on the Campisi brothers, under "Ruby's associations with Dallas Police".)

Testimony of Ralph Paul. In a Warren Commission deposition, Ruby's friend Ralph Paul told commission counsel Leon Hubert that he had loaned Ruby $1,650 to open the Carousel Club as a "burlesque house" on the same location as another club that Ruby had been operating. (WCHE, v.14, p.142) Paul had owned shares in the S&R corporation, which owned the Carousel Club. These shares had been given to Paul by Ruby as collateral or partial payment for previous loans that Paul had given Ruby. Paul told Hubert that he never made any money from the corporation, and Ruby never paid back the loans that he got from Paul.

HUBERT: Now, did you get any income from the corporation?
PAUL: No, sir.
HUBERT: Did you get any kind of pay?
PAUL: No, sir.
HUBERT: Of any sort? Jack never paid you any money through the years at all?
PAUL: He never paid me a dime.
HUBERT: And I gather from that that he stands owing you now $1,200, which was left from the original debt, about $2,200 that you loaned him for which you got a security – 500 shares of a corporation – and then another $1,650 that you loaned him in order to open up the Carousel?
PAUL: Right.
HUBERT: A total of about $5,050, and is it your thought that he still owes you that much money?
PAUL: Well, what am I going to do? (WCHE, v.14, p.143)

Either Ralph Paul is a very patient and understanding investor, or else these infusions of cash had nothing to do with investing for profit, but were simply designed to keep the business afloat so that it could be used as a front for other activities.

Testimony of Edward J. Pullman. Pullman was a friend and business associate of Ruby. Pullman's wife, Mary Ray, worked for Ruby as a hostess at the Carousel Club during the summer of 1963. In an FBI interview, Pullman said that his wife quit her job at the Carousel "mainly because Ruby allowed practically every employee he had to 'go into the cash register', and that his wife became somewhat discouraged when there would be questions raised as to the amount of money in the cash register." (WCHE, v.21, p.272) At his deposition on July 24, 1964, Pullman stated that his wife had previously managed a night club, and had tried to help Ruby run the Carousel in a more businesslike and profitable manner. Pullman added: "The confusion was constant and she couldn't do things the way they should be run, because she had a pretty good idea of how to run a club, and she would try to help him and it seemed like he didn't want to accept any help as far as his operations were concerned." (WCHE, v.15, p.224) Pullman himself tried offering Ruby business advice: "I tried to show him a lot of mistakes that were going on there but he didn't care. He just didn't care. Everyone had their finger in his till. Everybody went to the cash register, which was a very unusual thing, knowing what was going on in the other clubs [where] everything was accounted for every night." (WCHE, v.15, p.230)

Testimony of Thomas Palmer. Palmer was the branch manager for the American Guild of Variety Artists in Dallas. At the time of the assassination he had known Ruby for about a year and a half. He told the FBI that "he has recently learned, but cannot confirm, that Jack Ruby is not the owner of the Carousel Club but is instead a front man for Ralph Paul. . . . He said he does not know if Ralph Paul is the actual owner of the Carousel Club." (WCHE, v.22, p.870b) Palmer told the FBI agents that "it is inconceivable to him that Jack Ruby would shoot anyone as a result of any grief which he might feel as a result of the assassination of President Kennedy, since he feels it is not in keeping with the character of Ruby to have or to express any strong feelings in this regard, but that any strong feelings elicited from Ruby usually dealt with the question of whether someone tried to chisel him out of money." (WCHE, v.22, p.871b)

Ruby's association with known criminals

Association with Lewis McWillie. Ruby told the Warren Commission that Lewis McWillie was a close friend of his. In fact, Ruby testified, "I idolized McWillie. He is a pretty nice boy." Ruby admits to visiting McWillie in Havana, in August 1959, although he claims that it was just a vacation for pleasure. (WCHE, v.5, p.201) The HSCA concluded in 1978 that "vacationing was probably not the purpose for traveling to Havana, despite Ruby's insistence to the Warren Commission that his one trip to Cuba in 1959 was a social visit. The committee reached the judgment that Ruby most likely was serving as a courier for gambling interests when he traveled to Miami from Havana for one day, then returned to Cuba for a day, before flying to New Orleans." (HSCA, Final Report, p.152) Clarence Rector, an acquaintance of Ruby, met him at the Vegas Club in early 1960, and Ruby told him that "he had recently been to Cuba himself, as he and some associates were trying to get some gambling concessions at a casino there but it did not work out." (WCHE, v.22, p.858a) This was the trip that Ruby convinced the Warren Commission was a social visit, for pleasure only.

The Warren Report refers to McWillie as a "close friend" of Ruby, and characterizes him as a "known gambler". (WCR, p.370), and again as "a professional gambler". (WCR, p.801). The report also notes that McWillie "supervised gambling activities at Havana's Tropicana Hotel in 1959 and later was employed in a managerial capacity in a Las Vegas gambling establishment." (WCR, p.802) As far as the Warren Commission was concerned, Lewis McWillie was just an up-and-coming executive in the hospitality and entertainment industry.

An FBI report dated March 26, 1964 reveals that McWillie's "gambling activities" took place within a sinister context. A confidential source informed the FBI that in Dallas, "McWillie was a member of the 'so called gambling syndicate' operating in the Dallas area" before 1946. This report further reflects that "it would appear McWillie solidified his syndicate connections through his association in Havana, Cuba, with Santo Trafficante, well known syndicate member for Tampa, Florida; Meyer and Jake Lansky; Dino Cellini and others who were members of or associates of the 'syndicate'." The FBI report went on to state: "McWillie has been in Nevada since June, 1961. From 1941 to about 1948, he resided in the Dallas, Texas, area and was a prominent figure in illegal gambling in that area. He left Dallas and went to Havana, Cuba, where he was known to associate with nationally known gambling characters such as Willie Bischoff, also known as Lefty Clark, Jake Lansky, Trafficante, and others." (CD686d, p.2. Attachment (d) to CD686: FBI Letter from Director of 27 Mar 1964 re: Lewis McWillie.) In 1979, the House Select Committee on Assassinations noted that when Ruby visited McWillie in Havana in 1959, McWillie had been "working in an organized crime controlled casino." (HSCA Report, v.4, p.497) The HSCA reported that "law enforcement files indicate he [McWillie] had business and personal ties to major organized crime figures, including Meyer Lansky and Santos Trafficante." (HSCA Final Report, p.151) This was the man that Jack Ruby characterized as "a pretty nice boy".

Testimony of Elaine Mynier. Mynier knew both Lewis McWillie and Jack Ruby. She worked for National Car Rental at the Dallas airport. Mynier told the FBI on November 24, 1963 that "she has known McWillie for many years and has dated him in the past. She stated that prior to going to Cuba, he was a well-known Dallas and Fort Worth gambler and [she] is certain he paid off local police." (CD84, p.215) In a separate FBI interview two days later, Mynier described McWillie as "a big-time gambler who has always been in the big money and operated top gambling establishments in the United States and Cuba. . . . She frequently saw Ruby and McWillie at the Dallas airport, where she was employed." She stated that McWillie "ran the Tropicana Hotel in Cuba for about five years." (CD84, p.216) The HSCA reported that Florida crime boss Santo Trafficante "became heavily involved in various gambling casinos in Havana, including the Sans Souci and Tropicana, with his organized crime associates Meyer Lansky, Norman Rothman and Carlos Marcello." (NARA Record Number 180-10118-10142 in HSCA, Transcripts and Steno Tapes of Immunized Executive Session, "General Guidelines", p.12 of 64) Although the Warren Report acknowledged McWillie's managerial role at the Tropicana, the names of Trafficante, Lansky, and Marcello are nowhere to be found in its 800+ pages.

Testimony of Jack Hardee. During December 1963, Jack Hardee was an inmate in the Mobile County (Alabama) jail, incarcerated under federal custody. According to an FBI report, "Hardee stated that he has spent some time in Dallas, Texas, and he had met Jack Ruby during the course of his contacts in Dallas. He stated that approximately one year ago, while in Dallas . . . he [Hardee] attempted to set up a numbers game, and he was advised by an individual, whom he did not identify, that in order to operate in Dallas it was necessary to have the clearance of Jack Ruby. [Hardee] stated that this individual . . . told him that Ruby had the 'fix' with the county authorities." (WCHE, v.23, p.372b)

Testimony of Alonzo Hudkins. According to a Secret Service report of an interview with reporter Alonzo Hudkins of the Houston Post on December 17, 1963, Hudkins "stated that Ruby had a brother and a nephew who formerly worked for Jimmy Hoffa in Detroit, Michigan and he stated it was a 'wild guess' that the Hoffa organization could be behind the assassination." (CD320, p.116)

Robert F. Kennedy on Ruby's associations: In 2013, Robert F. Kennedy Jr. told reporters that his father "had investigators do research into the [JFK] assassination and found that phone records of Oswald and nightclub owner Jack Ruby . . . were like an inventory of mafia leaders the government had been investigating." ("RFK Children Speak about JFK Assassination", Associated Press report in USA Today, January 12, 2013)

HSCA investigation of Ruby's crime connections. The House committee concluded that "Ruby had probably talked by telephone to [Lenny] Patrick during the summer of 1963." The Committee found that Patrick and David Yaras both knew Ruby, and had both "been identified by law enforcement authorities as executioners for the Chicago mob." (HSCA Final Report, p.150-151)

A computer analysis of Ruby's long-distance telephone records for the month prior to the President's assassination "revealed that he either placed calls to or received calls from a number of individuals who may be fairly characterized as having been affiliated, directly or indirectly, with organized crime." The committee acknowledged that these calls could have been related to labor disputes that Ruby was having with some of the entertainers at his club, but noted that "the possibility of other matters being discussed could not be dismissed." (HSCA Final Report, p.154-155) The committee found that a number of Ruby's contacts had "dual roles" in the American Guild of Variety Artists and in organized crime. (HSCA Final Report, p.156)

Conclusions of the HSCA. The House Select Committee on Assassinations established that both Ruby and Oswald had connections to organized crime. The committee reported that "the evidence that has been presented by the committee demonstrates that Oswald did, in fact, have organized crime associations. Who he was and where he lived could have come to the attention of those in organized crime who had the motive and means to kill the President. Similarly, there is abundant evidence that Ruby was knowledgeable about and known to organized crime elements." (HSCA Final Report, p.179)

However, the HSCA, still working under the assumption that Oswald was the assassin, was perplexed that organized crime elements, who were anti-Castro, would form a conspiracy with a person like Oswald, who was ostensibly pro-Castro in his politics. Of course this apparent contradiction melts away when we realize that Oswald's pro-left politics were only a cover for his anti-subversive activity on behalf of U. S. intelligence and Federal law enforcement.

Ruby's associations with Dallas Police

The Warren Commission reviewed Ruby's associations with Dallas police officers, concluding indecisively that "the precise nature of his relationship to members of the Dallas Police Department is not susceptible of conclusive evaluation." (WCR, p.800) But the Warren Report did note that Police Chief Jesse Curry "testified that no more than 25 to 50 of Dallas's almost 1200 policemen were acquainted with Ruby." (WCR, p.801) As with Ruby's connections to organized crime, the commission's own files tell a different story. A number of witnesses testified that Ruby's association with the police was much closer and more extensive than Curry's testimony would suggest. His relationship with the police is important, as it may explain how Ruby was able to enter the city hall basement when the only persons authorized to enter were police officers and reporters carrying official press badges. If Ruby had help from members of the police department in entering the basement to kill Oswald, or was allowed to enter simply out of familiarity, then the police department is guilty of gross incompetence at best or, at worst, active complicity in a conspiracy to silence Oswald.

Testimony of Joe Campisi. Campisi, co-owner of the Egyptian Lounge in Dallas, told the FBI that he had known Ruby since about 1949, and that "Ruby made a practice of becoming acquainted with all police officers and he, Ruby, would cooperate with the police in the operation of his night club. . . . Campisi was of the opinion Ruby gained entrance to the City Hall basement on November 24, 1963, through this friendship with, and knowledge of, numerous Dallas police officers." (WCHE, v.23, p.357a) The House Select Committee on Assassinations in 1979 described Campisi himself as "an associate or friend of many Dallas-based organized crime members, particularly Joseph Civello, during the time he was the head of the Dallas organization." (HSCA Report, v.9, p.336)

Testimony of Walter C. Clewis. Clewis was manager of the Municipal Auditorium in Mobile, Alabama and was an acquaintance of Jack Ruby. Clewis told the FBI that Ruby had boasted that "he could do anything he wanted in Dallas, as he had enough information on the Police Department and judges that he could not be convicted." (WCHE, v.23, p.354b)

Testimony of Lewis McWillie: Ruby's gangster friend Lewis McWillie told the FBI that Ruby was "well acquainted with virtually every officer of the Dallas Police force and had an arrangement whereby off duty policemen were hired at Ruby's expense to maintain order in his night club." (WCHE, v.23, p.171a)

Testimony of Patricia Taylor. She became acquainted with Ruby after winning first prize in an amateur striptease contest at the Vegas Club in January 1963. In 1963, Taylor was dating Dallas Police officer J. W. Barnett. She told the FBI that "Ruby is acquainted with many police officers and due to this fact [she] feels that he had no trouble entering the police department on the day Lee Harvey Oswald was being transferred." (WCHE, v.22, p.875b)

Testimony of Reagan "Buddy" Turman. In an FBI interview, Turman stated that "during the time that he has known Ruby, it appears to him that Ruby was acquainted with at least 75 percent, and probably 90 percent, of the police officers on the Dallas Police Department. He stated that on many occasions, Ruby has told him that the only way a night club business can be operated successfully, is with the friendship of the police department and other city officials." (WCHE, v.22, p.886b) [As we saw above, there is no evidence that Ruby was interested in operating the Carousel Club "successfully".]

Testimony of Nancy Perrin Rich. On June 2, 1964, the Warren Commission took the deposition of Nancy Perrin Rich, a former bartender of Jack Ruby at the Carousel Club. She told the commission that there was a "standing order" to serve hard liquor to members of the Dallas police department. (WCHE, v.14, p.341) [The Carousel Club was not licensed to serve hard liquor. (WCHE, v.14, p.341 and CE1760 at WCHE, v.23, p.368b)]

On the question of how Ruby got into the basement of the City Hall to murder Oswald, Rich had a ready explanation.

> RICH: It was claimed that Ruby got in there by pretending to be a reporter. . . . Anyone that made that statement would be either a damn liar or a damn fool.
> HUBERT: Why?
> RICH: There is no possible way that Jack Ruby could walk in Dallas and be mistaken for a newspaper reporter, especially in the police department. . . . I don't think there is a cop in Dallas that doesn't know Jack Ruby. He practically lived at that station." (WCHE, v.14, p.358-359)

Then, in response to a question from Hubert, Rich switched to a different subject, describing a meeting with Ruby in which the subject of guns and Cuban refugees was discussed.

RICH: At the first meeting there were four people present. There was a colonel, or a light colonel, I forgot which. . . . There was my [former] husband, Mr. Perrin, myself, and a fellow named Dave, and I don't remember his last name. . . . At first it looked all right to me. They wanted someone to pilot a boat – someone that knew Cuba, and my husband claimed he did. . . . So they were going to bring Cuban refugees out into Miami. All this was fine, because by that time everyone knew Castro for what he appears to be, shall we say. So I said sure, why not – $10,000. I said that is fine. (WCHE, v.14, p.345);
HUBERT: Your husband was to receive $10,000?
RICH: Yes.
HUBERT: Who told him so?
RICH: The colonel.
HUBERT: Where did this meeting take place?
RICH: In Dallas at an apartment building." (WCHE, v.14, p.346)

Hubert asks some additional questions, trying to find out details about the apartment and its location, but Rich does not recall many specifics; The subject of the $10,000 again comes up:

RICH: It seemed awfully exorbitant for something like this. I smelled a fish, to quote a maxim.
HUBERT: You mean you thought that there was too much money involved for this sort of operation?
RICH: Yes, I did. (WCHE, v.14, p.348)

Then another meeting took place, 5 or 6 days after the first one, at the same place. At that meeting some additional people were present, and further details of the operation were revealed.

RICH: We were going to bring Cuban refugees out – but we were going to run military supplies and Enfield rifles in. . . . I believe it was the Latin-looking fellow that first made the statement. But the colonel clarified it. The colonel seemed to be the head of it and seemed to do all the talking.
HUBERT: He was in uniform?
RICH: Yes, he was." (WCHE, v.14, p.348)
. . . .
HUBERT: Did [the colonel] indicate in anyway that he was acting officially, in his official capacity.
RICH: No, he was not acting officially.
HUBERT: How do you know that?

RICH: Because of certain statements that were made – statements such as that the guns would have to come in via Mexico, meaning the Enfield rifles. Statements like 'We have been taking stuff off of the base for the last 3 months getting prepared for this' – meaning military equipment, I suppose small arms, or explosives, etc., as I understood it. . . .

HUBERT: So at that meeting it came out that the project had two purposes. One was to bring arms in, and the other was to take refugees out.

RICH: Yes, to make money both ways. (WCHE, v.14, p.349)

Having learned the scope of the project, Rich insisted on getting $25,000. This created some discomfort among the participants. Her testimony continues: "It was left that the bigwigs would decide among themselves. During this meeting I had the shock of my life. Apparently they were having some hitch in money arriving. No one actually said that that was what it was. But this is what I presumed it to be. I am sitting there. A knock comes on the door and who walks in but my little friend Jack Ruby. . . . And he took one look at me, I took one look at him, and we glared, we never spoke a word." (WCHE, v.14, p.349); Ruby and the colonel met in a separate room for about ten minutes. "When they came out, everybody looked relieved." She assumes that Ruby brought money to finance the operation. (WCHE, v.14, p.350) Rich's demand for $25,000 was going to be discussed among the higher bosses. A third meeting was scheduled. At the third meeting the colonel made a counter-offer of $15,000. Rich said, on behalf of her husband, that they needed time to think about it. Then the colonel said the project may need to be postponed anyway for 3 or 4 months. So Rich and her husband got out of this project. (WCHE, v.14, p.353) Rich feared the operation somehow involved organized crime figures, and she wanted nothing to do with such people. (WCHE, v.14, p.355)

The Warren Report makes no mention of Nancy Rich or her testimony linking Ruby to both the Dallas police and to international gun runners in Cuba. The report refers to her only in a footnote to the following statement: "No substantiation has been found for rumors linking Ruby with pro- or anti-Castro Cuban activities." (WCR, p.369, with Rich's testimony as a reference in footnote 1252). The report does not describe what efforts the commission made to check out Rich's story.

Finally, J. Edgar Hoover wrote, in an internal FBI memo, dated November 25, 1963: "I understood Ruby had been very close and had many friends among the men in the police department." (FBI 62-109060 JFK HQ File, Section 1, p.106)

Conclusion

The Warren Report paints a grossly misleading picture of Jack Ruby's associations with organized crime and the Dallas police, and it inadequately investigated possible ties between Ruby and anti-Castro Cubans. It also failed to look into the operation of the Carousel Club to verify that it was being run as a bona fide business venture, and not as a front business for criminal activities. Testimony from numerous witnesses, found in the Warren Commission's own evidence collection, show that the commission was derelict in pursuing leads that would have revealed Ruby's entanglement with both the police and the mob. Since Ruby's motivation for killing Oswald is of critical importance in explaining the assassination, these leads deserved more serious attention than the Warren Commission was willing to give them. All indications are that Ruby was heavily involved as a low-level operative of organized crime, with ties to Santo Trafficante's gambling operations at the Tropicana casino in Havana. This provides a prima facie case for Ruby acting as a mob hit man when he killed Oswald. Given the Kennedy brothers' vigorous prosecution of organized crime, the mob bosses had a strong motive for assassinating President Kennedy, and given Ruby's connections with and dependence on the mob, as well as his financial difficulties with the U. S. Internal Revenue Service, these criminal organizations would have had a powerful influence on Ruby, and could easily have exercised leverage over him to induce him to kill Oswald.

A conjecture

All indications are that Ruby was not the first choice for eliminating Oswald. Although it cannot be proven, it is consistent with the known evidence to hypothesize that Oswald was supposed to have been eliminated before he left the TSBD, possibly by police officer Marrion Baker, who was on the second floor of the TSBD a minute and a half after the last shot was fired, when most of the other officers and bystanders were headed for the railroad tracks behind the picket fence on the grassy knoll. But with Roy Truly standing nearby, Baker must have thought twice about gunning down an unarmed man who was not attempting to flee or resist arrest. Having escaped the TSBD alive, Oswald was next targeted by officer J. D. Tippit, who had reportedly been sitting in his patrol car for ten minutes at a service station, when he suddenly drove off at high speed. (Anthony Summers, *Not in your Lifetime,* (2013), p.109) Apparently Tippit had received word that Oswald was still at large. But Oswald got the drop on Tippit, killed him, and proceeded to the Texas Theatre, where he may have expected to meet a contact. Oswald might have been shot in the Texas Theatre while struggling to resist arrest, but officer McDonald was very likely not in on the plot, and he captured Oswald without firing a shot. With Oswald still very much alive, and needing to recruit another hit man, Ruby met for two or three hours with police officer Harry Olsen during the wee hours of Saturday morning, November 23. (WCHE, v.14, p.631) Ruby may have tried to persuade Olsen to get rid of Oswald while he was still in the custody of the Dallas police, but Olsen very likely refused the assignment. Finding no one else who could do the job, Ruby became the enforcer by default. This would explain Ruby's frustrated response when asked shortly after his arrest why he shot Oswald: "Somebody had to do it. You all couldn't do it." (Quoted by officer Barnard Clardy in WCHE, v.19, p.335, and confirmed by chief Jesse Curry who said that Secret

Service agent Forrest Sorrels told him that Ruby had said "somebody had to kill the son-of-a-bitch and the police department couldn't do it."(WCHE, v.4, p.197.) As I say, this scenario is conjecture, but it is consistent with the known evidence, and it goes some way toward explaining the movements of Tippit and Ruby, and it therefore cannot be ruled out.

TIPPIT

Less than an hour after President Kennedy was assassinated, Dallas police officer J. D. Tippit was shot to death in the Oak Cliff section of Dallas. Dr. Richard Liguori, who pronounced Tippit dead, identified "three wounds in the body; one being in the right temple, which in the opinion of Dr. Liguori could have caused instant death, one wound in the left chest, the bullet being deflected by a brass button of the uniform worn by Officer Tippit and the bullet being found only about one inch under the surface, and the third wound in the upper abdomen." (CD5, p.81) These same wounds are also cited in the official homicide report of the Dallas Police Department. (CD81.1, p.167) As we shall see, four bullets were recovered from Tippit's body, so we must infer that Dr. Liguori missed one of the wounds.

The Warren Commission concluded that Lee Oswald was Tippit's murderer. They were probably right. The evidence that Oswald shot Tippit is much stronger than the evidence that he killed the President. In reviewing the evidence we will see that Oswald would very likely have been found guilty beyond a reasonable doubt of killing the police officer. The Warren Report portrayed Tippit as having been cruising around Oak Cliff looking for the President's assassin, and having found him, being gunned down by Oswald, who then tried to hide in the nearby Texas Theatre. While the evidence by and large supports a guilty verdict against Oswald for the Tippit murder, Tippit's movements on that afternoon raise some interesting questions, and the awkward attempt by Tippit's supervising lieutenant to explain Tippit's presence in the vicinity of Tenth and Patton suggests that Tippit may have been stationed in that area for the specific purpose of intercepting Oswald and killing him. All other Dallas police units were advised to proceed downtown to the vicinity of Elm and Houston after the assassination. Tippit alone was advised to stay in Oak Cliff and to "be at large for any emergency". Author Anthony Summers quotes HSCA counsel Andy Purdy as suggesting "that Officer Tippit, by himself or with others, was involved in a conspiracy to silence Oswald. And when the attempt to kill Oswald by Tippit failed, then Jack Ruby was a fallback." (Quoted in Summers, *Not in your Lifetime,* (2013), p.109)

The Warren Report used the Tippit murder as "evidence" that Oswald also killed the President. The report states: "Oswald killed Dallas police patrolman J. D. Tippit approximately 45 minutes after the assassination. This conclusion *upholds the finding* that Oswald fired the shots which killed President Kennedy." (WCR, p.20) Of course, there is no logical connection between the two murders. Oswald could be guilty of killing Tippit, but innocent of the President's murder, or vice versa. Many conspiracists incorrectly assume that if Oswald was framed for the President's murder he must have been framed in the Tippit shooting, too – i.e., that Oswald was a totally innocent bystander and helpless victim. But this reasoning is faulty. Each case must be decided on its merits based on the evidence. Indeed, if you believe that Oswald was involved in a conspiracy to assassinate the President, either as a conspirator or an undercover informant, and if you believe that he was a U. S. intelligence asset or operative, then we must believe that his training would have equipped him to escape from threatening situations by using force if necessary. It is entirely possible, even likely, that Oswald killed Tippit in self-defense, realizing that Tippit may have been assigned to eliminate him in order to throw the blame for the assassination onto Oswald and protect the other conspirators. Oswald probably knew by the time he reached his rooming house that he was being set up to be the patsy for the President's murder. We have already reviewed the physical and eyewitness evidence in the President's assassination, and found that it points to an attack by at least three assassins, and that Oswald was probably not one of the shooters. It remains for us to determine whether Tippit's actions on November 22 are more consistent with a patrolman on the hunt for a Presidential assassin, or a conspirator out to silence a potential witness who could expose the conspiracy.

ESTABLISHING A TIMEFRAME FOR THE TIPPIT SHOOTING

Tippit's location at 12:54 p.m. At 12:45 p.m., Tippit received instructions from the dispatcher to "move into central Oak Cliff area." Officer R. C. Nelson (unit 87) received the same message. The police radio dispatcher called Tippit at 12:54, and asked "You are in the Oak Cliff area are you not?" Tippit responded that he was at Lancaster Avenue and 8th Street. The dispatcher ordered him, "You will be at large for any emergency that comes in." Tippit replied, "10-4". (DPD radio log transcript at WCHE, v.17, p.401) The intersection of Lancaster and 8th Street is about half a mile from the site of the shooting at 10th and Patton, according to Google maps. There are several routes Tippit could have taken to get to 10th and Patton. The shortest would have been to go west on 8th Street to Marsalis, then south on Marsalis to 10th Street, then right on 10th Street to Patton. But this would have left Tippit's car headed west, not east as the witnesses saw it. To enter 10th Street in the easterly direction, Tippit would have had to either take 8th Street west to Patton Avenue, then left on Patton and again left on 10th Street, or east on 8th Street to Ewing, south on Ewing to Jefferson, and then north on Patton to 10th Street. None of these routes would have left much time to scout around for an unknown assassin. It would appear from the times and distances that Tippit knew where he was headed, and wasted no time in getting there, after getting the 12:54 radio call.

Domingo Benavides happened to be driving near the scene of the Tippit shooting and witnessed the officer being shot from across the street. He saw the shooter discard two empty shells and disappear around the corner going south on Patton Avenue. Benavides stopped his car and got out to try to help the officer, but he was beyond help. Benavides testified that he used the police radio in the squad car to report the shooting. After some initial difficulty operating the radio, he got an acknowledgment from the dispatcher asking for the location. Benavides gave him the address of 410 East 10th Street. The police radio log records the time of this first report as 1:16 p.m. . (FBI transcript at WCHE, v.23, p.857b; DPD transcript at

WCHE, v.17, p.407); After the shooter disappeared around the corner, Benavides reports that he "sat there for just a few minutes. . . . I thought he went in back of the house or something. At the time, I thought maybe he might have lived in there and I didn't want to get out and rush right up. He might start shooting again." (WCHE, v.6, p.448)

T. F. Bowley was a passerby who happened upon the scene of Tippit's murder as he was driving to pick up his wife from work. He "noticed a Dallas police squad car stopped in the traffic lane headed east on 10th Street. I saw a police officer lying next to the left front wheel. I stopped my car and got out to go to the scene. I looked at my watch and it said 1:10 p.m." In an affidavit to Dallas police dated December 2, 1963, Bowley said he called police dispatch to report the shooting, using the radio in Tippit's patrol car. Bowley stated that another man had been trying to use the police radio to report the shooting, but this man was not able to get the radio to work. [This must have been Domingo Benavides, who, as noted above, was able to get through after all.] Bowley knew how to operate it and took the radio microphone from the other man and called the dispatcher. (WCHE, v.24, p.202a) Based on Benavides' testimony, Bowley's call must have been the second report, which appears transcribed just after the 1:19 timestamp in the police radio log. The transcript reads: "Hello, hello, hello. . . . from out here on 10th Street, 500 block. This police officer's just shot. I think he's dead." The dispatcher tells the citizen caller "we have the information. The citizen using the radio remain off the radio now." (FBI transcript: WCHE, v.23, p.859b; DPD transcript: v.17, p.409) Shortly before this second call the transcript has a timestamp of 1:19. The foregoing timestamps are all from the channel 1 radio log. Channel 1 was used for normal radio transmissions, while channel 2 was reserved for special occasions in which radio traffic was expected to be high. Channel 2 was in use on November 22, 1963 because of the motorcade. The channel 2 transcript records the following transmission at 1:18 p.m. – "All squads, we have a report that an officer has been involved in a shooting in the 400 E. 10th." (FBI transcript WCHE, v.23, p.920a; DPD transcript WCHE, v.17, p.467)

The Warren Report states that "at approximately 1:15 p.m., Tippit, who was cruising east on 10th Street, passed the intersection of 10th and Patton. . . . About 100 feet past the intersection Tippit stopped a man walking east along the south side of Patton." (WCR, p.165) If the police radio log is right about the time of the witnesses' first radio call being 1:16 p.m., then the commission's time of 1:15 for Tippit crossing the intersection cannot be right, as it would allow only one minute for Tippit to stop and confront the man, for the man to shoot him, discard two shells, and disappear around the corner, for the witnesses to gather, for Benavides to cower in his truck for "a few minutes" out of fear that the man might come back shooting, and for Benavides to make the first successful call on the police radio. It is not plausible that all this could have taken place within one minute. Either Tippit encountered the man earlier than 1:15, or the timestamp in the radio log is early.

We must be careful not to attribute too much precision to any of the times reported in the testimony. In 1963, people did not have cell phones or computers that could give them the exact time received from a central server. Clocks and watches could run fast or slow, and even in the police radio log transcripts, a timestamp of 1:16 p.m. cannot be assumed to mean *exactly* 1:16 p.m. but only an approximation. The cover memo of the FBI transcript of the radio log explains the imprecision in the recorded times of the radio log: "Lieutenant Gassett advised that each dispatcher has a time stamp clock before him and pointed out these clocks are not synchronized. He demonstrated by simultaneously time stamping a blank piece of paper, using two of the clocks. It was noted that one clock stamped the time as 11:16 a.m. and that the other clock stamped the time as 11:17 a.m. He stated this could explain a timestamp variation between channel 1 and channel 2. He further pointed out that the position of the hands on the clock appear different, depending on the angle of sight from which one is looking at the clock. He stated a short person would have a different angle of sight than a tall person. Lieutenant Gassett stated this quite probably could explain the time element variation of the shooting of officer J. D. Tippit with the channel 1 entry indicating the approximate time as 1:16 p.m. and the channel 2 entry indicating the approximate time as 1:18 p.m." (WCHE, v.23, p.833a) [Actually these are the times when the *report* of the shooting was received, not the times of the actual shooting, which would have been a few minutes earlier.]

Walking distance and time. A search on Google maps for the distance between Oswald's rooming house at 1026 N. Beckley and the site of the shooting at 10th and Patton, indicates that the distance is 8/10 of a mile. Assuming that a brisk walking pace is 15 minutes per mile, it would take approximately 12 minutes for Oswald to walk the distance from his rooming house to the scene of Tippit's shooting, *provided that* he immediately began walking in the direction of 10th and Patton.

Testimony of Earlene Roberts. Oswald's housekeeper, Earlene Roberts, testified that he came home "around 1:00, or maybe a little after" on that Friday afternoon. She said he stayed in his room no more than three or four minutes. (WCHE, v.6, p.440) If we estimate that Oswald left his rooming house at 1:05 p.m., and took 12 minutes to walk to the intersection of 10th and Patton, this already puts us at 1:17 p.m. which is a minute later than Benavides' call on the police radio. Either someone's time is off, or Oswald could not have walked the distance to 10th and Patton in time to be there when Tippit was shot. Or perhaps Oswald got a ride?

Mrs. Roberts, the housekeeper, testified that after Oswald came into the house, and while he was in his room, a police car stopped in front of the house and honked. She did not recognize the car as belonging to any of the officers she knew. She had no clear memory of this car's number, but said there were two uniformed officers in the car. After honking, this police car slowly went around the corner of Beckley onto Zangs Blvd., in the direction of downtown. (WCHE, v.6, p.443) After Oswald left the rooming house, Roberts saw him "standing on the curb at the bus stop just to the right, and on the same side of the street as our house. . . . I don't know how long Lee Oswald stood at the curb nor did I see which direction he went when he left there." (WCHE, v.7, p.439) If Oswald went to the right as he came out the front door, this would have taken him toward Zangs, and in the opposite direction from 10th and Patton. So it does not appear that Oswald immediately began walking toward the site of the Tippit killing. This makes it even more difficult that he could have walked to the site in time to have shot Tippit before 1:16 p.m. Given that the police car seen by Mrs. Roberts also went toward Zangs, the possibility exists that Oswald got a ride in the police car, and that it brought him to the vicinity of 10th and Patton. But the testimony of witnesses at the scene is consistent that there was no second officer in Tippit's police car and that his killer was walking along the sidewalk and was not seen to exit a police car.

Testimony of Helen Markham. On the day of the assassination, Markham gave a sworn affidavit to the Dallas police, stating that she saw Tippit's squad car stop in front of 404 E. 10th Street at approximately 1:06 p.m. (WCHE, v.24, p.215a) If this time is correct, it is much too early for Oswald to have arrived by walking from his rooming house, assuming that the testimony of Earlene Roberts is correct as to the time he left.

When Markham happened upon the scene of Tippit's shooting, she was on her way to catch a bus to work at Jefferson and Patton. The FBI was informed by the Dallas Transit System that "during the afternoon hours of every weekday a bus going to the downtown area of Dallas can be boarded about every ten minutes at the corner of Patton and Jefferson Streets. The bus is scheduled to pass this point at about 1:12 p.m. and every ten minutes thereafter." The FBI report quotes Markham as saying that before heading to catch her bus, she had used the pay phone at a nearby "washateria" in the building where she resided at 328 E. 9th Street. When she left the washateria, she noticed that the time was 1:04 p.m., according to the clock on the wall. (CD630c, p.1) The FBI determined that the walking time from the front door of the washateria to the northwest corner of the intersection at 10th and Patton Streets was two minutes and thirty seconds. (CD630h, p.1) Thus, Markham's arrival time of 1:06 p.m. at 10th and Patton is consistent with her having left the washateria at 1:04 p.m.

If Markham was expecting to catch a bus on Jefferson Blvd. at 1:12, then being at 10th and Patton at 1:06 would be reasonable, given that she had one more block to go to reach Jefferson. But another FBI interview taken on the day of the assassination, reports Markham as saying that she witnessed the Tippit shooting "possibly around 1:30 p.m." (CD5, p.79) This is clearly wrong, but whether it is wrong because the FBI agent (Bardwell Odum) incorrectly recorded her words, or because Markham is a confused and unreliable witness, cannot be established. In addition to identifying Oswald as Tippit's killer in a police lineup, FBI agents showed her a photo of Oswald on November 25, which she identified as the individual she saw shoot officer Tippit. (CD5, p.80)

Markham described the shooting of Tippit in an FBI interview dated March 16, 1964. She stated that when she stopped on the northwest corner of Patton and 10th Street a "police squad car was going east on 10th Street at a slow rate of speed. As it passed, she observed a young man, who she later identified at the Dallas Police Department as Lee Harvey Oswald, diagonally across the street from her, or on the southeast corner of the intersection of 10th and Patton Streets. Oswald was walking on the south side of the street and finally stopped at a point approximately 100 feet east of the intersection. Mrs. Markham could see that the officer, who was alone in the squad car, was talking to the man she identified as Oswald, but she could not hear what was being said. Oswald walked from the sidewalk over to the police car with his arms crossed. Oswald leaned forward, placing his arms on the window sill of the police car, and she could observe he was talking to the officer through an open window. (FBI report at CD630c, p.1) Markham said that after Tippit got out of the car, Oswald shot him three times across the hood of the car. She last saw Oswald running down the west side of Patton. (CD630c, p.2) Markham's FBI interview described in CD630 was taken on March 16, 1964, just ten days before she would testify in a session of the Warren Commission.

The only evidence we have from Tippit himself is his attempt to reach the police radio dispatcher at 1:08 p.m., but he received no response. This at least tells us that he was in his car at 1:08, perhaps about to get out and confront the man he saw walking. (DPD transcript of police radio log at WCHE, v.17, p.406)

Putting the above sources together, we can construct the following timeline:

12:45	Tippit is ordered to move into central Oak Cliff.
12:54	Tippit reports that he is at Lancaster and 8th in Oak Cliff.
1:00	Oswald arrives at rooming house.
1:04	Helen Markham leaves the washateria at her apartment building.
1:05	Oswald leaves rooming house wearing zip-up jacket.
1:06	Markham arrives at corner of 10th and Patton.
1:08	Tippit calls police radio dispatcher, but receives no answer.
1:10	T. F. Bowley arrives at the scene to find Tippit lying next to his patrol car.
1:12	Markham's bus due at Patton and Jefferson.
1:15	Warren Report says Tippit cruised past 10th and Patton. This is also the approximate time that the report says Oswald would have reached 10th and Patton "walking at a brisk pace". (WCR, p.165)
1:16	Warren Report says Tippit was shot. (WCR, p.157)
1:16	First report (Benavides) of shooting using Tippit's police radio.
1:17	Earliest time when Oswald could have arrived at 10th and Patton, walking at 15 minutes per mile from his rooming house, assuming he left the rooming house at 1:05.
1:18	Channel 2 broadcast to all units advising an officer has been shot.

1:19   Second report (Bowley) of shooting using Tippit's police radio; Ambulance reported en route to scene.

It is clear that this time line raises considerable doubt as to Oswald's ability to have been in the right place at the right time to shoot Tippit – if he walked to the site from his rooming house, and especially if he did not proceed right away toward the vicinity of 10th and Patton but instead headed to the right, in the opposite direction, and stood at the bus stop for a while as Earlene Roberts reported. If he got a ride for part of the way from the two policemen who were described by Roberts as having stopped and honked while Oswald was inside his room, then he could have made it in time. The time of the shooting seems to be fixed by the testimony of these witnesses as occurring between 1:06 and 1:10. Markham's departure from the washateria and Bowley's arrival at the intersection were established by the witnesses looking at a clock or watch. Markham's two minute walk from the washateria to the intersection was timed by the FBI. Given that Benavides remained in his car for an undetermined time after the shooting before going to Tippit, the shooting had to take place at least a few minutes before the 1:16 radio call. The Warren Commission's guess of 1:15 for when Tippit arrived at the intersection seems untenable, and the Warren Report gives no reference for this claim.

WHERE WAS OSWALD GOING?

We have already noted above that Oswald was walking in the general direction of Jack Ruby's apartment at 223 S. Ewing. Another possible destination for Oswald comes from an FBI document dated August 24, 1977 (NARA Record Number 124-10370-10012, p.128-130) which quotes an informant to the Dallas Police as saying that a certain Max Long told him that "Oswald was on his way to 324 East 10th Street after the assassination of President Kennedy. Long told the source that 324 East 10th Street was supposed to have been a 'safe house' for Oswald to go to. Long advised the source that by letting Oswald come to this house located at 324 East 10th Street . . . this was supposed to wipe out an unspecific debt that Long had with some people in New Orleans." The FBI letter quotes Dallas Police Lieutenant James E. Hobbs as saying that the department's offense report for the Tippit shooting reflects the fact that "Oswald was walking west on East 10th Street which would have been in the direction of the 324 East 10th Street address." (FBI letter August 24, 1977, NARA record number 124-10370-10012, p.128-129) (A Dallas police intelligence report on Max Long immediately follows the FBI letter, on page 130 of this record.)

Seth Kantor relates another possible explanation for Oswald's destination provided by Warren Commission attorney David Belin. Based on the bus transfer in Oswald's pocket, and the proximity of the Tippit shooting scene to other bus routes on Jefferson Avenue, one of which could have "taken him to a point on

Lancaster Road where the first southbound Greyhound bus was scheduled to stop for passengers around 3:30 p.m.", Belin concludes that Oswald was likely headed to the stop on Jefferson Avenue where he could board the city bus that would take him to the Greyhound stop and from there to points south, including Mexico. (Kantor, *The Ruby Cover-up*, p.388) However, this argument is based only on possibility. There is no actual evidence that Oswald was headed for the Greyhound stop. This plan would seem to be too risky if Oswald had really killed the President. It would have left him out in the open for too long along busy streets and public places, making it all the more likely that he would have been spotted and picked up by the police.

In an interview with Anthony Summers, former Dallas Assistant District Attorney Bill Alexander noted that Oswald had been walking close to the road that led to Red Bird Airport. Alexander speculated that "Oswald may have expected to be picked up and taken to the airport, but that something went wrong at the rendezvous, and the getaway failed." (Quoted in Summers, *Not in your Lifetime*, p.500)

Oswald's movements make sense if he was going to meet Ruby, or headed for a CIA safe house, or meeting a contact to pick him up and help him escape Dallas. But all these scenarios require that Oswald have accomplices and be involved in a conspiracy to kill the President. The Warren Commission's theory of Oswald as lone gunman does not mesh with Oswald's Friday afternoon stroll through Oak Cliff. If Oswald alone had really shot Kennedy and if he was trying to escape on his own, it makes no sense at all that he would be wandering around in broad daylight in his own neighborhood, knowing that police from all over town would be looking for him, given that his absence from the Book Depository would surely have been discovered by the time he reached his rooming house.

THE EYEWITNESS TESTIMONY IN THE TIPPIT MURDER

Although the timeline suggests that Oswald could not have arrived at the intersection of 10th and Patton in time to have shot Tippit, the eyewitness testimony is overwhelming that he did just that. The eyewitnesses all described Tippit pulling up next to a man fitting Oswald's description walking along 10th Street, getting out of his car, and being shot at least three times by the man. No witness described seeing a second officer or any other person in the patrol car. No one saw Oswald get out of the patrol car or any other car, as might have been the case if Oswald had hitched a ride to the scene in Tippit's car or in some other car.

Other witnesses not interviewed in the Warren Commission's investigation have suggested that there may have been a third man at the scene. One of these witnesses is Frank Wright, who was described in an article by George and Patricia Nash in *The New Leader* as having seen "a man standing in front of the police car wearing a long coat, and getting into a little old gray coupe, possibly a 1950 or 1951 Plymouth, which had been parked behind Tippit's police car headed west and immediately driving away." (FBI Airtel memo dated October 21, 1964, FBI 105-82555 Oswald HQ File, Section 218, p.68) This FBI memo concluded that the witness testimony already collected on the Tippit murder was more than sufficient to conclude that Oswald was Tippit's murderer and there was no further need to continue interviewing new witnesses such as Wright. The memo noted that "the possibility of ever identifying the person and/or car described by Frank Wright as being in the immediate area of the Tippit murder scene on November 22, 1964 [sic], seems extremely remote, if not impossible, due to the passage of time." (FBI Airtel, p.69)

Another possible dissenting witness was said to be Acquilla Clemons, who told independent interviewers that she had seen two men near the patrol car just before the shooting. Anthony Summers quotes from an interview with Clemmons:

INTERVIEWER: Was there another man there?
CLEMONS: Yes, there was one, other side of the street. All I know is, he tells him to go on.
INTERVIEWER: Mrs. Clemons, the man who had the gun, did he make any motion at all to the other man across the street?
CLEMONS: No more than tell him to go
INTERVIEWER: He waved his hand and said, "Go on"?
CLEMONS: Yes, said, "Go on." (Summers, *Not in your Lifetime* (2013), p.105)

The FBI Airtel memo cited above reports that a search for Acquilla Clemons found that "such a person's name does not appear in the current Dallas City Directory. The Nashes even noted in their aforementioned article [in The New Leader] that 'her version of the slaying was rather vague, and she may have based her story on second-hand accounts of others at the scene'. In view of the above, it is not felt that an investigation at this time to identify and locate Acquilla Clemmons is warranted." (FBI Airtel memo, p.69) [Summers gives the citation for the Nash article as George and Patricia Nash, *New Leader,* November 12, 1964, while the FBI memo gives the date October 12, 1964.]

In contrast to these isolated witnesses, the record contains eyewitness testimony from roughly a dozen witnesses who placed Oswald, or a man closely resembling him, at the scene of Tippit's murder. These witnesses told a remarkably consistent story of hearing shots, and then seeing this man flee the scene headed south on Patton street, dropping empty revolver shells along the way and reloading as he ran.

Testimony of Helen Markham. Although Markham's testimony before the commission was shaky, and she had difficulty saying whether or not she identified Oswald in a police lineup, Markham did identify Oswald from a photo shown to her by the FBI as the man she saw shoot Officer Tippit. In an interview just 3 days after the assassination, she told the FBI agents that "she is positive that he is the individual who killed the police officer." (CD5, p.80) She told the FBI that the officer "was shot twice in the head by the young man." (CD5, p.79) In her testimony before the commission, she testified that she heard three shots. (WCHE, v.3, p.308)

If Markham were the only witness to identify Oswald we might be hesitant to rely on her word alone, but her identification of Oswald as Tippit's killer is corroborated by several other witnesses.

Testimony of W. W. Scoggins. Scoggins was a witness to the shooting while sitting in his taxi cab eating his lunch at the corner of 10th and Patton. Scoggins told the commission that he heard 3 or 4 shots. (WCHE, v.3, p.325) He identified Oswald in a police lineup as the man he saw fleeing the scene. (WCHE, v.3, p.334)

Testimony of Ted Callaway. While working at his used car lot on Jefferson Avenue, Callaway heard what sounded like five shots. (WCHE, v.3, p.352) He looked up to see what was going on, and saw a man running south on Patton with a pistol in his hand. He identified Oswald (the "number 2 man") in a police lineup as the man he saw running. (WCHE, v.24, p.204a)

Testimony of Sam Guinyard. An employee at Harris Motor Company on East Jefferson Avenue, Guinyard heard three shots from the direction of 10th and Patton. He saw Oswald running down Patton (WCHE, v.7, p.396) and identified him in a police lineup. (WCHE, v.7, p.400)

Testimony of Domingo Benavides. Benavides heard three shots, but did not see them being fired. (WCHE, v.6, p.447) He was hesitant to positively identify the shooter as Oswald (WCHE, v.6, p.452), but testified that the man looked like Oswald, and the description he gave sounds like Oswald: 5'10", about 25 years old, wearing a light-colored zipper jacket, and needing a haircut (WCHE v.6, p.450-451). Recall that Earlene Roberts saw Oswald putting on a zippered jacket as he left the rooming house. (WCHE, v.6, p.440; v.7, p.439), and TSBD employee Danny Arce testified that on the morning of the assassination several of the TSBD employees teased Oswald about needing a haircut. (CD205, p.7)

Testimony of Barbara Jeanette Davis. She lived at 400 E. 10th Street. Shortly after 1:00 she heard two shots. (WCHE, v.3, p.343) She looked out and saw a man running across her yard emptying revolver shells into his hand. She later found one of the shells and her sister-in-law Virginia found another. She identified Oswald in a police lineup as the man she saw running through her yard. (WCHE, v.3, p.345-346)

Testimony of Virginia Davis. She is Barbara Jeanette Davis's sister-in-law and lived in the same house. After hearing two shots (WCHE, v.6, p.456), she looked out and saw a man running across her yard emptying shells into his hand from a revolver. (WCHE, v.6, p.458-459) She identified Oswald as the man she saw running across her yard with the gun. (WCHE, v.6, p.462)

Testimony of B. M. "Pat" Patterson. On the afternoon of November 22, Patterson was standing at Johnny Reynolds' used car lot when he heard an unspecified number of shots from the direction of 10th and Patton. Soon afterwards, he saw a man running south on Patton holding a revolver and trying to reload it. In an FBI interview on January 23, 1964, "Patterson was shown a photograph of Lee Harvey Oswald at which time he identified said photograph as being identical with the individual he had observed on the afternoon of November 22, 1963, running south on Patton Avenue with a weapon in his hand." (CD385, p.90)

Testimony of Warren Reynolds. While sitting in his office at the Johnny Reynolds Used Car Lot, Reynolds heard shots from the vicinity of 10th and Patton. He is uncertain how many shots he heard. He testified, "I would say four or five or six. I just would have no idea. I heard one, and then I heard a succession of some more." (WCHE, v.11, p.435) Shortly thereafter, he "observed an individual running south on Patton Avenue toward Jefferson Street and then walking at a fast rate of speed west on Jefferson. As the individual was running down Patton Avenue, he had a pistol or an automatic in his possession and was apparently attempting to conceal same in his belt while he was running. . . . [Reynolds] attempted to follow the individual in order that he could inform the Dallas Police Department of the individual's location. . . . Reynolds was shown a photograph of Lee Harvey Oswald, at which time he advised he is of the opinion Oswald is the person he had followed on the afternoon of November 22, 1963. However, he would hesitate to definitely identify Oswald as the individual." (CD385, p.86) At his deposition on July 22, 1964, Reynolds said that he could now positively identify the fleeing man as Lee Oswald. (WCHE, v.11, p.435) In the meantime, Reynolds had been shot in the head by an unknown gunman, but he survived the attack. (WCHE, v.11, p.438)

Testimony of Harold Russell. Russell was employed at Johnny Reynolds Used Car Lot. Shortly after hearing an unspecified number of shots from the vicinity of 10th and Patton, Russell "observed a young white man running south on Patton Avenue carrying a pistol or revolver which the individual was attempting to either reload or place in his belt line." (CD385, p.87) "Russell positively identified a photograph of Lee Harvey Oswald . . . taken August 9, 1963 as being identical with the individual he had observed at the scene of the shooting of Dallas Police Officer J. D. Tippit on the afternoon of November 22, 1963 at Dallas." (CD385, p.88)

Testimony of Mary Brock. At about 1:30 p.m. she was at the Ballew Texaco Service Station on Jefferson when "a white male described as approximately 30 years of age, 5 feet, 10 inches, light-colored complexion, wearing light clothing, came past her walking at a fast pace, wearing a light-colored jacket and with his hands in his pockets. . . . Mrs. Brock was shown a photograph of Lee Harvey Oswald [taken by the New Orleans police] dated August 9, 1963, which she identified as being the same person she observed on November 22, 1963, at Ballew's Texaco Service Station." She does not report hearing any shots. (CD385, p.93)

Testimony of Jack Tatum. In 1978 the House Select Committee on Assassinations uncovered a new witness, Jack Ray Tatum, who told of hearing four shots. "Tatum stated that on the afternoon of November 22, 1963, he was driving north on Denver Street and stopped at Tenth Street. At that point he saw a police squad car, and a young white male walking on the sidewalk near the squad car. Both the police car and the young man were heading east on Tenth Street. [Witnesses are not all agreed on whether the man was walking in an easterly or a westerly direction on 10th Street. The homicide report of the Dallas Police Department says the assailant was walking west on 10th Street, while Tippit was driving east.] As Tatum approached the squad car, he saw the young male leaning over the passenger side of the police car with both hands in his zippered jacket. Tatum said that as he drove through the intersection of Tenth and Patton Streets he heard three shots in rapid succession. Tatum said he went through the intersection, stopped his car and turned to look back. At that point he saw the police officer lying on the ground near the front of the police car, with the young male standing near him. Tatum said the man ran toward the back of the police car with a gun in his hand. The man then stepped back into the street and shot the police officer as he was lying on the ground. The man then started to run in Tatum's direction. Tatum said he then sped off in his car and last saw the man running south on Patton toward Jefferson." (HSCA, v.12, p.41.)

Conclusion:

The eyewitness testimony is clear, consistent, and overwhelming that Lee Oswald was the man seen running away from the scene of the Tippit shooting, carrying a revolver which he was trying to reload after ejecting spent shells, which were recovered from the scene. This testimony is reinforced by the ballistic evidence linking Oswald's revolver to the crime.

BALLISTICS EVIDENCE IN THE TIPPIT CASE

The physical evidence in the Tippit shooting

The expert ballistics witness for the Tippit case is FBI firearms expert Cortlandt Cunningham. As with the Kennedy assassination, we will be interested in the chain of possession for the ballistic evidence in the Tippit murder, specifically for the bullets and shells and their connection to Oswald's revolver. Of course it must also be proven that the revolver in evidence, CE143, is actually Oswald's revolver which was taken from him at the time of his arrest.

Commission Exhibit 594 consists of four cartridge cases (shells) found in the vicinity of the Tippit shooting. Cunningham testified that "those four cartridge cases, Commission Exhibit 594, were fired in the revolver, Commission Exhibit 143, to the exclusion of all other weapons." (WCHE, v.3, p.466) Cunningham notes that two of these shells are Remington-Peters .38 Special cartridge cases. The other two shells are Western .38 Special cartridge cases." (WCHE, v.3, p.465) The chain of possession for these shells is discussed in the following section.

Cunningham also examined four bullets which were said to have been recovered from Tippit's body. These are designated as Commission Exhibits 602-605. The FBI refers to them as C13, C251, C252, and C253. One slug, C13, was removed from Tippit's body by Dr. Paul Moellenhoff. This was identified by Patrolman R. A. Davenport as having the mark he put on it when he received it from Dr. Moellenhoff on 11/22/63. Davenport said he observed the slug being removed from the body. Dr. Earl Rose identified his mark on three slugs C251, C252, and C253 which he removed from Tippit's body on 11/22/63. (WCHE, v.24, p.415b) The chain of possession is thus established for these bullets.

Cunningham observed that CE604 "is a .38 Special Remington-Peters lead bullet, which has been fired from a barrel having five lands and grooves, right twist." CE602, 603, and 605 are ".38 Special, copper-coated lead bullets of Winchester-Western manufacture, which had been fired from a barrel having five lands and grooves, right twist." Cunningham was not able to determine from microscopic examination whether any of these bullets were definitely fired from the revolver, CE143. He noted that the revolver was not producing consistent markings on the test bullets, and thus it was not possible to obtain a match between the test bullets and the bullets recovered from Tippit's body. (WCHE, v.3, p.475) The bullets from Tippit's body therefore cannot be shown to have come from Oswald's revolver, although it cannot be ruled out that they were fired from it.

Also in evidence are six loaded revolver cartridges found in Oswald's revolver at the time of his arrest. Sgt. Jerry Hill of the Dallas police department identified his mark on the 6 cartridges removed from the revolver. Hill witnessed the revolver being taken from Oswald and kept the gun in his possession until he returned to Dallas police headquarters, where he marked them with his name. Four of these cartridges were given to FBI agent Vincent Drain for delivery to the FBI lab. The other two were released to the Secret Service on 11/26/63. These cartridges were designated by the FBI as C51-C54 and C137-C138. (WCHE, v.24, p.416a) The Warren Commission exhibit numbers are CE145 (2 cartridges) and CE518 (4 cartridges). Cunningham testified that there was no indication that any of these cartridges had been struck by a firing pin. (WCHE, v.3, p.461, 463) This would seem to rule out a misfire of Oswald's revolver, which was reported by some of the officers present during his capture at the Texas Theatre. (WCHE, v.24, p.241b; v.24, p.820b-821a)

Five revolver cartridges were found in Oswald's pocket after he was arrested. These are designated by the FBI as C55-C59, and by the commission as a single exhibit, CE592. Detective Elmer Boyd identified his mark on each of the five cartridges "and stated these are the same five cartridges which he removed from the pocket of Lee Harvey Oswald at the Dallas Police Department on November 22, 1963." (WCHE, v.24, p.416b; WCHE, v.7, p.126)

Rep. Boggs summarizes the key points of Cunningham's testimony:

> BOGGS: So that while you can establish the fact that the cartridge cases, the four that we have, were fired in that gun . . . you cannot establish the fact that the bullets were fired in that gun?

CUNNINGHAM: That is correct.
BOGGS: And you cannot – having the cartridge case and the bullet – you cannot match them up?
CUNNINGHAM: No, you cannot . . .
BOGGS: But there is no doubt about the fact that the four cartridge cases came from firing in that weapon?
CUNNINGHAM: They were fired in that weapon to the exclusion of all other weapons. (WCHE, v.3, p.476)

A slight problem: Mismatched shells and bullets

Commission counsel Melvin Eisenberg questions Cunningham about the fact that the cartridge cases and the bullets do not match in terms of the brand. Eisenberg refers to this as a "slight problem". (WCHE, v.3, p.473)

EISENBERG: Now, you said that there were three bullets of Winchester-Western manufacture, those are 602, 603, and 605, and one bullet of Remington-Peters manufacture.
CUNNINGHAM: That is correct.
EISENBERG: However as to the cartridge cases, Exhibit 594, you told us there were two Remington-Peters cartridge cases and two Western cartridge cases.
CUNNINGHAM: That is correct.
EISENBERG: So that the recovered cartridge cases, there is one more recovered Remington-Peters cartridge case than there was recovered bullet?
CUNNINGHAM: Yes.
EISENBERG: And as to the bullets, there is one more recovered Winchester-Western bullet than there is Winchester-Western cartridges?
CUNNINGHAM: That is correct.
BOGGS: How would you account for that?
CUNNINGHAM: The possibility exists that one bullet is missing. Also, they may not have found one of the cartridge cases. (WCHE, v.3, p.476)
. . . Inasmuch as there are three Western bullets, you would be missing one Western cartridge case, and one Remington bullet. You are missing one of each. He could have missed one of the shots." (WCHE, v.3, p.477)

Given the testimony of those who heard the shots, the possibility of there being a lost bullet seems remote. Most witnesses heard three shots, but we have seen that Jack Tatum heard and saw a fourth shot being fired. Since four bullets were recovered from Tippit's body, a missing Remington bullet would mean that the shooter fired five shots, one of which missed, and there is no firm testimony from any of the witnesses that more than four shots were fired. Eisenberg offers a hypothesis to explain the discrepancy without having to assume a lost bullet. He says that if the revolver had an empty Remington cartridge case already in the cylinder, then one of the recovered Remington cases is not connected with the Tippit shooting. In that case there only needs to be a missing Western cartridge case which was not found, in order to explain the discrepancy. (WCHE, v.3, p.478)

Establishing the chain of possession for the Tippit ballistics evidence

Since the bullets removed from Tippit's body cannot be matched with the revolver, they will not figure in our discussion here, although the chain of possession for these bullets was established in the preceding section. The key evidence linking the revolver to Tippit's murder is the set of four cartridge cases designated as CE594. Before being accepted into evidence, these cartridge cases were individually designated as C47-C50, and in the FBI's designation as Q74-Q77. In order to establish a foundation for this evidence it must be shown that these cartridges were the ones recovered at the scene of the crime, and that the revolver, CE143, was the one found on Oswald at the time of his arrest.

The chain of possession for the cartridge cases (and for other items of physical evidence) is presented in CE2011, an FBI report dated July 7, 1964. The report tells us that Capt. G. M. Doughty of the Dallas police identified his mark on cartridge case Q76 when it was shown to him on June 12, 1964. "Captain Doughty stated this is the same shell which he obtained from Barbara Jeanette Davis at Dallas, Texas, on November 22, 1963." (WCHE, v.24, p.414b) Also on June 12, Dallas Detective C. N. Dhority of the Homicide Division identified the mark he placed on the cartridge case marked Q75, and told FBI agents that this is the same cartridge case which he obtained from Virginia Davis on November 22, 1963. The four cartridge cases were also shown to Dallas police officer J. M. Poe. Poe stated that he had received two such cases from Domingo Benavides on November 22, 1963 and had given them to Pete Barnes of the DPD crime lab. Poe recalled marking these two shells with his initials before giving them to Barnes, but after examining the cases on June 12, 1964, Poe was not able to find his initials on any of them. "Therefore, he cannot positively identify any of these cartridges as being the same ones he received from Benavides." These shells were shown to Pete Barnes, and he identified his mark on Q74 and Q77, and stated that "these are the same two cartridge cases which he received from Officer J. M. Poe of the Dallas Police Department at Dallas, Texas on November 22, 1963." (WCHE, v.24, p.415a)

It appears, then, that these four cartridges can be traced back to the day they were found, with a clear chain of possession, except for the missing initials from Officer Poe. Assuming that the officers are giving truthful information to the FBI, we can state that sufficient foundation has been laid for accepting these four cartridge cases into evidence. Thus, Cunningham's expert testimony regarding the cartridge cases meets the foundational requirements.

The revolver itself was entered into evidence as Commission Exhibit 143 on the basis of an identification by Marina Oswald. Upon being shown the revolver, she recognized it as a pistol belonging to her husband, Lee Oswald. (WCHE, v.1, p.120)

This does not prove that it was the same gun found on Oswald at the time of his arrest, but only that it belonged to Oswald. We turn to the testimony of officer M. N. McDonald for proof that the revolver CE143 was the one found on Oswald when he was captured in the Texas Theatre. McDonald told the commission that he took the revolver from Oswald during a scuffle, and gave it to Detective Bob Carroll, after Oswald was taken outside, McDonald marked the revolver with his initial "M". During McDonald's testimony, Joseph Ball presented the revolver CE143 to McDonald for identification. McDonald found his mark on the gun and testified that this was the gun he took from the man he arrested in the Texas Theatre. (WCHE, v.3, p.301)

Conclusion

In contrast to the evidence from the Kennedy assassination, the physical evidence from the Tippit shooting shows a clear chain of possession, showing that the evidence is what it is purported to be, and that the four cartridge cases were fired in Oswald's revolver to the exclusion of all other weapons. Cunningham's expert testimony regarding this evidence has probative value. The physical evidence supports the eyewitness testimony that Lee Oswald shot Officer Tippit, and fled the scene by running south on Patton Avenue. But the timeline suggests that Oswald could not have walked to the scene at 10th and Patton by the time Tippit was shot. How can we reconcile these two sets of evidence? Something has to give. The simplest way to do this is to discard the assumption that Oswald walked to the site. This would mean that he got a ride for part of the way with someone else. This assistance may have been given to him by the police car that Mrs. Roberts saw stop and honk in front of the rooming house. It was the kind of short honk that a person makes if they are signaling to someone that their ride is there. "Just kind of a 'tit-tit' – twice" is how Earlene Roberts described it. (WCHE, v.6, p.444) The presence of the police car in front of the rooming house, the horn signal, Oswald's departure in the direction of the police car, and the impossibility of Oswald arriving at 10th and Patton in time to encounter Tippit, all point to the conclusion that Oswald got a ride to the scene, or near the scene, in the police car that signaled to him in front of the rooming house. It was probably not Tippit himself who picked up Oswald. Mrs. Roberts said she saw two officers in the car, And none of the witnesses at the scene saw a second man getting out of Tippit's car, Instead, Tippit was alone in the car, driving slowly as he approached Oswald.

So why would these officers have dropped Oswald off near 10th and Patton? We can only speculate. Perhaps they were taking him to the safe house at 324 East 10th Street, but didn't want a police car to be seen directly in front of that house so dropped him off a couple of blocks away, where Oswald just happened to run into Tippit. The two officers in the car may or may not have known that Tippit would be in the vicinity. Given Tippit's movements, which we will examine shortly, it is likely that he was looking for Oswald as Oswald, not as the President's assassin. The two officers who picked Oswald up may have knowingly delivered him into

Tippit's hands, or may have thought they were just delivering him to a safe house, or to a bus stop, while Tippit was acting according to other instructions. One thing is certain: Oswald could not have walked the distance from his rooming house to 10th and Patton in time to shoot Tippit at the time testified to by the eyewitnesses and by the radio log.

Postscript: Was Roscoe White the Tippit shooter?

There is a story that Dallas Police Officer Roscoe White was involved in the assassination and in the murder of Officer Tippit. This story is based on the alleged discovery of some diary entries made by White which seem to suggest that he was the grassy knoll shooter, and that he also shot Tippit. This diary was said to have been discovered by White's son, Ricky. The alleged diary says that after the assassination, White "ran around back of fence, down embankment to car. Drove to Oak Cliff, met officer. Told officer not to drive by house. Something was at this point wrong. Forced to take out officer at 10th and Patton. Not going as planned. Back tracked to car, drove back to the area of take out to locate other passenger. Failed to transport subject to Redbird [Airport]. Realized what a mistake I had made." (Quoted in Jim Marrs, *Crossfire,* 2013, pp.300-302, citing as source an unpublished manuscript by White's son Ricky, as well as Marrs' own interviews with Ricky.)

The Roscoe White story suffers from lack of hard evidence. The diary entry, even if genuine, is too vague to draw definite conclusions from it. The grassy knoll shooter is identified only by a code name ("Mandarin") which supposedly refers to White. The description of the Tippit incident is vague, does not explain what was "wrong" in the situation or why the writer was "forced to take out" the officer at 10th and Patton. Worse still, the description of the Tippit incident is at odds with the testimony of the many eyewitnesses to the shooting. Eventually a second diary turned up, but was shown to be a forgery. Given the many uncertainties in the Roscoe White story, we need not consider it further. It poses no credible challenge to the story that we get from the eyewitness testimony and ballistics evidence in the Tippit killing. This does not mean that White had no role to play in the Kennedy assassination, just that the alleged diary entries are not sufficient to make us change our view of the Tippit killing based on the other evidence discussed above.

TIPPIT'S MOVEMENTS FOLLOWING THE ASSASSINATION

Tippet's actions and movements during the afternoon of November 22, 1963 raise many suspicions. The attempts by Dallas Police officials to explain these movements during the Warren Commission hearings and depositions raised even more suspicions. When we find that these explanations contradict the police radio transcripts, and that one of the transcripts prepared by the police department contains wording different from the original Dictabelt recordings, then we are led to suspect that something was being covered up. Unlike all other Dallas police officers, Tippit had received special instructions to remain in Oak Cliff following the President's assassination, and to "be at large for any emergency" while all other squads were ordered downtown to Elm and Houston. Why was Tippit given different instructions from all other Dallas police squads? The only plausible explanation that suggests itself is that Tippit was a backup for eliminating Oswald when it became known that Oswald had escaped the TSBD alive after Kennedy was killed.

The Dallas Police radio log transcripts

The Dallas police radio log is a key source for understanding Tippit's movements on the afternoon of the assassination. The communications recorded in the log are reproduced as transcripts in the Warren Commission's hearings and exhibits, but there are three versions of the log, which appear in three different volumes with no cross references:

Police radio log version 1 is in the WCHE as Sawyer Exhibits A and B (WCHE, v.21, pp.388-400). Sawyer exhibit A is an abridged transcript of channel 2 communications (generally used for special events, such as the Presidential motorcade) and Sawyer exhibit B is a highly abridged transcript of channel 1 communications (ordinary police radio traffic) from November 22, 1963. The channel 2 transcript is dated December 3, 1963, and the channel 1 transcript is dated December 5, 1963. They were produced by Sgt. G. D. Henslee, DPD Radio Dispatcher.

Police radio log version 2 is designated as Commission Exhibit 705 and is found at WCHE, v.17, pp.361-494. It consists of separate transcripts of radio communications by the State Police (pp.363-366), Dallas Sheriff's Department (pp.368-387) and Dallas Police (pp.390-485), with the DPD providing background information on radio signal codes and officer call numbers in pages 487-494. These transcripts were provided to the Warren Commission in letters dated March 16, 1964 for the State Police, and March 23, 1964 for the Dallas Sheriff and Police departments.

Police radio log version 3 was compiled by the FBI by listening directly to the DPD's Dictabelt tapes on which the original transmissions were recorded. The commission requested in a letter dated July 16, 1964 that the FBI produce such a transcript, "in view of the importance of these transcripts". This transcript is designated as Commission Exhibit 1974 and is found at WCHE, v.23, pp.832a-939. In addition to being compiled directly from the original Dictabelt tapes, the FBI transcript has the advantage of listing the name of each caller next to the recorded conversation. The FBI transcript was provided to the commission on August 11, 1964 and consists of Channel 1 and 2 transmissions of the Dallas Police Department.

210

(Note that these transcripts include some communications with Patrolman W. W. Tippett, who should not be confused with officer J. D. Tippit, who was shot in Oak Cliff.)

Police radio communications with Tippit on the afternoon of the assassination

All of Tippit's communications with police radio dispatchers on the afternoon of November 22, 1963 are presented below. Tippit's radio call number is 78, since he was assigned that afternoon to patrol district 78. Unit 87 is identified in the FBI transcript as Patrolman R. C. Nelson. (WCHE, v.23, p.860b) The following excerpt picks up the thread of the conversation just before 12:45 p.m. (WCHE, v.17, p.397) The first excerpts are from the version 2 DPD transcript, as identified above.

Version 2 transcript (DPD full transcript)
DISPATCHER: Attention all squads, report to downtown area code 3 to Elm and Houston, with caution. . . . Attention all squads, attention all squads. At Elm and Houston reported to be an unknown white male, approximately 30, slender build, height 5 ft 10 inches, 165 pounds. Reported to be armed with what is believed to be a 30 caliber rifle. . . . No further description or information at this time. (timestamp: 12:45 p.m.) . . . [Units] 87 [and] 78 [Tippit] move into Central Oak Cliff area. (WCHE, v.17, p.397) . . .

(timestamp 12:54 p.m.)
DISPATCHER: 78.
UNIT 78: 78
DISPATCHER: You are in the Oak Cliff area are you not?
UNIT 78: Lancaster and 8th.
DISPATCHER: You will be at large for any emergency that comes in.
UNIT 78: 10-4
(timestamp 12:55) (WCHE, v.17, p.401)

DISPATCHER: 78 location
(78 does not respond. There is some interference on the channel. This transmission has no timestamp – it occurs sometime between 12:55 and 1:04 p.m., and appears to be closer to 1:04, so probably around 1:00 to 1:02.)
(WCHE, v.17, p.404)

UNIT 78: 78 . . .
UNIT 78: 78 [calling dispatcher twice, but dispatcher is conversing with unit 15 and does not respond to 78] (timestamp 1:08) (WCHE, v.17, p.406)

211

(timestamp 1:16)
CITIZEN: Hello, police operator
DISPATCHER: Go ahead, go ahead, citizen using the police [radio]
CITIZEN: We've had a shooting out here.
DISPATCHER: Where's it at? . . .
CITIZEN: On 10th Street
DISPATCHER: What location on 10th Street?
CITIZEN: It's a police officer. Somebody shot him. . . . 404 10th Street.
(background voice said "78 squad car number 10")
(WCHE, v.17, p.407-408)

It was customary for Dallas police officers to contact the dispatcher when they were going to be out of their car. The call by Tippit at 1:08 indicates that he was still alive and in his car at that time, but according to the usual procedure, he may have been intending to inform the dispatcher that he was about to get out of his patrol car, probably to confront Oswald. If so, this would fix the time of his death at around 1:08 or 1:09, understanding that even the police clocks are not necessarily exact. As we saw above, this time conforms well to the reports of eyewitnesses, and puts Tippit's radio call to the dispatcher in between Helen Markham's arrival at the intersection (1:06) and T. F. Bowley's arrival on the scene (1:10) where he found Tippit lying in the street next to his patrol car.

The DPD transcript (our version 2) shown above is mostly consistent with the transcript made by the FBI from the original recordings (version 3). But there are a few minor differences which are worth noting. Also, the correspondence between version 2 and version 3 provide evidence of falsification in the transcript of version 1 (the first radio log transcript provided by the police department), since the FBI transcript confirms that the dispatcher instructed *all squads* to report to Elm and Houston, not just those squads already in the downtown area. Here are the excerpts from the FBI transcript which differ in detail from the version 2 excerpt given above (with differences in italics).

Version 3 transcript (FBI)
DISPATCHER: Attention all squads, report to downtown area, code 3 [red lights and sirens] to Elm and Houston, with caution. . . . Attention all squads, at Elm and Houston reported to be an unknown white male, approximately 30, slender build, height 5 feet 10 inches, weight 165 pounds, reported to be armed with what is believed to be a .30 caliber rifle. . . . No further description or information at this time. (timestamp 12:45 p.m.) (WCHE, v.23, p.843b-844a) . . .
DISPATCHER: 87, 78, move into central Oak Cliff area.
UNIT 78 [TIPPIT]: I'm at Kiest and Bonnieview.

212

UNIT 87 [NELSON]: I'm going north of Marsalis on R. L. Thornton. (WCHE, v.23, p.844b)

(timestamp 1:08) [*Garbled transmission noted.* This is where the DPD transcript reports two attempts by Tippit to call the dispatcher.] (WCHE, v.23, p.855b)

We cannot say why the DPD transcript has omitted the transmissions from Tippit and Nelson in response to the dispatcher's instructions to "move into central Oak Cliff area". It is potentially important because it tells us where Tippit was at 12:45. Kiest and Bonnieview would be in Tippit's assigned district 78.

The contrast between version 1 of the radio transcript and the other two versions is striking. Not only is version 1 much shorter, with no attempt to be complete, but the key instruction to all units following the assassination is doctored to give a much different picture of who was being asked to report downtown. At the 12:43 timestamp on channel 1, where versions 2 and 3 have "*Attention all squads*, report to downtown area, code 3 to Elm and Houston", version 1 has "Attention all squads *in the downtown area* code three to Elm and Houston." The version 1 transcript then continues on with the description of the suspect as the other versions do. (WCHE, v.21, p.398) Version 1 cannot be reporting a correct transcription. It is two witnesses against one, and the FBI transcript was prepared directly from the original Dictabelt recordings. The version 1 transcript must be false, and perhaps deliberately so. We must ask what could be the purpose of this distorted record.

This discrepancy in the transcripts is not a trivial difference, because the version 1 transcript can be used, and was used, to justify the claim that Tippit, like all officers in the outer reaches of the city, was only supposed to move *closer* to downtown, remaining on the lookout for the suspect, while filling in for those units in the downtown area who had been called to Elm and Houston. Versions 2 and 3 of the transcript make it clear that *all units* were instructed to report downtown to Elm and Houston. This is reflected in the fact that Patrolman M. N. McDonald reported downtown to Elm and Houston, even though he had been working in district 95, which was even farther out than Tippit's district 78. (WCHE, v.7, p.82) Why wasn't McDonald instructed to simply move in closer to fill in for downtown units called to Elm and Houston? Why wasn't McDonald told to "be at large for any emergency"? The same goes for Officer J. L. Angel, who also was working in Oak Cliff and who likewise reported to Elm and Houston. (WCHE, v.7, p.82) If an officer was needed to be at large in Oak Cliff, why not let Officer Angel stay in Oak Cliff and send Tippit downtown with all the other units?

Inexplicably, the Warren Report adopts the version 1 wording of the radio communication, even though at the time the report was written, the commission had both of the more complete versions of the radio log. The Warren Report tells us that "about 12:44 p.m. on November 22, the radio dispatcher on channel 1 ordered *all downtown patrol squads* to report to Elm and Houston." (WCR, p.165) As we have seen, this order was actually issued to *all squads,* not just to those in the downtown area. Yet when the Warren Report cites the source for this misquoted broadcast, it not only quotes the inaccurate version 1 transcript (Sawyer Exhibit B), but claims the FBI transcript made from the Dictabelt recordings as a source for the report's inaccurate wording – despite the fact that the wording of the FBI transcript is directly opposed to the Warren Report's quote on p.165. (The footnote is number 496.)

By adopting the fiction that only the downtown units were called to Elm and Houston, it is possible to interpret Tippit's instructions to remain in Oak Cliff as being part of normal procedure, in that he was called in to Oak Cliff to fill in for other units which had been called downtown. But Tippit was the only officer who received such an instruction. Why weren't any other officers told to remain in an outlying neighborhood and to "be at large for any emergency"? What led the dispatcher to think that Oak Cliff, out of all Dallas neighborhoods, might be the scene for an "emergency"?

What was Tippit doing in Oak Cliff?

Sgt. Calvin "Bud" Owens was Acting Lieutenant in the Oak Cliff section on the afternoon of November 22, 1963, and thus was Tippit's supervisor. In an interview with FBI agents on May 15, 1964, Owens told the agents that on that day Tippit was assigned to patrol District 78, which is an area bordered by the Trinity River on the east and northeast, Southerland Avenue on the northwest, Sunnyvale and Keats Streets on the west, and Loop 12 or Ledbetter on the south. (A map of the DPD patrol districts is reproduced as Putnam Exhibit 1 at WCHE, v.21, p.274)

Owens told the FBI agents that "due to the extreme emergency of November 22, 1963, numerous patrol units were assigned to different areas" and he mentioned as an example two units (95 and 81) which "had been sent to the downtown area of Dallas immediately after the shooting of President Kennedy." Owens however, could not tell the agents "when or how Tippit's assignment from District 78 had been changed as he, Owens, had gone to lunch and had not returned during the time that Tippit's assignment had been changed." (WCHE, v.24, p.1a) In other words, Owens had no idea what he was talking about, since he had not been monitoring radio traffic during the time following the assassination. Owens cannot cite any examples of other officers who were moved to a different district outside of downtown on the afternoon of the assassination.

Owens had previously been interrogated in a deposition on April 9, 1964, and must have felt that he had some explaining to do after being grilled by commission staffer John Hart Ely about the districts where Tippit had been present on November 22, 1963. During his questioning, Ely showed Owens a map of the Dallas police districts. Owens says that Tippit was assigned to district 78, and his radio call number would thus have been 78. Ely calls Owens' attention to the police radio log, using what we have designated as version 1, in Sawyer Exhibits A and B. (The DPD radio log transcript (version 2) had been provided to the Warren Commission more than two weeks before Owens' deposition, so we have to wonder why Ely was using the heavily edited and abridged (and inaccurate) version of the transcript when he questioned Owens.) The wording of the version 1 transcript allows Owens to explain that Tippit would naturally have moved closer to downtown, but would not have headed directly for Elm and Houston, since he was not a downtown unit.

> ELY: Am I correct in saying that at 12:54 p.m., according to this log, Officer Tippit reported by radio that he was then at the corner of Lancaster and Eighth?
> OWENS: That's right.
> ELY: Now, in which district on this map would the corner of Lancaster and Eighth fall?
> OWENS: In district 109.
> ELY: Now, we would like to have your opinion as to why Officer Tippit, who was assigned to district 78, would have been in district 109 at 12:54 p.m. and then later in district 91?
> OWENS: It says here on channel 1 . . . *"Attention all squads in the downtown area,* code 3 to Elm and Houston with caution. . . . Any officer would proceed as near that location as possible to try to apprehend whoever had done it.
> ELY: Well, would somebody in an outlying district head for Elm and Houston itself or would he just come in closer?"
> OWENS: He would move in that direction, and when they had ordered all downtown squads to proceed to Elm and Houston, knowing that he was going to have to answer calls in the downtown area while they are there, and if you know that in all probability you may get called in, and – instead of the district you are in, you are going to head down there so it won't take you near as long, and also you can still be in the area if the suspect comes your way, you will have a better chance of apprehending him.
> ELY: So, you think Tippit might have been filling in for the people whom he knew had been pulled in to Elm and Houston? [helpfully leading the witness]
> OWENS: That's what I think. Not only filling in, but also looking for the suspect. (WCHE, v.7, p.80-81)

Ely points out that Tippit, who was assigned to district 78, was reported to have been in district 109 at 12:54 p.m. and was later found shot in district 91. Ely notes that these districts do not seem to be on a direct route for moving closer to the downtown area. Owens explains that this would be a logical route for Tippit to take if he were headed downtown to Elm and Houston as it would avoid routes with heavy traffic. But the call to report downtown specified to proceed under code 3 (red lights and sirens), so traffic should not have been a concern for any officer headed downtown. Nor did any witnesses report hearing sirens or seeing flashing red lights on Tippit's patrol car as he drove through Oak Cliff. Furthermore, we have seen that Tippit received explicit instructions to move into central Oak Cliff and to remain in Oak Cliff while being "at large for any emergency". So Owens' explanation that Tippit was headed downtown and was on the lookout for the assassination suspect does not hold water. The radio instruction for Tippit to "be at large for any emergency" sounds almost like a code of some kind, as it stands out in the transcript as being a very unusual instruction, unlike anything given to the other officers that day. Was this a phrase that signaled to Tippit that Oswald was still at large and that the backup plan was to be implemented for eliminating Oswald?

In a letter to the commission dated July 17, 1964, Police Chief Jesse Curry tried to explain Tippit's movements of November 22. He noted in the letter that Tippit and Nelson (units 78 and 87) had received explicit instructions from the dispatcher to move into central Oak Cliff, which included district 91 where Tippit was shot. Curry says this explains why Tippit was out of his usual district when he was shot, but it does not explain why Tippit received instructions to "be at large for any emergency" when no other officers and no other sections of the city were the subject of similar instructions. (WCHE, v.22, p.597b) Nor does it explain why the dispatcher had such an intense interest in Tippit's location, trying to reach him again around 1:00 to 1:02 p.m., even though Tippit was supposedly not one of the units told to report to the main action at Elm and Houston.

So we now have two conflicting explanations from the police for Tippit's movement to Oak Cliff: Owens, who says Tippit was just following standard procedure by moving into Oak Cliff, to fill in for downtown units who were called to Elm and Houston; and Curry, who says that *all* units were ordered downtown, except for Tippit and Nelson who headed for Oak Cliff on specific instructions from the dispatcher.

Conclusion

The testimony from Dallas police officials goes to great lengths to explain Tippit's whereabouts on November 22 as being a result of normal department procedures. Except for the late latter from Curry on July 17, 1964, the police department's story is that Tippit was moving closer to downtown to fill in for squads which were summoned to Elm and Houston following the President's assassination. In doing so, according to this story, he remained on the lookout for a suspect fitting the description of the President's assassin. Having encountered Oswald walking along 10th Street, Tippit confronted him and was shot by Oswald, proving, by the commission's reasoning, that Oswald had killed the President and that he shot Tippit because he was afraid of being arrested for Kennedy's murder. According to this story, Tippit died in the line of duty, as he tried to apprehend the President's assassin.

The radio log transcripts reveal a different story. *All* units were ordered to report to Elm and Houston. Only Tippit and Nelson received specific instructions to move from their normal districts into central Oak Cliff, which included the neighborhood around 10th Street and Patton Ave. This move did not bring Tippit closer to the downtown area as a replacement for officers who had been removed from their normal districts, and this is shown by the patrol district map reproduced as Putnam Exhibit 1 at WCHE, v.21, p.274. Tippit was given the highly unusual instruction to "be at large for any emergency". What could this possibly mean for a police patrolman? Aren't they *always* at large for any emergency when they are patrolling a neighborhood?

Tippit's movements on the afternoon of November 22 admit of only one reasonable explanation. He was on alert as the backup killer of Oswald in case Oswald escaped alive from the TSBD. Given that Oswald did just that, Tippit was looking for Oswald specifically, not just for a generic assassin. He may have been tipped off about Oswald being headed for the safe house at 324 E. 10th Street, so knew exactly where he needed to be in order to confront Oswald. But Oswald, who already suspected that he had been set up as the disposable patsy, got Tippit before Tippit got him. Oswald then proceeded to the Texas Theatre, following his own backup plan, where he perhaps expected to meet an intelligence contact who would help him escape Dallas.

PREDICTIONS

If it could be shown that certain individuals had foreknowledge of the assassination, that would in itself prove that a conspiracy existed, since there is no claim that Oswald as lone gunman would have announced his intentions of shooting Kennedy to anyone else. We have already seen that when Air Force Sergeant Robert Vinson was conferring with Colonel Chapman about his promotion, Chapman took a phone call in which he warned the caller that "we have information, and I strongly recommend that the president not go to Dallas." This was on November 21, the day before the assassination. Were there others who knew in advance that an assassination plan was in the works?

The prediction of Joseph Milteer

One of the best documented examples of foreknowledge is in a tape recorded phone conversation between Joseph Milteer and Miami police informant William Somersett. Milteer was a racist activist with ties to white supremacist groups across the south. He spoke to Somersett about a plan which was in the works to assassinate Kennedy "from an office building with a high powered rifle." A partial transcript of this recorded conversation, which occurred on November 9, 1963, less than two weeks before the assassination, is printed in HSCA, v.3, p.447-450. In this call, Somersett told Milteer that Kennedy was coming to Miami around November 18 to make a speech. The conversation continued:

> MILTEER: The more bodyguards he has, the easier it is to get him.
> SOMERSETT: Well, how in the hell do you figure would be the best way to get him?
> MILTEER: From an office building with a high powered rifle. . . .
> SOMERSETT: They are really going to try to kill him?
> MILTEER: Oh yeah, it is in the working. . . . They will pick up somebody within hours afterwards, if anything like that would happen just to throw the public off. (HSCA, v.3, pp.447-450)

An FBI report says that "the U. S. Secret Service was advised" of this information. (CD1347, p.118) Milteer was quoted as saying the day after the assassination to a "reliable informant" (presumably Somersett), that he was "very jubilant" about Kennedy's death. "Milteer stated, 'Everything ran true to form. I guess you thought I was kidding you when I said he would be killed from a window with a high-powered rifle.' When questioned as to whether he was guessing when he originally made the threat regarding President Kennedy, Milteer is quoted as saying, 'I don't do any guessing.'" (CD1347, p.119)

The prediction of Rose Cheramie

The story of Rose Cheramie is told in an HSCA interview with Lt. Francis Fruge of the Louisiana State Police. (Fruge interview, NARA Record Number 180-10106-10014) and in an HSCA Staff Report at HSCA, v.10, pp.199-204. Cheramie had previously worked for Jack Ruby as a stripper. The HSCA Staff Report on her describes her as "a heroin addict and prostitute with a long history of arrests." (HSCA, v.10, p.199)

Interview with Lt. Francis Fruge: Fruge was a lieutenant with the Louisiana State Police from 1947 to 1967. (Fruge interview, p.1) Fruge was called to the emergency ward of Moosa Memorial Hospital in Eunice, Louisiana at about 10:00 p.m. on November 20, 1963, about a patient, Rose Cheramie, who had been struck by a car on highway 190 in front of the Silver Slipper Lounge. She was not seriously injured, but because hospital personnel thought she was on drugs, Lt. Fruge was called. He brought her to the local jail until she sobered up. After allegedly bizarre behavior in her cell, possibly due to heroin withdrawal, Cheramie was taken to the East Louisiana State Hospital for examination. It was a two hour drive to the state hospital, and during the drive Cheramie appeared calm, and engaged in conversation with Fruge. (Fruge interview, p.2) The HSCA report of Fruge's interview continues: "During the trip from Eunice to Jackson, Rose Cheramie stated that she was just passing through town from Miami and on her way to Dallas and Houston. She stated, 'We're going to kill President Kennedy when he comes to Dallas in a few days.' She talked about traveling with a couple of guys, but Lt. Fruge did not take any of the conversation as serious due to her condition." (Fruge interview, p.3) Lt. Fruge admitted Cheramie to the hospital at Jackson and went back home.

After hearing about President Kennedy's assassination two days later on November 22, Fruge called the hospital at Jackson and found that Cheramie was in a hysterical state, but he was able to visit her the following Monday, November 25. "She stated that she was coming from Miami with two men that were either Cubans or Italians and she was going to go to Dallas, then to Houston. The men were going to kill Kennedy and she was going to check into the Rice Hotel, where reservations were already made for her, and pick up 10 kilos of heroin from a seaman coming into Galveston. She was to pick up the money for the dope from a man who was holding her baby. She would then take the dope to Mexico." (Fruge interview, p.3) Fruge later confirmed the name of the ship and the seaman's name with the chief U. S. customs agent in Port Arthur, Texas. Colonel Morgan of the Louisiana State Police phoned Captain Will Fritz of the Dallas Police Department to inform him about the Cheramie story, and the fact that it had been partly corroborated by the customs information. Fritz told Morgan that the case was in the hands of the federal agents and he gave Morgan a name to call. When Morgan called this agent, he was told that "they weren't interested at that time." (By now, Oswald was dead, and no one was looking for additional assassins or conspirators.)

Further investigation by the Louisiana State Police and Customs agents confirmed additional details of Cheramie's story: "The Customs people checked the Rice Hotel and reservations were made just as Cheramie had said. The man that allegedly had the money and her baby was checked and his name showed that he was an underworld, suspected narcotics dealer." (Fruge interview, p.4) Cheramie, who accompanied the customs agents in a government plane, told the agents that Oswald and Ruby were "bed partners" when Cheramie had worked for Ruby as a stripper. But FBI agents were not interested in pursuing Cheramie's assassination story, so the matter was dropped. (Fruge interview, p.5)

In 1966, Fruge was asked to locate Rose Cheramie in connection with the Jim Garrison investigation into the assassination. He found that she had been struck by a car and killed in 1965. The circumstances of the accident were unclear and never followed up on. Fruge tried to investigate her death, but local officials were uncooperative, and nothing ever came of his efforts. (Fruge interview, p.7)

HSCA investigation: The HSCA's Staff Report on the Rose Cheramie incident confirms several aspects of Lt. Fruge's statement. The committee found that "Cheramie's condition upon initial examination indicated heroin withdrawal and clinical shock." One of the doctors on the staff at East Louisiana State Hospital, Dr. Victor Weiss, was asked by another physician, Dr. Bowers, on Monday, November 25, 1963, "to see a patient who had been committed November 20 or 21. Dr. Bowers allegedly told Weiss that the patient, Rose Cheramie, had stated before the assassination that President Kennedy was going to be killed. Weiss questioned Cheramie about her statements. She told him she had worked for Jack Ruby. She did not have any specific details of a particular assassination plot against Kennedy, but had stated the 'word in the underworld' was that Kennedy would be assassinated. She further stated that she had been traveling from Florida to her home in Texas when the man traveling with her threw her from the automobile in which they were riding." (HSCA, v.10, p.200-201)

The committee had limited success in verifying the claims of prior assassination knowledge by Rose Cheramie. The committee tells us that "Cheramie's allegations were eventually discounted." (HSCA, v.10, p.199) This judgment appears to be based more on the committee's inability to find key documents and witnesses fifteen years after the fact, than on any actual refutation of her story.

The story of Richard Case Nagell

Author Dick Russell wrote about Nagel in his book *The Man Who Knew Too Much.* The Assassination Records Review Board looked into the Nagell story in 1995 and sent Nagell a letter asking him to contact the Board's Executive Director to discuss any assassination records he might have. The Board later found out that Nagell was found dead in his apartment the day after the ARRB's letter was mailed. The coroner ruled that he died as a result of natural causes. (Final Report of the Assassinations Records Review Board, p.133) (Note that the ARRB's purpose was to identify and collect records related to the assassination. It was not an investigative body and did not draw substantive conclusions about the assassination.)

As summarized by the ARRB, Nagell allegedly told Dick Russell that he:

- had conducted surveillance on Lee Harvey Oswald for both the CIA and the KGB;
- had been recruited by a KGB agent (masquerading as a CIA operative) to persuade Oswald *not* to participate in a plot against President Kennedy;
- had been instructed by the KGB to kill Oswald if he could not dissuade him from participating in the plot;
- was in possession of a Polaroid photograph that had been taken of himself with Lee Harvey Oswald in New Orleans;
- had audio tape recordings of Oswald and others discussing a forthcoming assassination attempt on President Kennedy; and
- had sent a letter, via registered mail, to FBI Director J. Edgar Hoover in September 1963, warning of a conspiracy to kill President Kennedy in late September 1963 in Washington, D.C. (ARRB Final Report, p.133)

In Russell's book, we learn that Nagell fired shots in a bank in El Paso on September 20, 1963 in order to be arrested so that he could get out of his assignment to kill Oswald. He said he preferred to be incarcerated than to "commit murder and treason". "He was convicted of armed robbery and served four and one-half years in prison." (James W. Douglass, *JFK and the Unspeakable* (2008), p.155, citing Dick Russell, *The Man Who Knew Too Much*.)

After Nagell's death, a staff member from the ARRB searched Nagell's Los Angeles apartment and a Phoenix storage unit with Nagell's son and niece, searching for assassination records. None of the items that Nagell claimed to have possessed turned up in these searches. (ARRB Final Report, p.133) However, the board did find "a considerable amount of documentary material on Nagell from the U. S. Secret Service and the U. S. Army". This material on Nagel, along with some CIA files, was designated by the ARRB as an assassination record.

As for the KGB's alleged efforts to neutralize Oswald, Yuri Nosenko, a KGB officer who defected to the United States in early 1964, told the FBI that the KGB had had no interest in Oswald when he tried to defect to the Soviet Union, and especially after Oswald tried to commit suicide the KGB "washed its hands of Oswald". (CD434 – FBI Memorandum Report of 28 Jan 1964 re: Yuri Ivanovich Nosenko, p.2) Nosenko told the FBI that after Oswald left Russia, "no further word was received at the KGB headquarters concerning Oswald until he appeared at the Soviet Embassy [in] Mexico City, Mexico, and sought to return to the Soviet Union." (CD434, p.3) Nosenko, whose reliability had not yet been established at the time of this FBI interview, was later determined by the CIA to be a legitimate defector, and not a KGB plant, and that he "is the person he claims to be." (CIA Study: Conclusions and Comments in the Case of Yuriy Ivanovich Nosenko, dated

10/1/68, released (1998) with deletions; originally classified as "secret"; NARA Record Number: 104-10210-10009, p.4)

According to a CIA summary of Nagell's career, he had survived a plane crash in 1954, after achieving a "brilliant Korean War record". On December 15, 1962 he advised the FBI in Jacksonville, Florida that "he had been approached shortly before in Washington, D.C. by [an] individual believed to be working for [the] Soviets. Nagell at this time was noted to be in an inebriated condition – vague in answering questions." Shortly after this incident, Nagell was diagnosed as having "chronic brain syndrome associated with brain trauma with behavioral reaction characterized by passive aggressive and paranoid features".(CIA Security File on Richard Case Nagell, NARA Record number 104-10305-10005, p.15-16)

Nagell's revelations to Dick Russell sound tantalizing, but in the end there is little or no corroboration of his story. The lack of corroborating documentation, along with Nagell's erratic behavior, require us to suspend judgment about his alleged assignment to block the assassination by removing the patsy Oswald. It is not at all clear that by eliminating the patsy the plot would have been foiled. Nor is it plausible that if the KGB wanted to block the assassination they would have chosen to go after the patsy rather than the actual perpetrators. Nosenko's report that the KGB had no interest in Oswald may or may not be true, but his assessment that "Oswald was not regarded by the KGB as being completely normal mentally nor was he considered to be very intelligent" rings true, and it strains the imagination to think that the KGB believed that by eliminating such an insignificant player, the forces behind the assassination would have just given up and gone home, instead of coming up with another patsy to fill the role.

The prediction of John Martino

John Martino was an organized crime figure, "an electronics expert, particularly specializing in the gambling machines employed in Havana casinos run by organized crime." After the Cuban revolution, Martino spent three years in a Cuban prison. After he was released, he wrote a book: "I Was Castro's Prisoner". (See "John Martino's Confessions" at maryferrell.org)

After Martino's death, author Anthony Summers interviewed his wife Florence, and son Edward, about "what her husband said and did on November 22, 1963." Florence Martino told Summers, "John insisted he wanted to paint the breakfast room that day. . . . We were supposed to go out to the Americana [in Miami Beach] for lunch. . . . But it was on the radio about [the visit to] Dallas. . . . And he said, 'Flo, they're going to kill him. They're going to kill him when he gets to Texas.'" Edward Martino told Summers, that after the news of the assassination broke on television, "my father went white as a sheet. But it wasn't like 'Gee whiz!' – it was more like confirmation." "Then," according to Mrs. Martino, "John was on the phone. . . . He got I don't know how many calls from Texas. I don't know who called him, but he was on the phone, on the phone, on the phone." (Summers, *Not in Your Lifetime* (2013), p.429)

According to Martino's close business associate Fred Claasen, Martino told him, "The anti-Castro people put Oswald together. Oswald didn't know who he was working for – he was just ignorant of who was really putting him together. Oswald was to meet his contact at the Texas Theater. They were to meet Oswald in the theater and get him out of the country, then eliminate him. Oswald made a mistake. . . . There was no way we could get to him. They had Ruby kill him." (Summers, *Not in Your Lifetime,* p.431, citing a 1978 article by Earl Golz in the Dallas Morning News.)

Conclusion:

These reports of foreknowledge of the assassination are suggestive but not conclusive. Several of them are well attested (e.g., Milteer, Cheramie, Martino), but contain little detail beyond a general expectation that an assassination plot against Kennedy was in the works. However, we would not expect that persons in the position of these witnesses would have access to all the details of the plot. Indeed, any conspiracy of this type would share as little information as possible with lower level actors, so that many people might know that something is being planned, but not have detailed knowledge of it. Also, Presidents often receive threats and it would not necessarily indicate specific knowledge if someone said that "so-and-so is going to get the President".

Of the examples cited above, Martino's words quoted by his widow are the most specific, pinpointing the date and the place of the assassination, which followed only hours afterward. Therefore, his prediction seems most likely to be based on specific knowledge of the plot. Many details of Cheramie's story were confirmed by police and customs agents, but her prediction is vague and general, indicating that she may have been relying on "word in the underworld" rather than on any specific knowledge from her traveling companions. Milteer may have heard rumors from his associates in the Klan and other such organizations, but there is no serious research to suggest that white supremacist groups were active in planning the assassination.

But taken together, these stories suggest that something indeed was "in the works", and that word to that effect had gotten around in the milieu of organized crime, right-wing extremists, CIA, and anti-Castro Cuban exiles. While not conclusively proving foreknowledge, these stories represent evidence which must be weighed in the balance along with all the other evidence, and which tips the scales a bit more toward the existence of a conspiracy to kill President Kennedy. They add to the probability, but do not by themselves prove the case for conspiracy.

POSTSCRIPTS

A conspiracist scenario

Since November 22, 1963, the government's media trolls have continued with their gaslighting of the American public by trying to convince us that what we can plainly see before our eyes is nothing more than a phantom of our weak and feeble minds. But we are not seeing phantoms. The conspiracy is real. The Warren Commission's own evidence is overwhelming and obvious that President Kennedy was killed by at least three assassins firing in Dealey Plaza. The Warren Commission's records cannot tell us the names of the assassins, or who hired them, or who conceived and orchestrated the plot. But research by many journalists and scholars, and revelations by participants and eyewitnesses have gradually, over the course of more than 50 years, filled in many gaps in our knowledge, so that today the broad outlines of the crime can be sketched with reasonable confidence. For readers who have not yet immersed themselves in this followup research, we offer the following synopsis of the leading conspiracist scenario, which has emerged as the view best supported by the evidence, although many uncertainties remain to be resolved.

From Congressional investigations in the 1970s it is now known that at an operational level, the CIA, organized crime, and anti-Castro Cuban exile groups were intertwined in such a way that distinctions between the lowest levels of these organizations had become blurred. Evaluating the dynamics of this interaction and the possible role of these organizations in the Kennedy assassination is a complex task and beyond the scope of this book. Many excellent books have been written since the 1960s investigating this topic. To briefly summarize the prevailing viewpoint, we can say that the dominant conspiracy scenario explains the assassination as a collaboration among elements of the CIA, Cuban exiles, and organized crime, all of whom had strong motives for wanting to eliminate President Kennedy. The anti-Castro Cubans felt betrayed by Kennedy's failure to support the Bay of Pigs invasion with U. S. air support. Certain elements of the CIA were heavily involved in training and supporting these anti-Castro rebels and also felt betrayed by Kennedy's lack of military support, and beyond this even at higher levels of the CIA and the U. S. military establishment Kennedy was seen as a possible national security risk, or even as a traitor, for his failure to vigorously pursue a military solution to overthrow the Castro regime and even to wage a preventive war against the Soviet Union while the United States still possessed nuclear superiority over the Soviets. Major organized crime figures had also been involved in the anti-Castro invasion plans, with mobster Johnny Rosselli acting as the go-between between the mob and the CIA. Moreover, organized crime had lost lucrative sources of income when Castro closed down their casinos in Havana. New Orleans crime boss Carlos Marcello had personal reasons for hating the Kennedys, as he had been summarily deported and ignominiously airlifted into the Guatemalan jungles at the direction of Attorney General Robert Kennedy, who had continued to vigorously prosecute the mob even after his brother had received financial support from various crime families for his successful presidential campaign. In addition to Marcello, a number of other crime figures were under intense pressure from the Attorney General's campaign against organized crime. These figures included Jimmy Hoffa of Detroit, Sam Giancana of Chicago, and Santo Trafficante of Tampa. On a number of fronts, the crime bosses felt betrayed and double crossed by both Bobby and Jack Kennedy. In 2013, the attorney general's son, Robert F. Kennedy Jr., told reporters that his father "had investigators do research into the assassination and found that phone records of Oswald and nightclub owner Jack Ruby . . . were like an inventory of mafia leaders the government had been investigating." ("RFK children speak about JFK assassination", Associated Press report in USA Today, January 12, 2013)

There are strong indications that Oswald had connections to this world of anti-Castro Cubans, U. S. intelligence, and organized crime. Some of these connections have been outlined in the foregoing pages. These connections are relevant in deciding whether Oswald should be viewed as a lone gunman, a Castro agent, a right-wing extremist, or an unwitting dupe. From the evidence collected by the Warren Commission, as well as by later government investigations and by independent journalists and researchers, we can now conclude that Oswald was in all likelihood not a communist, and not a Castro agent. The weight of the evidence indicates that his pro-communist profile, including his non-existent New Orleans chapter of the Fair Play for Cuba Committee, was a ruse, and that he was working as a U. S. intelligence operative, and possibly as an informant to the FBI, infiltrating subversive organizations such as the FPCC in the role of an *agent provocateur* and creating damaging publicity for them.

There is no serious evidence that either the Soviet or the Cuban governments were behind the Kennedy assassination or that they were directing Oswald's actions. Neither of these countries would have had anything to gain from Kennedy's death, and Castro in particular would have been running the risk of a U. S. invasion of his island if he were ever even suspected of ordering Kennedy to be assassinated, by Oswald or anyone else. While he was president, Kennedy had opened secret channels of communication with both Cuba and the Soviet Union, and had indicated a desire to bring about a peaceful coexistence with both countries. Neither the Russians nor the Cubans would have benefited from eliminating an apparently conciliatory Kennedy, only to replace him with Lyndon Johnson, who had close ties with the U. S. military establishment and who would be likely to adopt a more hawkish posture with both these adversaries.

No serious conspiracist today thinks that Oswald was just an innocent book order filler who was framed for both the Kennedy assassination and the Tippit murder by persons unknown to him. No serious conspiracist today thinks that Oswald was an assassin hired by Castro or the Russians. The evidence laid out in this book has shown that Oswald was probably not a shooter in the Kennedy assassination, although he was very likely involved in the plot. Whether his involvement was as a conspirator or as an infiltrator and informant cannot be firmly established, but it is not likely that a serious conspiracy would have tapped Oswald as a shooter, because, regardless of his marksmanship skills, Oswald was not, and never had been, a professional assassin. It is not likely that the groups behind the Kennedy assassination would have entrusted such a high stakes, high profile job to an amateur assassin, when they had professional talent at their disposal, especially if they had any doubts about Oswald's loyalty to the conspirators. More likely, Oswald was pretending to go along with the plot, in whatever role the conspirators had assigned him, all the while feeding information about the conspiracy to his FBI contacts, in hopes of foiling the plot. But these contacts were themselves, in all likelihood, part of the conspiracy. So that by playing along with the conspirators and pretending to cooperate with them, Oswald was in fact laying a trail of evidence that would implicate himself as the President's assassin, even though he may never have touched a rifle on November 22, 1963. In infiltrating the conspiracy, Oswald was probably freelancing, rather than carrying out an undercover assignment given to him by bona fide FBI or CIA handlers. He may have expected to win fame and fortune for preventing the President's assassination, by exposing the plot to his FBI contacts. When he realized on the afternoon of November 22 that the plot against Kennedy had succeeded, it is no wonder that Oswald's movements after the assassination had an improvised quality about them, indicating that he was at that point reacting to an unexpected situation and was resorting to plan B, C, or D to avoid playing the patsy role which he now realized had been assigned to him. For about an hour on the afternoon of November 22, Oswald succeeded in evading those who sought to silence him before he could talk. But the conspirators had their backup plans, too, and succeeded in cutting off his escape routes and eventually trapping him in the Texas Theatre.

A historically flawed theory of assassinations

During the Warren Commission's early meetings, Allen Dulles distributed to commission members copies of a book, *The Assassins*, by Robert J. Donovan, a Washington journalist. (David Talbot, *The Devil's Chessboard* (2015) p.576) In this book, Donovan put forth a theory that American assassinations have been the work of single individuals, while European assassinations were often committed by political zealots working together in pursuit of political or ideological goals. (FBI 105-82555 Oswald HQ File, Section A-2, p.10) Dulles's purpose in distributing this book was obviously to implant in the minds of the commission members that the laws of history rule out an American assassination conspiracy.

But the premises of Donavan's argument conflict with the actual history, and his argument also contains a logical mistake. As for the history, Lincoln's assassin John Wilkes Booth was the head of a conspiracy whose goal was to avenge the Confederacy by murdering the President, Vice-President, and Secretary of State. Both President Lincoln and Secretary of State Seward were attacked, but only

Lincoln was killed. So the very first U. S. presidential assassination was the result of a conspiracy, and does not conform to Donovan's stated premise. Also, the failed assassination attempt against President Truman in 1950 involved at least two Puerto Rican nationalists, so also was not the work of a single assassin. (Contrary to the popular saying, exceptions do not "prove" the rule, they refute it.)

Dulles's introduction of Donovan's theory into the Warren Commission's deliberations was a clear attempt to limit the possible outcomes by imposing a theoretical constraint based on which country the assassination occurred in. Donovan's logical mistake is to infer a general law ("American assassins act alone") from a very small sample. Before Kennedy, only three U. S. presidents had been assassinated: Lincoln, Garfield, and McKinley. Lincoln was the victim of a conspiracy, the other two were killed by gunmen apparently acting alone. So there are really only two data points in support of Donovan's general "law". There is nothing wrong with tentatively drawing hypothetical conclusions from a data set, but subsequent events must be used to confirm or refute the hypothesis, rather than using the hypothesis to constrain the events, especially when the hypothesis is based on insufficient data. Also, historical "laws" are not like the laws of physics. Whatever generalizations may be drawn from history, subsequent events can always contradict them.

It is easy to illustrate the flaws in Donovan's theory by the following argument: Before Kennedy, all presidential assassinations were committed with handguns. Therefore, Kennedy could not have been killed with a rifle. He must have been killed with a handgun, since history shows that this is how American presidents are killed. The argument is, of course, absurd, but in logical form it is no different from Donovan's flawed theory of lone American assassins which Dulles tried to foist upon the commission.

Consistency and possibility

A search in the online version of the Warren Report on the maryferrell.org website turns up 46 page hits for the phrase "consistent with". When the evidence was not strong enough to prove the point they wanted to establish, the commission fell back on the argument that the evidence is "consistent with" their preferred conclusion. Criminal guilt must, of course, be proven beyond a reasonable doubt – at least in a real criminal proceeding, which the Warren Commission was not. Offering evidence which is "consistent with" a proposition does not prove the proposition. The only legitimate use of the consistency argument is to rebut a positive defense. Here is an example where the consistency argument is valid:

> PROSECUTION: Oswald was on the sixth floor at the time of the assassination.
> DEFENSE: That's impossible. There wasn't time for him to get from the sixth floor to the second floor lunchroom, where Officer Baker saw him just a minute and a half after the shooting.

PROSECUTION: But we timed the route and it only took a minute and a half. Therefore, Oswald being on the sixth floor during the shooting is *consistent with* his being on the second floor a minute and a half later.

This is a valid rebuttal of the defense that Oswald's presence on the second floor within 1 minute 30 seconds of the shooting was *inconsistent* with his having shot from the sixth floor window. "Consistent with" is only a valid argument when it is offered in rebuttal to a claim of *inconsistency*. But it cannot be used as a primary argument to prove the fact of guilt. The reason, of course, is that evidence is usually "consistent with" a variety of conditions and circumstances, in addition to the condition of guilt. The possibility of escaping from the sixth floor to the second floor in a minute and a half is also consistent with Oswald's having been on the second floor all along.

Despite the weakness of the consistency argument, the Warren Report uses it throughout its 800+ pages, and it is impossible to avoid the impression that it appears so often because the evidence for the commission's position is weak. A few examples will illustrate the use made of this argument in trying to establish the commission's case:

- "The location of the cartridge cases was therefore consistent with the southeast window having been used by the assassin." (WCR, p.557) (The location of the cartridge cases was also consistent with their having been planted in order to frame Oswald.)

- "The dimensions of that [small] wound were consistent with having been caused by a 6.5 mm bullet fired from behind and above which struck at a tangent. (WCR, p.86) (It was also consistent with a head shot from the front, since nothing precludes Kennedy having been hit in the head from both the front and the rear.)

- [The calculated angle through the President's body] "was consistent with the trajectory of a bullet passing through the President's neck and then striking Governor Connally's back." (WCR, p.106) (It was also consistent with the two men having been hit by separate bullets.)

- "Oswald's movements, as described by these witnesses, are consistent with his having been at the window at 12:30 p.m." (WCR, p.149) (They were also consistent with his having been downstairs the whole time.)

- "Oswald's palmprint on the bottom of the paper bag . . . was consistent with the bag having contained a heavy or bulky object when he handled it." (WCR, p.135) (However, there was no positive evidence that the makeshift bag had actually contained a rifle or any other heavy object.)

- The testimony of Fischer and Edwards "is of probative value . . . because their limited description is consistent with that of the man who has been found by the Commission, based on other evidence, to have fired the shots from the window." (WCR, p.147) (Translation: Only those witnesses whose testimony is consistent with our predetermined conclusion are credible.)

A variation on the consistency argument is the argument from "possibility". This is subject to the same criticisms. To say that it is "possible" for an event to occur does not mean that it probably occurred, or that it actually did occur.

- "It is entirely possible that [Connally] heard the missed shot and that both men were struck by the second bullet." (WCR, p.112) (It is also possible that Connally's recollection is accurate and that they were shot by two separate bullets.)
- "If Altgens' recollection is correct that he snapped his picture at the same moment as he heard a shot, then it is possible that he heard a second shot which missed." (WCR, p.115) (It is also possible that Altgens was correct in saying that he snapped his picture with the first shot.)
- "According to expert witnesses, exacting tests conducted for the Commission demonstrated that it was possible to fire three shots from the rifle within 5½ seconds." (WCR, p.645) (However, these tests did not demonstrate that it was likely that a gunman would fire the rifle that fast. Most of the marksmen who conducted these tests did not achieve this rate of fire, and none of the marksmen who attained this rate of fire managed to hit all three targets when placed at intervals corresponding to the assassination distances. See the detailed results in the chapter "The Experts".)
- "A series of time tests made by investigators and by Roy S. Truly and Patrolman M. L. Baker . . . show that it was possible for Oswald to have placed the rifle behind a box and descended to the lunchroom on the second floor before Patrolman Baker and Truly got up there." (WCR, p.648) (It was also "possible" that he was on the second floor the whole time.)

The point should be clear from these examples. An argument based on "consistency" or "possibility" does not prove the truth, or even the likelihood, of any positive fact. It can only be used to rebut specific defenses based on a claim of impossibility or inconsistency with the facts.

Ten questions for the Commission:

1. Why wouldn't a lone assassin have shot the President as he rode along Houston Street, before making the turn to Elm Street? This would have been a much clearer shot for a sniper waiting in the sixth floor window. (See the photo in CE875 at WCHE, v.17, p.875)
2. Why would Oswald shoot the President with a mail-order rifle that could be easily traced to his name and post office box, when he could have bought a rifle for cash at any gun store in Dallas, without showing any identification?

3. How could Oswald have missed a clear shot through a lighted window at a sitting General Walker, yet be a good enough shot to land at least two hits on targets in the car, which was moving away and downhill?

4. If Oswald was seeking notoriety and a place in history, why did he deny shooting Kennedy?

5. Why would a shooter be hanging out the TSBD window (as witnesses described) when it would be just as easy to take the shot from farther inside, where he could remain concealed, unless the scene in the window was just a decoy?

6. If, on the morning of November 22, Oswald was planning to assassinate the President, why did he leave his revolver at home so that he would have to delay his escape by coming back to get it?

7. Why was no rifle ammunition found at Oswald's rooming house or on his person? Why was no evidence presented showing where he obtained his 6.5 mm Mannlicher-Carcano ammunition? How could he have practiced his marksmanship with the rifle without purchasing ammunition?

8. Why did none of the Dealey Plaza witnesses who saw the man shooting from the window report seeing him operate the bolt of the rifle?

9. Why was a seating arrangement chosen for the Presidential limousine that prevented Secret Service agent Roy Kellerman from leaping back to cover Kennedy with his body, as Rufus Youngblood did for Vice-President Johnson? Why wasn't Kennedy seated in the jump seat directly behind Kellerman, instead of Connally?

10. Why was Officer J. D. Tippit the only officer told to "remain at large" rather than proceeding downtown as all other units were ordered to do?

Made in United States
Orlando, FL
22 February 2024

43985211R00137